Bloom's Classic Critical Views

MARY SHELLEY

Bloom's Classic Critical Views

Bloom's Classic Critical Views

MARY SHELLEY

Edited and with an Introduction by
Harold Bloom
Sterling Professor of the Humanities
Yale University

 BLOOM'S
LITERARY CRITICISM
An imprint of Infobase Publishing

Bloom's Classic Critical Views: Mary Shelley

Copyright © 2008 Infobase Publishing

Introduction © 2008 by Harold Bloom

All rights reserved. No part of this publication may be reproduced or utilized in any form or by any means, electronic or mechanical, including photocopying, recording, or by any information storage or retrieval systems, without permission in writing from the publisher. For more information contact:

Bloom's Literary Criticism
An imprint of Infobase Publishing
132 West 31st Street
New York NY 10001

Library of Congress Cataloging-in-Publication Data
Mary Shelley / edited and with an introduction by Harold Bloom.
    p. cm. — (Bloom's classic critical views)
  Includes bibliographical references and index.
  ISBN 978-1-60413-137-6 (acid-free paper) 1. Shelley, Mary, 1797–1851--Criticism and interpretation. I. Bloom, Harold. II. Title. III. Series.

PR5841.W8Z75625 2008
828'.609—dc22

2008019293

Bloom's Literary Criticism books are available at special discounts when purchased in bulk quantities for businesses, associations, institutions, or sales promotions. Please call our Special Sales Department in New York at (212) 967-8800 or (800) 322-8755.

You can find Bloom's Literary Criticism on the World Wide Web at
http://www.chelseahouse.com

Contributing editor: Janyce Marson
Series design by Erika K. Arroyo
Cover design by Takeshi Takahashi
Printed in the United States of America
Bang EJB 10 9 8 7 6 5 4 3 2 1

This book is printed on acid-free paper.

All links and Web addresses were checked and verified to be correct at the time of publication. Because of the dynamic nature of the Web, some addresses and links may have changed since publication and may no longer be valid.

Contents

Series Introduction

Bloom's Classic Critical Views is a new series presenting a selection of the most important older literary criticism on the greatest authors commonly read in high school and college classes today. Unlike the Bloom's Modern Critical Views series, which for more than 20 years has provided the best contemporary criticism on great authors, Bloom's Classic Critical Views attempts to present the authors in the context of their time and to provide criticism that has proved over the years to be the most valuable to readers and writers. Selections range from contemporary reviews in popular magazines, which demonstrate how a work was received in its own era, to profound essays by some of the strongest critics in the British and American tradition, including Henry James, G.K. Chesterton, Matthew Arnold, and many more.

Some of the critical essays and extracts presented here have appeared previously in other titles edited by Harold Bloom, such as the New Moulton's Library of Literary Criticism. Other selections appear here for the first time in any book by this publisher. All were selected under Harold Bloom's guidance.

In addition, each volume in this series contains a series of essays by a contemporary expert, who comments on the most important critical selections, putting them in context and suggesting how they might be used by a student writer to influence his or her own writing. This series is intended above all for students, to help them think more deeply and write more powerfully about great writers and their works.

Introduction by Harold Bloom

I have, through the years, read all of Mary Shelley's fictions, but even *The Last Man* (1826) does not sustain rereading. Her first narrative, *Frankenstein* (1818), composed when she was nineteen, was to be her only canonical contribution to imaginative literature. The subtitle of *Frankenstein* is *The Modern Prometheus*, and the reader needs to remember that is the role of Victor Frankenstein. His achievement, the New Adam he had brought to life, ought not to be called the "monster" and perhaps even not the "creature." Think of him rather as the "daimon" first expounded by Empedocles. The daimon wandered through the cosmos, seeking to expiate previous incarnations with all their transgressions of bloodletting.

Victor Frankenstein's daimon is also his antithetical self, in a familiar Romantic pattern that was to culminate in Nietzsche and in W.B. Yeats. Ironically, the daimon is both more intelligent and more passionate than his maker, with more capacity both for good and for evil. Compared to the daimon, Victor Frankenstein is a dreadful egomaniac, so solipsistic that he is incapable of understanding the moral enormity of what he has done. This crime is augmented when Frankenstein finds his creation abhorrent, rejects the daimon, and flees from him.

The poet Shelley, though he admired his wife's novel, necessarily was troubled by its implicit criticism of High Romantic Byronic-Shelleyan Prometheanism. Young as she was, the daughter of William Godwin and Mary Wollstonecraft had inherited their radical vision of social realities, and therefore resisted her husband's various transcendentalisms. Not that Victor Frankenstein was a portrait of Shelley; Clerval rather resembles the poet of *Prometheus Unbound*, and his murder by the daimon prompts my own uneasy reflections.

By any standard, Victor Frankenstein is a moral monster. We are moved by the daimon's pleas, but Frankenstein is not, even when they are eloquent with plangency:

> Oh, Frankenstein, be not equitable to every other, and trample upon me alone, to whom thy justice, and even thy clemency and affection, is most due. Remember that I am thy creature; *I ought to be thy Adam, but I am rather the fallen angel, whom thou drivest from joy for no misdeed.* Everywhere I see bliss, from which I alone am irrevocably excluded. I was benevolent and good; misery made me a fiend. Make me happy, and I shall again be virtuous.

The passage I italicize is the heart of the novel, deliberately recalling its epigraph from *Paradise Lost*, where the fallen Adam laments his creation:

> Did I request thee, Maker, from my clay
> To mold me man? Did I solicit thee
> From darkness to promote me?

Like the God of *Paradise Lost,* Victor Frankenstein manifests what I have to regard as moral idiocy:

> During these last days I have been occupied in examining my past conduct; nor do I find it blameable. In a fit of enthusiastic madness I created a rational creature, and was bound towards him, to assure, as far as was in my power, his happiness and well-being. This was my duty; but there was another still paramount to that. My duties towards the beings of my own species had greater claims to my attention, because they included a greater proportion of happiness or misery.

Peculiarly appalling, this self-revelation by the Modern Prometheus could not have been lost on the subtle and sensitive Shelley. We have debased the daimon in our ghastly series of filmed travesties called *Frankenstein*. For all his murderousness, the daimon remains the severe poet of the moral climate Mary Shelley created for him.

BIOGRAPHY

Mary Shelley
(1797–1851)

On July 28, 1814, Mary Godwin, only seventeen years of age, and the radical poet-philosopher, Percy Bysshe Shelley, twenty-one at the time, decided to elope to France, a country still recovering from defeat in war. Their actions were considered scandalous. Beside the fact that they were not married to one another, Percy was still married to another woman, Harriet Shelley. Still, the passion and attraction that drew the two together were overwhelming and, when William Godwin became aware of the relationship, he argued with his daughter about the affair. By the time they eloped, Mary was pregnant by Shelley, a situation rendered even more scandalous by Shelley's desertion of his first wife, Harriet, who was also pregnant with his child. Godwin refused to communicate with his daughter for a period of more than two years. However, given her parents' personal histories, her father's admonition failed to deter Mary. When they left for mainland Europe, they took their companion, Jane Clairmont, with them. Jane too wished to get away from her mother's ever-watchful eye and, given her penchant for reading romances and ghost stories, she longed to travel. Furthermore, Jane had been the agent for arranging secret meetings for the lovers in the weeks leading up to their elopement. Once in Paris, they settled into cheap lodgings at the Hôtel de Vienne while planning a journey to Switzerland. The three had left behind many distressed relatives, among them Percy's wife, who was awaiting the birth of their second child, Charles Shelley, while caring for their daughter, Ianthe Shelley, then only one year old. The list of unhappy family members also included Mary's stepmother, who rushed to Calais in an attempt to dissuade her stepdaughter, and William Godwin, who, despite his radical views, was concerned about the notoriety that this unconventional marriage would bring to his daughter. Indeed, the rift with his daughter would create a three-and-a-half-year estrangement.

Mary had met Percy less than two years before their marriage when the poet paid a visit to her father, whom he greatly admired. Godwin was in a great deal of business debt, and Percy Shelley, who also needed money, had pledged to pay the totality of Godwin's indebtedness over time and was visiting to discuss the terms of a loan they were negotiating. When his business discussion with Godwin was concluded, Percy Shelley visited Mary at her schoolroom to discuss politics and women's rights. Before he left for home a few days later, Percy bought Mary a notebook to use for a translation of the *Aeneid* she was about to begin. The two were falling in love, though Percy was still married. At the time of his first visit to the Godwins, Percy was accompanied by his wife, who despite her education was deemed by her husband to be one-dimensional. When Percy's father later insisted that his son give up his radical views as the condition for financial assistance, the poet refused and the relationship with his wife became even more difficult. The couple separated amid rumors of infidelity, including the contention that Harriet's lover Captain Ryan was the biological father of her second child. Percy Shelley never knew for sure but assumed that the child was his, as it would have been financially disadvantageous for him not to be the father.

Both before and after meeting Percy, Mary had been living in Scotland where she was introduced to Scottish traditions and myths and was encouraged to write stories. She delved into the occult aspects of Scottish culture and became enamored of its legends, including dealings with the devil, the raising of spirits, and humanoid monsters. At this time, Mary's favorite older poets were Spenser, Sidney, Shakespeare, and Milton, while Wordsworth, Coleridge, South, and Byron were her favorite modern ones. She had met Percy during a brief trip to London and soon returned to Scotland with her traveling companion, Isabella Baxter, the daughter of William Thomas Baxter, a prosperous sailcloth manufacturer. During her sixteen months at the spacious Baxter residence, Mary was able to live according to her own values: privacy, intellectual and loving companionship, and a close proximity to nature. When she next met Percy on May 5, 1814, he was estranged from his wife and even more transfixed by Mary, whom he described as "a child of love and light." He admired Mary for her bold and fearless ways as well as for her knowledge of and interest in abstruse subjects. Mary's family name and parentage were an additional allure for the handsome young poet. For her part, Mary loved Shelley, seeing him as the living embodiment of her parents' radical ideals. Percy was dedicated to human betterment and great generosity, sentiments for which Mary had a great sympathy. Percy was also an accomplished classical scholar.

While traveling in Switzerland with Percy and Jane Clairmont, Mary Shelley wrote her *History of a Six Weeks' Tour* (published in 1817), a record of her response to the grandeur of the Alps with a vision that appreciated the vital and life-giving elements among the frozen wastes. "The scenery of this day's journey was divine, exhibiting piny mountains barren rocks, and spots of verdure surpassing imagination." And at the desolate summit of Montanvert, she surveyed the barren ice fields in order to discover how the meager forms of life struggled to survive. "We went on the ice; it is traversed by irregular crevices. . . . The air is very cold, yet many flowers grow here, and, among others, the rhododendron, or *Rose des Alpes*, in great profusion."

During the eight years the Shelleys spent together, they were often on the move, with stints in England, France, Italy, and elsewhere, at times relocating several times a year. Between 1815 and 1819, Mary lost three of her four children. In February 1815, Mary's first child, a daughter, was born prematurely, and in January 1816, her son William was born and died three years later in 1819; finally, in September 1817, a third child, Clara, was born, and she died in 1818, just barely more than a year old. Their fourth child, a son named Percy Florence, was born on November 12, 1819.

Despite their domestic problems at the time—a period that saw the suicides of Fanny Imlay and Harriet Shelley—the Shelleys continued to work hard, reading widely and writing assiduously. They mixed with a number of the most significant cultural figures of the times, in particular Lord Byron. While living in Switzerland, Mary's first and best-known work, *Frankenstein*, was famously composed as a result of a ghost story competition during a long, wet summer in Geneva. The novel, first published in 1818, incorporates many details from her familial experiences and disappointments as well as her unique education and acquaintance with some of the most gifted writers and thinkers of her time. Each element of the novel, from the explorer's paternal reverence of Victor Frankenstein to Victor's own tortured relationship with his creation, represents a familial bond, ruptured or otherwise. In *Frankenstein*, Mary Shelley succeeded not only in creating an enduring myth but also in expressing the dangers of driving scientific activity to its limits without considering the possible human consequences. Ultimately, Mary's fascination with scientific radicalism in the book brought her criticism, and she was forced to bowdlerize her own work for later editions.

Mary Godwin was born on August 30, 1797, the daughter of William Godwin, the writer and philosopher, and his feminist activist wife, Mary Wollstonecraft. Tragically, Mary Wollstonecraft died of puerperal fever eleven days after giving birth to her daughter. Wollstonecraft, best known for her *Vindication of the Rights of Woman with Strictures on Political and Moral Subjects* (1792), argued for the rightful education and value of women. By the time of Mary's birth, William Godwin had written *An Enquiry Concerning Political Justice* (1793), advocating a republican and minimal form of government, and a novel, *Caleb Williams* (1794), a fictional attack on current social values. Both Wollstonecraft and Godwin lent their voices to the revolutionary passions of their day and rejected the status quo. From 1793 to 1815, Great Britain and France were at war, and the British government took action to silence the radical elements, while Wollstonecraft, Godwin, and their adherents envisioned a renewed world as a result of the French Revolution. However, even with this group of reformers there were differences of opinion as to how society should be reenvisioned. While Godwin was in favor of a gradual, evolutionary form of change based on universal education, the first generation of Romantic poets had, initially, called for a replacement of old values with new ones. But the dreams of the early 1790s never came to fruition. Repressive measures were enacted by the British government, while the French Revolution had bloody consequences. Following this, the Napoleonic wars brought widespread unemployment along with social and political upheaval. By the second decade of the nineteenth century, Great Britain's agrarian society faced radical changes, with large segments of the population flooding into the cities to earn their living in industry and commerce.

Mary Godwin's life was difficult from the outset. On December 21, 1801, her father remarried, and Mary Jane Clairmont became her stepmother. The new Mrs. Godwin was obnoxious and unethical, opening other people's mail, acting behind their backs, and slandering them. Mary would forever resent her stepmother, accusing her of taking her father away. Her stepmother also succeeded in removing from the household Mary's allies and supporters, including her nursemaid and Wollstonecraft's former maid. Godwin's friends felt bad for Mary. As a result of the union, Mary Godwin inherited a household consisting of Fanny Imlay (the daughter of Mary Wollstonecraft by Gilbert Imlay), and a stepsister and stepbrother (Jane, later called Claire) and Charles Clairmont.

Mary Godwin was educated at home by her father, who advocated the cultivation of knowledge and feeling through the liberal arts, which he had studied at the Dissenting schools. His instruction was rigorous and ambitious, his primary interests being history and literature, especially the Latin and Greek classics, Shakespeare, Milton, and acclaimed poets writing in other languages. He likewise encouraged his daughter in literary pursuits. Godwin published Mary's light verse; "Mounseer Nongtongpaw" was issued in 1808 and was later pirated in the United States. Her enduring mythological hero was Prometheus, the same god whose name becomes the subtitle for *Frankenstein*. Mary was also given considerable access to the diverse reading matter in Godwin's own library.

Another important part of her education consisted of family outings to adult lectures, theaters, and other events in London. When she was only five years old, she observed the first parachute jump in England. Mary Godwin had the additional advantage of being able to travel. Her education was also enhanced by a multitude of illustrious visitors to the Godwin residence, including Wordsworth, the painters Thomas Lawrence and James Northcote, the actor-manager Charles Kemble, the scientist Humphrey Davy, and Maria Edgeworth.

Early in June 1822, Mary suffered a miscarriage and only survived because Percy immediately immersed her in a bath of freezing water to staunch the bleeding. Then on July 8, 1822, the final tragedy of their marriage occurred when Percy and Edward Williams drowned in a storm during a boating trip. The boat they were on was new and had been christened the *Don Juan* by Byron. The loss was a defining moment for Mary. The consequence of her husband's untimely death left a burden of guilt, and Mary alleviated her trauma by publishing Shelley's poems and writing his biography. From this point on, Mary Shelley was driven to write different fictionalized versions of her life with Percy. However, her plans to write a formal biography of her husband never came to fruition, mainly because she could never have gotten her father to sanction it. On October 2, 1822, Mary began to write what she referred to as her "Journal of Sorrow," in which she approached the painful subject of the terms on which she and Percy had parted and, in so doing, constructed a romantic fiction, a story that was happy yet troubled:

> For eight years I communicated with unlimited freedom with one whose genius, far transcending mine, awakened & guided my thoughts. . . . Now I am alone! Oh, how alone. . . . How often during those happy days, happy though chequered, I thought how superiorly gifted I had been in being united to one to whom I could unveil myself, & who could understand me.

In June 1824, in an attempt to restore Percy's reputation, sullied by a largely hostile public, and after expending an enormous amount of editorial effort, Mary published the *Posthumous Poems of Percy Bysshe Shelley*. However, when Percy's father, Timothy Shelley, demanded that Mary relinquish custody of all manuscript material and that the book be suppressed, or he would discontinue his financial support of Mary and his grandson, Mary capitulated to his ultimatum, withdrawing the 200 remaining copies.

The task of writing about Shelley's life continued in her next novel, *The Last Man* (published in 1826), which celebrated her experience as part of a very gifted and intellectual company of Shelley and Byron. The latter had died in April 1824 in Missolonghi during his attempt to aid the Greeks in their struggle for independence, although it was not until May that news of his death had reached England. Mary reflected on the death of these two luminaries while she, at twenty-six years old, was "doomed to live on seeing all expire before her . . . in the condition of an aged person," all her old friends having died. *The Last Man* takes place on a vast scale and moves through the destruction of humanity by war and plague until only one man remains. A far lesser work than the seminal *Frankenstein*, it is still affecting and conceptually powerful; nor was *The Last Man* without its literary and cultural influences. Foremost among these would be Byron himself. Before leaving Italy, Mary spent a good deal of time transcribing Byron's poetry, in which she would have confronted his ideas on the decline of civilization, a notion that was influenced by his reading of the work of the French geologist Georges Cuvier. *The Last Man* may also have been influenced by the work of the German poet and dramatist Johann

Schiller, whom both Shelleys had read. Schiller had prophesied the fragmentation of society in apocalyptic terms as "a patching together of a vast number of lifeless parts [from which] a collective mechanical life results." Thomas Malthus's *Essay on the Principles of Population* struck a similar doomsday tone, the author warning of the catastrophic consequences that would result from the overpopulation of cities. Malthus's *Essay* first appeared in 1798, and, by 1817, his work was in its fifth edition. Significantly, in *The Last Man*, the deaths of the Byron and Shelley characters, both of whom are portrayed as irremediably flawed, are not from the plague that wipes out the rest of humankind but instead follow the tragedies of their real lives. At the time, like many of Mary Shelley's works, it was mocked on the grounds of its author's gender, "The Last Woman" being the cruel and chauvinistic title of one review.

Following Percy's death, Mary returned to England with her son, Percy Florence. Money continued to be a constant problem, despite Percy having been the heir to a rich baronetcy and Percy Florence becoming the sole heir in 1826 following the death of Percy Bysshe's elder half-brother Charles. Mary was by then earning her living as an early Victorian woman of letters, and she occasionally hovered on the brink of poverty. Added to her financial woes was her own scandalous past, which, despite the anxious conformity of manner in which she raised her son, continued to plague her so that she never became entirely assimilated into the middle-class mainstream. Finally, her depressive tendencies meant that she felt slights and social rejections keenly, and relations marked by conflict and ultimate estrangement far outweighed those friendships in which others were happy to accept Mary's own terms. In the 1840s, Mary Shelley was subjected to two particularly cruel blackmail attempts. In 1845 an itinerant Italian political rebel, who Mary had initially supported both emotionally and financially, attempted to extort money from her on the basis of some affectionate letters she had written to him. A year later, Thomas Medwin, an old friend of Shelley, threatened Mary with the publication of a life of Percy that would expose some of the obfuscations and distortions Shelley's friends and admirers had considered necessary to promote in order to win public recognition for the poet. In her later years, Mary's depression would be exacerbated by an undiagnosed brain tumor. She died in 1851 at the home of her son and his wife.

PERSONAL

The opinions represented here, attempting to define Mary Shelley's personality and demeanor, are all positive, ranging from evaluations of her character, appearance, and social graces to her writing abilities. There is one notable exception, however, in the bitter exchange between Mary Shelley's father-in-law, Sir Timothy Shelley, and Mary's rejoinder to his biting criticism. In response to Sir Timothy's accusation that Mary is responsible for Percy Shelley's estrangement from his family and obligations as well as being morally suspect for having been a part of Percy's life while he was still married to his first wife, Mary in turn accuses Sir Timothy of being mean-spirited in his willingness to offer assistance to a stranger who will take charge of his grandson. The commentary from another family member, however, her father, William Godwin, is in the form of a loving and supportive letter in which he encourages her not to be despondent about her circumstances and to remain independent, offering what financial assistance he can provide. Godwin also firmly believes that *Frankenstein* is a masterpiece, all the more impressive given her age at the time of writing it, and attributes her success to her pursuing a diligent reading program.

Percy Bysshe Shelley's "Dedication: to Mary ___ ___" was written in 1817 as a preface to a poem titled "The Revolt of Islam." It can best be characterized as a panegyric—a poem written in praise of an individual. In essence, Shelley's poem, which recalls events from their life together, speaks to Mary as a partner and soul mate. In the first stanza, in lines that are influenced by Spenser's *Faerie Queen*, Percy refers to his homecoming as that of a knight returning to his queen. "And I return to thee, mine own heart's home; / As to his Queen some victor Knight of Faery, / Earning bright spoils for her enchanted dome." Percy had been away from Mary for some time and returned once he had finished the poem, his "summer task [now] ended." Addressing Mary as his truest friend, Percy views her as the healing balm to his overwhelming feelings of loneliness and despair, while acknowledging her courage in defying convention and bitter social criticism in order to be with him. "Thou Friend, whose presence on my wintry heart / Fell, like bright Spring upon some herbless plain; / How beautiful and calm and free thou wert / In thy young wisdom, when the mortal chain / Of Custom thou didst burst and rend in twain. / . . . Let scorn be not repaid with scorn." Written at a time before their children died, Percy tells Mary how grateful he is to have achieved a time of peace and contentment in his life. "And from thy side two gentle babes are born / To fill our home with smiles, and thus are we / Most fortunate beneath life's beaming morn; / And these delights, and thou, have been to me / The parents of the Song I consecrate to thee," he writes, concluding that, despite the troubled world around them, they can look back as "two tranquil stars."

Turning our attention to the positive reviews, Edward Trelawny, an English writer and close friend of the Shelleys and of Byron, praises Mary Shelley as a "rare genius, striking in looks and intellectual abilities," while noting her exceptionally accomplished use of language. Robert Dale Owen finds her to be quite different from the radical he expected, commenting on her congeniality, sympathy, and femininity, a young woman mature beyond her years. Mary Cowden Clarke extols Mary Shelley's physical attributes and demeanor, seeing the author as a decorous young woman who always presented herself as a mature intellectual, patiently considering what others had to say. Clarke's commentary includes a detailed description of the most minute of physical attributes, making much of Mary's hands: "her exquisitely-formed, white, dimpled, small hands" with fingers that "tapered into tips as slender and delicate as those in a Vandyk portrait." Florence Ashton Marshall praises Mary Shelley's beauty of character, her ability to mellow with the passage of time, even though her perspective on life was not rooted in the conventional world. Most significantly, in addressing the issue of Mary's spiritual sensibility, Marshall maintains that, while neither her life nor her writings should be judged according to traditional notions of religious affiliation or biblical associations, her spirituality was nevertheless solid and firmly anchored in a belief in God and an afterlife, despite Percy Shelley's atheism. Marshall also raises the matter that repeatedly marks early criticism of Mary Shelley, namely the extent to which she was influenced by her poet husband. From Marshall's perspective, Mary had a positive influence on Percy vis-à-vis her patient and nurturing nature, which served as a foil to Percy's more extravagant and emotional personality. "The indirect, unconscious power of elevation of character is great, and not even a Shelley but must be the better for association with it. . . . We owe him, in part," she writes, "to her."

Percy Bysshe Shelley "Dedication: to Mary _____ " (1817)

There is no danger to a man, that knows
What life and death is: there's not any law
Exceeds his knowledge; neither is it lawful
That he should stoop to any other law.
                    (Chapman)

So now my summer task is ended, Mary,
    And I return to thee, mine own heart's home;
As to his Queen some victor Knight of Faery,
    Earning bright spoils for her enchanted dome;
    Nor thou disdain, that ere my fame become
A star among the stars of mortal night,
    If it indeed may cleave its natal gloom,
Its doubtful promise thus I would unite
With thy beloved name, thou Child of love and light.

The toil which stole from thee so many an hour,
    Is ended,—and the fruit is at thy feet!
No longer where the woods to frame a bower
    With interlaced branches mix and meet,
    Or where with sound like many voices sweet,
Waterfalls leap among wild islands green,
    Which framed for my lone boat a lone retreat
Of moss-grown trees and weeds, shall I be seen:
But beside thee, where still my heart has ever been.

Thoughts of great deeds were mine, dear Friend, when first
    The clouds which wrap this world from youth did pass.
I do remember well the hour which burst
    My spirit's sleep: a fresh May-dawn it was,
    When I walked forth upon the glittering grass,
And wept, I knew not why; until there rose
    From the near schoolroom, voices, that, alas!
Were but one echo from a world of woes—
The harsh and grating strife of tyrants and of foes.

And then I clasped my hands and looked around—
    —But none was near to mock my streaming eyes,

Which poured their warm drops on the sunny ground—
  So, without shame, I spake:—'I will be wise,
  And just, and free, and mild, if in me lies
Such power, for I grow weary to behold
  The selfish and the strong still tyrannise
Without reproach or check.' I then controlled
My tears, my heart grew calm, and I was meek and bold.

And from that hour did I with earnest thought
  Heap knowledge from forbidden mines of lore,
Yet nothing that my tyrants knew or taught
  I cared to learn, but from that secret store
  Wrought linked armour for my soul, before
It might walk forth to war among mankind;
  Thus power and hope were strengthened more and more
Within me, till there came upon my mind
A sense of loneliness, a thirst with which I pined.

Alas, that love should be a blight and snare
  To those who seek all sympathies in one!—
Such once I sought in vain; then black despair,
  The shadow of a starless night, was thrown
  Over the world in which I moved alone:—
Yet never found I one not false to me,
  Hard hearts, and cold, like weights of icy stone
Which crushed and withered mine, that could not be
Aught but a lifeless clod, until revived by thee.

Thou Friend, whose presence on my wintry heart
  Fell, like bright Spring upon some herbless plain;
How beautiful and calm and free thou wert
  In thy young wisdom, when the mortal chain
  Of Custom thou didst burst and rend in twain,
And walked as free as light the clouds among,
  Which many an envious slave then breathed in vain
From his dim dungeon, and my spirit sprung
To meet thee from the woes which had begirt it long!

No more alone through the world's wilderness,
  Although I trod the paths of high intent,

I journeyed now: no more companionless,
    Where solitude is like despair, I went.—
    There is the wisdom of a stern content
When Poverty can blight the just and good,
    When Infamy dares mock the innocent,
    And cherished friends turn with the multitude
To trample: this was ours, and we unshaken stood!

Now has descended a serener hour,
    And with inconstant fortune, friends return;
Though suffering leaves the knowledge and the power
    Which says:—Let scorn be not repaid with scorn.
    And from thy side two gentle babes are born
To fill our home with smiles, and thus are we
    Most fortunate beneath life's beaming morn;
And these delights, and thou, have been to me
The parents of the Song I consecrate to thee.

Is it that now my inexperienced fingers
    But strike the prelude of a loftier strain?
Or, must the lyre on which my spirit lingers
    Soon pause in silence, ne'er to sound again,
    Though it might shake the Anarch Custom's reign,
And charm the minds of men to Truth's own sway
    Holier than was Amphion's? I would fain
Reply in hope—but I am worn away,
And Death and Love are yet contending for their prey.

And what art thou? I know, but dare not speak:
    Time may interpret to his silent years.
Yet in the paleness of thy thoughtful cheek,
    And in the light thine ample forehead wears,
    And in thy sweetest smiles, and in thy tears,
And in thy gentle speech, a prophecy
    Is whispered, to subdue my fondest fears:
And through thine eyes, even in thy soul I see
A lamp of vestal fire burning internally.

They say that thou wert lovely from thy birth,
    Of glorious parents, thou aspiring Child.

I wonder not—for One then left this earth
   Whose life was like a setting planet mild,
   Which clothed thee in the radiance undefiled
Of its departing glory; still her fame
   Shines on thee, through the tempests dark and wild
Which shake these latter days; and thou canst claim
The shelter, from thy Sire, of an immortal name.

One voice came forth from many a mighty spirit,
   Which was the echo of three thousand years;
And the tumultuous world stood mute to hear it,
   As some lone man who in a desert hears
   The music of his home:—unwonted fears
Fell on the pale oppressors of our race,
   And Faith, and Custom, and low-thoughted cares,
Like thunder-stricken dragons, for a space
Left the torn human heart, their food and dwelling-place.

Truth's deathless voice pauses among mankind!
   If there must be no response to my cry—
If men must rise and stamp with fury blind
   On his pure name who loves them,—thou and I,
   Sweet friend! can look from our tranquillity
Like lamps into the world's tempestuous night,—
   Two tranquil stars, while clouds are passing by
Which wrap them from the foundering seaman's sight,
That burn from year to year with unextinguished light.

—Percy Bysshe Shelley,
"Dedication: to Mary _____ _____,"
The Revolt of Islam, 1817

SIR TIMOTHY SHELLEY (1823)

Mrs. Shelley was, I have been told, the intimate friend of my son in the lifetime of his first wife, and to the time of her death, and in no small degree, as I suspect, estranged my son's mind from his family, and all his first duties in life; with that impression on my mind, I cannot agree with your Lordship that, though my son was unfortunate, Mrs. Shelley is innocent; on the contrary, I think that her conduct was the very reverse of what it ought to have been, and I must, therefore, decline all interference in matters in which Mrs. Shelley is interested. As to the child, I am inclined to afford the means of a suitable protection and care of him in this country, if he shall be placed with a person I shall approve; but your Lordship will allow me to say that the means I can furnish will be limited, as I have important duties to perform towards others, which I cannot forget.

—Sir Timothy Shelley, letter to Lord Byron, February 6, 1823, cited in Florence Ashton Marshall, *The Life and Letters of Mary Wollstonecraft Shelley*, 1889, vol. 2, p. 66

Mary Shelley (1823)

It appears to me that the mode in which Sir Timothy Shelley expresses himself about my child plainly shows by what mean principles he would be actuated. He does not offer him an asylum in his own house, but a beggarly provision under the care of a stranger.

Setting aside that, I would not part with him. Something is due to me. I should not live ten days separated from him. If it were necessary for me to die for his benefit the sacrifice would be easy; but his delicate frame requires all a mother's solicitude; nor shall he be deprived of my anxious love and assiduous attention to his happiness while I have it in my power to bestow it on him; not to mention that his future respect for his excellent Father and his moral well-being greatly depend upon his being away from the immediate influence of his relations.

This, perhaps, you will think nonsense, and it is inconceivably painful to me to discuss a point which appears to me as clear as noonday; besides I lose all—all honourable station and name—when I admit that I am not a fitting person to take charge of my infant. The insult is keen; the pretence of heaping it upon me too gross; the advantage to them, if the will came to be contested, would be too immense.

As a matter of feeling, I would never consent to it. I am said to have a cold heart; there are feelings, however, so strongly implanted in my nature that, to root them out, life will go with it.

—Mary Shelley, letter to Lord Byron,
February 1823, cited in Florence Ashton
Marshall, *The Life and Letters of Mary
Wollstonecraft Shelley,* 1889, vol. 2, p. 67

WILLIAM GODWIN (1823)

Do not, I entreat you, be cast down about your worldly circumstances.
You certainly contain within yourself the means of your subsistence. Your
talents are truly extraordinary. *Frankenstein* is universally known, and though
it can never be a book for vulgar reading, is everywhere respected. It is the
most wonderful work to have been written at twenty years of age that I
ever heard of. You are now five and twenty, and, most fortunately, you have
pursued a course of reading, and cultivated your mind, in a manner the most
admirably adapted to make you a great and successful author. If you cannot be
independent, who should be?

Your talents, as far as I can at present discern, are turned for the writing of
fictitious adventures.

If it shall ever happen to you to be placed in sudden and urgent want of a
small sum, I entreat you to let me know immediately; we must see what I can
do. We must help one another.

—William Godwin, letter to
Mary Shelley, February 18, 1823,
cited in Florence Ashton Marshall,
*The Life and Letters of Mary Wollstonecraft
Shelley,* 1889, vol. 2, pp. 68–69

EDWARD JOHN TRELAWNY (1858)

Such a rare pedigree of genius was enough to interest me in her, irrespective
of her own merits as an authoress. The most striking feature in her face was
her calm, grey eyes; she was rather under the English standard of woman's
height, very fair and light-haired, witty, social, and animated in the society of
friends, though mournful in solitude; like Shelley, though in a minor degree,
she had the power of expressing her thoughts in varied and appropriate words,
derived from familiarity with the works of our vigorous old writers. Neither
of them used obsolete or foreign words. This command of our language
struck me the more as contrasted with the scanty vocabulary used by ladies

in society, in which a score of poor hackneyed phrases suffice to express all that is felt or considered proper to reveal.

—Edward John Trelawny, *Recollections of the Last Days of Shelley and Byron*, 1858

ROBERT DALE OWEN (1874)

I expected to find Mrs. Shelley a radical reformer, probably self-asserting, somewhat aggressive, and at war with the world; more decidedly heterodox in religion and morals than I myself was; endorsing and enforcing the extreme opinions of her father and mother, and (as I then understood them) of her husband. 1 found her very different from my preconceptions.

Genial, gentle, sympathetic, thoughtful and matured in opinion beyond her years, for she was then but twenty-nine; essentially liberal in politics, ethics, and theology, indeed, yet devoid alike of stiff prejudice against the old or ill-considered prepossession in favor of the new; and, above all, womanly, in the best sense, in every sentiment and instinct; she impressed me also as a person with warm social feelings, dependent for happiness on loving encouragement; needing a guiding and sustaining hand.

I felt all this, rather than reasoned it out, during our too brief acquaintance; and few women have ever attracted me so much in so short a time. Had I remained in London I am sure we should have been dear friends. She wrote me several charming letters to America.

In person, she was of middle height and graceful figure. Her face, though not regularly beautiful, was comely and spiritual, of winning expression, and with a look of inborn refinement as well as culture. It had a touch of sadness when at rest; yet when it woke up in animated conversation, one could see that underneath there was a bright, cheerful, even playful nature, at variance, I thought, with depressing circumstances and isolated position.

—Robert Dale Owen, *Threading My Way: An Autobiography*, 1874, pp. 322–323

MARY COWDEN CLARKE (1878)

Mary Wollstonecraft Godwin Shelley, with her well-shaped, golden-haired head, almost always a little bent and drooping; her marble-white shoulders and arms statuesquely visible in the perfectly plain black velvet dress, which the customs of that time allowed to be cut low, and which her own taste adopted (for neither she nor her sister-in-sorrow ever wore the conventional "widow's weeds" and "widow's cap"); her thoughtful, earnest eyes; her short upper lip and intellectually curved mouth, with a certain close-compressed and decisive expression while she listened, and a relaxation into fuller redness and mobility when speaking; her exquisitely-formed, white, dimpled, small hands, with rosy palms, and plumply commencing fingers, that tapered into tips as slender and delicate as those in a Vandyk portrait—all remain palpably present to memory. Another peculiarity in Mrs. Shelley's hand was its singular flexibility, which permitted her bending the fingers back so as almost to approach the portion of her arm above her wrist. She once did this smilingly and repeatedly, to amuse the girl who was noting its whiteness and pliancy, and who now, as an old woman, records its remarkable beauty.

—Mary Cowden Clarke, *Recollections of Writers*, 1878, pp. 37–38

Florence Ashton Marshall (1889)

The true success of Mary Shelley's life was not, therefore, the intellectual triumph of which, during her youth, she had loved to dream, and which at one time seemed to be actually within her grasp, but the moral success of beauty of character. To those people—a daily increasing number in this tired world—who erect the natural grace of animal spirits to the rank of the highest virtue, this success may appear hardly worth the name. Yet it was a very real victory. Her nature was not without faults or tendencies which, if undisciplined, might have developed into faults, but every year she lived seemed to mellow and ripen her finer qualities, while blemishes or weaknesses were suppressed or overcome, and finally disappeared altogether.

As to her theological views, about which the most contradictory opinions have been expressed, it can but be said that nothing in Mrs. Shelley's writings gives other people the right to formulate for her any dogmatic opinions at all. Brought up in a purely rationalistic creed, her education had of course, no tinge of what is known as "personal religion," and it must be repeated here that none of her acts and views were founded, or should be judged as if they were founded on Biblical commands or prohibitions. That the temper of her mind, so to speak, was eminently religious there can be no doubt; that she believed in God and a future state there are many allusions to show. Perhaps no one, having lived with the so-called atheist, Shelley, could have accepted the idea of the limitation, or the extinction of intelligence and goodness.

Her liberality of mind, however, was rewarded by abuse from some of her acquaintance, because her toleration was extended even to the orthodox.

Her moral opinions, had they ever been formulated, which they never were, would have approximated closely to those of Mary Wollstonecraft, limited, however, by an inability, like her father's, *not* to see both sides of a question, and also by the severest and most elevated standard of moral purity, of personal faith and loyalty. To be judged by such a standard she would have regarded as a woman's highest privilege. To claim as a "woman's right" any licence, any lowering of the standard of duty in these matters, would have been to her incomprehensible and impossible. But, with all this, she discriminated. Her standard was not that of the conventional world.

At every risk, as she says, she befriended those whom she considered "victims to the social system." It was a difficult course; for, while her acquaintance of the "advanced" type accused her of cowardice and worldliness for not asserting herself as a champion of universal liberty, there were more who were ready to decry her for her friendly relations with Countess Guiccioli, Lady Mountcashel, and others not named here; to say nothing of Clare, to whom much of her happiness had been sacrificed. She refrained from pronouncing judgment, but reserved her liberty of action, and in all doubtful cases gave others the benefit of the doubt, and this without respect of persons. She would not excommunicate a humble individual for what was passed over in a man or woman of genius; nor condemn a woman for what, in a man, might be excused, or might even add to his social reputation. Least of all would she secure her own position by shunning those whose case had once been hers, and who in their after life had been less fortunate than she. Pure herself, she could be charitable, and she could be just.

The influence of such a wife on Shelley's more vehement, visionary temperament can hardly be over-estimated. Their moods did not always suit or coincide; each, at times, made the other suffer. It could not be otherwise with two natures so young, so strong, and so individual. But, if forbearance may have been sometimes called for on the one hand, and on the other a charity which is kind and thinks no evil, it was only a part of that discipline from which the married life of geniuses is not exempt, and which tests the temper and quality of the metal it tries; an ordeal from which two noble natures come forth the purer and the stronger.

The indirect, unconscious power of elevation of character is great, and not even a Shelley but must be the better for association with it, not even he but must be the nobler, "yea, three times less unworthy" through the love of such a woman as Mary. He would not have been all he was without her sustaining and refining influence; without the constant sense that in loving him she loved his ideals also. We owe him, in part, to her.

Love—the love of Love—was Shelley's life and creed. This, in Mary's creed, was interpreted as love of Shelley. By all the rest she strove to do her duty, but, when the end came, that survived as the one great fact of her life—a fact she might have uttered in words like his—

> And where is Truth?
> On tombs; for such to thee
> Has been my heart; and thy dead memory
> Has lain from (girlhood), many a changeful year,
> Unchangingly preserved, and buried there.

—Florence Ashton Marshall, *The Life and Letters of Mary Wollstonecraft Shelley*, 1889, vol. 2, pp. 322–325

GENERAL

The criticism contained in these general assessments of Mary Shelley examines her personal life and the many ways in which it influenced her writing. The commentary expresses a range of positive to negative opinions and more often than not is preoccupied with the influence of Percy Bysshe Shelley on his wife's writings. While discussing her literary talents, these writers express opinions on several works and are therefore separate from the reviews of individual works that follow.

George Gilfillan begins with an idealized portrait of Mary and Percy Bysshe Shelley's marriage, a relationship that he believes to have been inevitable, going so far as to cite Shelley's doctrine of preexistence in discussing a marriage that he believes was foreordained, while framing the beauty of their relationship in extravagantly lush imagery. "They met at last, like two drops of water—like two flames of fire—like two beautiful clouds which have crossed the moon, the sky and all its stars, to hold their midnight assignation over a favorite and lonely river." Gilfillan also muses on the romantic influence of her time at Broughty Ferry. As to the issue of Percy's influence on Mary Shelley's writing, though Gilfillan extols Mary's genius, he is quick to point out that it in no way compares to that of Percy's, stating that she lacks his subtlety, spontaneity, and breadth of imagination "and is never caught up (like Ezekiel by his lock of hair) into the same rushing whirlwind of inspiration." Gilfillan finds Mary's creativity to be tedious and narrowly focused, consumed with the gloomier aspects of nature and devoid of a sense of humor. Though he believes *Frankenstein* exhibits her true strengths in exploring the more dismal aspects of human nature, he cites *The Last Man* and *Perkin Warbeck* as failures. As for *Frankenstein*, Gilfillan is willing to bestow accolades for her portrait of a monster that had no equal in the literature that came before her, congratulating her on the sublime conception of a creature who is at once physically terrifying while at the same time being pathetic and affectionate in his abject loneliness. Still he does not refrain from pointing out the more preposterous elements of the story such as the monster's education. In the final analysis, Gilfillan finds *Frankenstein* exceptional given the youthful age of its author, while at the same time he deems it a work that represents the pinnacle of her writing, a complexity and clarity of vision that was never again to be achieved in subsequent novels. The rest of Gilfillan's essay can be characterized as a tribute to Percy Shelley at the expense of Mary, portraying her as a diminutive version of her husband, "the resemblance which Laone did to Laon," a reference to Canto X of Percy Shelley's "The Revolt of Islam": "Let Laon and Laone on that pyre, / Linked tight with burning brass, perish!— then pray / That with this sacrifice the withering ire / Of Heaven may be appeased." Always melodramatic, Gilfillan argues that those who came in contact with such a rarified and visionary poet as Percy Bysshe could not help but have their originality subordinated to his, a supposition that he then offers as an explanation for the trauma of Mary losing her husband while he was in his prime. Gilfillan believes that Shelley's early demise left Mary with no other recourse than to idolize him in death and goes so far as to give us a somewhat histrionic account of Mary rushing to the scene of the tragic accident.

> But in the mind of "Mary" there must lurk a feeling of a still stronger kind toward that element which *he,* next to herself, had of all things most passionately loved—which he trusted as a parent . . . how can she, without horror, hear the boom of its waves, or look without a shudder, either at its stormy or its smiling countenance? What a picture she presents to our imagination, running with dishevelled hair, along the seashore, questioning all she met if they could tell her of her husband—nay, shrieking out the dreadful question to the surges, which, like a dumb murderer, had done the deed, but could not utter the confession!

Unlike Gilfillan, Thornton Hunt focuses on Mary Shelley's positive influence on Percy, her tranquil nature serving as a restorative to his moral condition. Hunt presents a flattering and sympathetic portrait of Mary and the trials and tribulations of her early years. "She was, indeed, herself a woman of extraordinary power, of heart as well as head. Many circumstances conspired to conceal some of her natural faculties." Hunt identifies Mary's affinity for and facility with academic study as a male trait, instilled at an early age. He admires her skills in the genre of historical fiction in such works as *Valperga* but is especially effusive in his praise of *Frankenstein*, a work that demonstrates her "daring originality." Hunt asserts that her genius is derived from her extraordinary parents and aided, of course, by her association with Shelley, as evidenced by a deeper understanding of the issues that most interested her husband. Hunt also finds a greater magnanimity and maturity manifest in her, as the result of losing her husband in a tragic accident.

Writing on *Frankenstein* and other works by Mary Shelley, Helen Moore finds that the sum total of her literary output does not do justice to her intellectual prowess, with the result that Moore is generally dissatisfied with most of Mary's writing, except for *Frankenstein* and a few short biographical pieces on Tasso and Galileo. As for *Frankenstein*, Helen Moore has the highest praise and maintains that it is a masterpiece, citing its immediate commercial success and the fact that it engaged both littérateurs and ordinary readers alike as further proof of its uniqueness.

> We have intimated that there was a dual quality in it, to which it owed its singular power and place in literature. One element is doubtless the horror of the tale and the weird fancy of the author's imagination in the ordinary acceptation of the word. But it is to an entirely different department of mental conception that we must look for the secret of its peculiar influence.... Profoundly considered, it is that function of the mind which formulates, as though real, a state of things which if present would so appear. It is the power of projecting the mind into unhappened realities.

Moore spends considerable time explaining the allegorical aspects of *Frankenstein*, the hidden story submerged beneath the ostensible narrative, and views the novel as a tale of a man's inclination to subvert the natural order of things and to supplant it with his own conception. The work is, therefore, an account of the dire consequences resulting from an extreme hubris. "[T]he chief allegorical interest in the narrative concerns itself about that tendency in the human being to discard the established order of things and to create for itself a new and independent existence." Moore also argues that *Frankenstein*, written by the daughter of highly unconventional parents, most especially Mary Wollstonecraft, is a political allegory as well. "The whole story is but the elaboration of the embarrassment and dangers which flow from departure from the ordinary course of nature; ... She has not failed to learn the lesson of her mother's history; time analyzes rather than destroys." Moore also discusses the circumstances at the Villa Diodati in the summer of 1816 and the types of ghost stories the circle of friends was reading. In her assessment of

Frankenstein, Moore carefully examines its generic qualities so as to be able to classify Mary Shelley's masterpiece.

With respect to *Valperga*, Moore makes it clear that the only justification for reading this novel is "the curiosity to know Mrs. Shelley's most serious endeavor at romance." Declaring the work limpid and utterly unable to engage the reader, Moore nevertheless grants it importance on the grounds that it is an exposition of Mary Shelley's cognitive abilities and mental status.

> As an illustration of its author's mental and moral development it has a place and a purpose. For although she has a certain sympathetic insight into the imaginative, the emotional; although she delights in the deeply tragical,—page follows page of unmitigated melancholy—it is totally without the light and shade which would make us feel the pathos of the story intensely. Indeed, one could not call it pathetic; it is simply tragical.

Moore further draws an analogy between Victor Frankenstein and Beatrice, declaring that both characters exhibit aberrant and skewed, narcissistic behavior. "Like Frankenstein, Beatrice is the result of an abnormal and one-sided development. Like him, she creates for herself a strange and unnatural state of existence. Like him, she suffers the fatal consequence of an intense absorption to one idea,—the idea of her divine inspiration." Thus Moore, it can be concluded, views *Valperga* as another allegory of the individual who pits herself against society, in this instance flaunting orthodox religion.

Lucy Madox Rossetti focuses on three of Mary Shelley's novels, *The Last Man*, *Lodore* and *Falkner*. Rossetti finds the theme of *The Last Man*, about the outbreak of a devastating plague in London in the distant future of the twenty-first century, to have left a wide field in which Mary Shelley's imagination took flight. Most impressive for Rossetti is the description of a desolate landscape and the meticulous chronology through which the fortunes of Lionel Verney, who will become the last man, are traced through various phases of the plague as it spreads across England. Perhaps most poignant in Rossetti's review of this futuristic tale of disease gone out of control is the terrible price that humans must pay in seeking desperate companionship yet at a distance deemed safe from exposure to infection and death. Rossetti also identifies the correlation between Mary Shelley's travels, especially regarding her visit to the Cumaean cave, and this work of science fiction. The Cumaean Sibyl was the priestess presiding over the Apollonian oracle at Cumae, a Greek colony located near Naples, Italy. According to Virgil, she wrote her prognostications on leaves and scattered them among the hundred mouths to her cave, where others could find them and read her prophecies or from where they would be scattered by the wind.

> Mrs. Shelley avails herself of reminiscences of her own travelling with Shelley some few years before; and we pass the places noted in her diary.... At one moment a dying acrobat, deserted by his companions, is seen bounding in the air behind a hedge in the dusk of evening. At another, a black figure mounted on a horse, which only shows itself after dark, to cause apprehensions soon calmed by the death of the poor wanderer, who wished only for distant companionship through dread of contagion.

In her introduction to *The Last Man*, Mary describes her visit to this site:

> We visited the so called Elysian Fields and Avernus: and wandered through various ruined temples, baths, and classic spots; at length we entered the gloomy cavern of the Cumaean Sibyl.... [It was] a large, desert, dark cavern, which the Lazzeroni assured us was the Sibyl's Cave. We were sufficiently disappointed—Yet we examined it with care, as if its blank, rocky walls could still bear trace of celestial visitant.

With respect to *Lodore*, Rossetti sees a very definite link between the events of the novel and events surrounding the estrangement of Percy Bysshe Shelley from his first wife, Harriet Westbrook. "She is charmingly described, and shows a great deal of insight on Mary's part into the life of fashionable people of her time, which then, perhaps more than now, was the favourite theme with novelists." Among the other autobiographical elements she identifies are the complex financial dealings in the novel, which bear a strong resemblance to Percy Bysshe's financial troubles, and Mary's feelings toward Emilia Viviani, a woman with whom a seventeen-year-old Percy was once romantically involved. Most impressive to Rossetti are the character portraits in *Lodore,* which she sees as both drawing from and providing a window into the brilliant circle of poets and thinkers that Mary Shelley was privileged to call her friends.

As for *Falkner*, Mary's last novel, Rossetti's opinion is that this work exhibits a lack of inspiration attributable to Mary's ill health and dejection while writing it. Still, Rossetti again expresses an appreciation for the way in which the narrative affords us an opportunity to engage with the more inspired aspects of Mary's life, as evidenced by the beauty of certain evocative passages. The story of "a little deserted child in a picturesque Cornish village," who in turn becomes the instrument of Falkner's salvation, is a highly imaginative work. Rossetti spends a great deal of time summarizing the plot and admires the novel for its expansive scope, powerful emotions, and insight into human nature, though she feels its impact is somewhat attenuated by its daunting three-volume length, a story inspired by Godwin's *Caleb Williams*, in which a man leads a life shrouded in secrets. She asserts that "Elizabeth's grandfather in his dotage is quite a photograph from life; old Oswig Raby, who was more shrivelled with narrowness of mind than with age, but who felt himself and his house, the oldest in England, of more importance than aught else he knew of."

Richard Garnett also takes up the theme of influence. Believing Godwin had a more profound influence on *Frankenstein* than Percy Bysshe did, he easily recognizes the individual expression that marks her work, despite its extravagant flaws, declaring that she possesses "the insight of genius." It is highly significant and insightful that Garnett goes so far as to compare the monster to Shakespeare's hideous and revengeful Caliban and the misshapen malcontent Richard the Third, stating that Mary Shelley has brought these characters into a contemporary context. "The conception of a character at once justly execrable and truly pitiable is altogether modern. Richard the Third and Caliban make some approach towards it but the former is too self-sufficing in his valour and his villainy to be deeply pitied, and the latter too senseless and brutal." Garnett sees Mary Shelley as offering a balance to these two Shakespearean characters, while also noting other contemporary manifestations of this type of character in alluding to *The Hunchback of Notre Dame*, a work that he believes suffers from being too heavily influenced by *Frankenstein*. With respect to Mary's subsequent writings, Garnett constantly refers to the "languor" that besets her later works, attributing this enervation to the tragic death of her infant son in 1819. While he believes *Valperga* presents some beautiful passages, it is, nevertheless, "laboriously dug."

C.H. Herford also focuses on Godwin's influence on *Frankenstein*, particularly his novel, *St. Leon*, praising Shelley's work for its enthusiastic inquiry into philosophic and scientific matters. The critic then pays tribute to Mary Shelley's daring to continue a Renaissance tradition, stating that the gothic romances of Lewis and others were negations of weightier concerns. As to Mary's subsequent forays into historical romance, Herford finds them lacking, while *The Last Man* is indicative of her feelings of desolation. "*The Last Man* (1826) which so deeply impressed the not very susceptible Jefferson Hogg, has a pathetic significance as shadowing her own tragic loneliness,—the 'loneliness of Crusoe'—as she herself long afterwards declared it to have been."

Clara Helen Whitmore's brief essay on Mary Shelley begins with a discussion of the extraordinarily powerful nature of *Frankenstein,* which she maintains is derived, most especially, from the fact that the monster is so closely allied to human nature, eliciting our sympathy despite his acts of vengeance. As to *Valperga*, Whitmore celebrates the two heroines, Euthanasia and Beatrice, while expressing profound respect for the latter's deep spiritual convictions. "But more beautiful than the intellectual character of Euthanasia, is the spiritual one of Beatrice, the adopted daughter of the bishop of Ferrara, who is regarded with feelings of reverence by her countrymen, because of her prophetic powers." Her opinion of *The Last Man*, however, is far different, as Whitmore finds the plot to be awkward and the characterization weak, though she finds validity in Mary Shelley's expression of emotions. Whitmore opines that Mary's biggest error was in writing the novel in the first person. As to the next novel, *Lodore*, Whitmore's opinion is consistent with her views of *The Last Man,* though she finds the plot and characterization to be more distinct. Whitmore is particularly interested in the way in which Lady Lodore's personality evolves over the course of the narrative to resemble that of Shelley's first wife, Harriet. Finally, *Falkner* and *Perkin Warbeck* are summarily dismissed as possessing no merit.

ROBERT BROWNING (1845)

Mrs. Shelley found Italy for the first time, real Italy, at Sorrento, she says. Oh that book *(Rambles in Germany and Italy)*—does one wake or sleep? The "Mary dear" with the brown eyes, and Godwin's daughter and Shelley's wife, and who surely was something better once upon a time—and to go thro' Rome & Florence & the rest, after what I suppose to be Lady Londonderry's fashion: the intrepidity of the commonplace quite astounds me.

—Robert Browning, letter to
Elizabeth Barrett Browning,
September 11, 1845

GEORGE GILFILLAN "MRS. SHELLEY" (1848)

It is not at all to be wondered at, that two such spirits as Shelley and Mary Godwin, when they met, should become instantly attached. On his own doctrine of a state of preexistence, we might say that the marriage had been determined long before, while yet the souls were waiting in the great antenatal antechamber! They met at last, like two drops of water—like two flames of fire—like two beautiful clouds which have crossed the moon, the sky and all its stars, to hold their midnight assignation over a favorite and lonely river. Mary Godwin was an enthusiast from her childhood. She passed, by her own account, part of her youth at Broughty Ferry, in sweet and sinless reverie, among its cliffs. The place is, to us, familiar. It possesses some fine features—a bold promontory crowned with an ancient castle jutting far out the Tay, which here broadens into an arm of the ocean—a beach, in part smooth with sand, and in part paved with pebbles—cottages lying artlessly along the shore, clean, as if washed by the near sea—sandy hillocks rising behind—and westward, the river, like an inland lake, stretching around Dundee, with its fine harbor and its surmounting Law, which, in its turn, is surmounted by the far blue shapes of the gigantic Stuicknachroan and Benvoirlich. Did the bay of Spezia ever suggest to Mrs. Shelley's mind the features of the Scottish scene? That scene, seen so often, seldom fails to bring before us her image—the child, and soon to be the bride, of genius. Was she ever, like Mirza, overheard in her soliloquies, and did she bear the shame, accordingly, in blushes which still rekindle at the recollection? Did the rude fishermen of the place deem her wondrous wise, or did they deem her mad, with her wandering eye, her rapt and gleaming countenance, her light step moving to the music of her maiden meditation? The smooth sand retains no trace of her young feet—to the present race she is altogether unknown; but we have more than once seen the man, and the lover of genius, turn round and look at the spot, with warmer interest, and with brightening eye, as we told them that she had been there.

We have spoken of Mrs. Shelley's similarity in genius to her husband—we by no means think her his equal. She has not his subtlety, swiftness, wealth of imagination, and is never caught up (like Ezekiel by his lock of hair) into the same rushing whirlwind of inspiration. She has much, however, of his imaginative and of his speculative qualities—her tendency, like his, is to the romantic, the ethereal, and the terrible. The tie detaining her, as well as him, to the earth, is slender—her protest against society is his, copied out in a fine female hand—her style is carefully and successfully modelled upon his—she bears, in brief, to him, the resemblance which Laone did to Laon, which Astarte did to Manfred. Perhaps, indeed, intercourse with a being so peculiar, that those who came in contact with, either withdrew from him in hatred, or fell into the current of his being, vanquished and enthralled, has somewhat affected the originality, and narrowed the extent of her own genius. Indian widows used to fling themselves upon the funeral pyre of their husbands; she has thrown upon that of hers her mode of thought, her mould of style, her creed, her heart, her all. Her admiration of Shelley was, and is, an idolatry. Can we wonder at it? Separated from him in the prime of life, with all his faculties in the finest bloom of promise, with peace beginning to build in the crevices of his torn heart, and with fame hovering ere it stooped upon his head—separated, too, in circumstances so sudden and cruel—can we be astonished that from the wounds of love came forth the blood of worship and sacrifice? Wordsworth speaks of himself as feeling for "the Old Sea some reverential fear."

But in the mind of "Mary" there must lurk a feeling of a still stronger kind toward that element which *he,* next to herself, had of all things most passionately loved—which he trusted as a parent—to which he exposed himself, defenceless—(he could not swim, he could only soar)—which he had sung in many a strain of matchless sweetness, but which betrayed and destroyed him—how can she, without horror, hear the boom of its waves, or look without a shudder, either at its stormy or its smiling countenance? What a picture she presents to our imagination, running with dishevelled hair, along the seashore, questioning all she met if they could tell her of her husband—nay, shrieking out the dreadful question to the surges, which, like a dumb murderer, had done the deed, but could not utter the confession!

Mrs. Shelley's genius, though true and powerful, is monotonous and circumscribed—more so than even her father's—and, in this point, presents a strong contrast to her husband's, which could run along every note of the gamut—be witty or wild, satirical or sentimental, didactic or dramatic, epic or lyrical, as it pleased him. She has no wit, nor humor—little dramatic talent. Strong, clear description of the gloomier scenes of nature, or the darker passions of the mind, or of those supernatural objects which her fancy, except in her first work, somewhat *laboriously* creates, is her *forte*. Hence her reputation still rests upon *Frankenstein;* for her *Last Man, Perkin Warbeck,* &c, are far inferior, if not entirely unworthy of her talents. She unquestionably made him; but, like a mule or a monster, he has had no progeny.

Can any one have forgot the interesting account she gives of her first conception of that extraordinary story, when she had retired to rest, her fancy heated by hearing ghost tales; and when the whole circumstances of the story appeared at once before her eye, as in a camera obscura? It is ever thus, we imagine, that truly original conceptions are produced. They are cast—not wrought. They come as wholes, and not in parts. It was thus that "Tarn o' Shanter" completed, along Burns' mind, his weird and tipsy gallop in a single hour. Thus Coleridge composed the outline of his *Ancient Mariner,* in one evening walk near Nether Stowey. So rapidly rose *Frankenstein,* which, as Moore well remarks, has been one of those striking conceptions which take hold of the public mind at once and forever.

The theme is morbid and disgusting enough. The story is that of one who finds out the principle of life, constructs a monstrous being, who, because his maker fails in forming a female companion to him, ultimately murders the dearest friend of his benefactor, and, in remorse and despair, disappears amid the eternal snows of the North Pole. Nothing more preposterous than the meagre outline of the story exists in literature. But Mrs. Shelley deserves great credit, nevertheless. In the first place, she has succeeded in her delineation; she has painted this shapeless being upon the imagination of the world forever; and beside Caliban, and Hecate, and Death in Life, and all other weird and gloomy creations, this nameless, unfortunate, involuntary, gigantic unit stands. To succeed in an attempt so daring, proves at once the power of the author, and a certain value even in the original conception. To keep verging perpetually on the limit of the absurd, and to produce the while all the effects of the sublime, this takes and tasks very high faculties indeed. Occasionally, we admit, she does overstep the mark. Thus the whole scene of the monster's education in the cottage, his overhearing the reading of the *Paradise Lost,* the *Sorrows of Werter,* &c, and in this way acquiring knowledge and refined sentiments, seems unspeakably ridiculous. A Cacodemon weeping in concert with Eve or Werter is too ludicrous an idea—as absurd as though he had been represented as boarded at Capsicum Hall. But it is wonderful how delicately and gracefully Mrs. Shelley has managed the whole prodigious business. She touches pitch with a lady's glove, and is not defiled. From a whole forest of the "nettle danger" she extracts a sweet and plentiful supply of the "flower safety." With a fine female footing, she preserves the narrow path which divides the terrible from the disgusting. She unites, not in a junction of words alone, but in effect, the "horribly beautiful." Her monster is not only as Caliban appeared to Trinculo—a very pretty monster—but somewhat poetical and pathetic withal. You almost weep for him in his utter insulation. Alone! dread word, though it were to be alone in heaven! Alone! word hardly more dreadful if it were to be alone in hell!

Alone, all, all alone,
Alone on a wide, wide sea,
And never a saint took pity on
My soul in agony.

Thus wrapt around by his loneliness, as by a silent burning chain, does this gigantic creature run through the world, like a lion who has lost his mate, in a forest of fire, seeking for his kindred being, but seeking forever in vain.

He is not only alone, but alone because he has no being like him throughout the whole universe. What a solitude within a solitude!—solitude comparable only to that of the Alchemist in *St. Leon,* when he buries his last tie to humanity, in his wife's grave, and goes on his way, "friendless, friendless, alone, alone."

What a scene is the process of his creation, and especially the hour when he first began to breathe, to open his ill-favored eyes, and to stretch his ill-shapen arms, toward his terrified author, who, for the first time, becomes aware of the enormity of the mistake he has committed; who has had a giant's strength, and used it tyrannously like a giant, and who shudders and shrinks back from his own horrible handy-work! It is a type, whether intended or not, of the fate of genius, whenever it dares either to revile, or to resist, the common laws and obligations, and conditions of man and the universe. Better, better far be blasted with the lightnings of heaven, than by the recoil, upon one's own head, of one false, homeless, returning, revenging *thought.*

Scarcely second to her description of the moment when, at midnight, and under the light of a waning moon, the monster was born, is his sudden apparition upon a glacier among the high Alps. This scene strikes us the more, as it seems the fulfilment of a fear which all have felt, who have found themselves alone among such desolate regions. Who has not at times trembled lest those ghastlier and drearier places of nature, which abound in our own Highlands, should bear a different progeny from the ptarmigan, the sheep, the raven, or the eagle—lest the mountain should suddenly crown itself with a Titanic spectre, and the mist, disparting, reveal demoniac forms, and the lonely moor discover its ugly dwarf, as if dropped down from the overhanging thunder cloud—and the forest of pines show unearthly shapes sailing among their shades—and the cataract overboil with its own wild creations? Thus fitly, amid scenery like that of some dream of nightmare, on a glacier as on a throne, stands up before the eye of his own maker, the miscreation, and he cries out, "Whence and what art thou, execrable shape?"

In darkness and distance, at last, the being disappears, and the imagination dares hardly pursue him as he passes amid those congenial shapes of colossal size, terror, and mystery, which we fancy to haunt those outskirts of existence, with, behind them at midnight, "all Europe and Asia fast asleep, and before them the silent immensity and Palace of the Eternal, to which our sun is but a porch-lamp."

Altogether, the work is wonderful as the work of a girl of eighteen. She has never since fully equalled or approached its power, nor do we ever expect that she shall. One distinct addition to our original creations must be conceded her—and it is no little praise; for there are few writers of fiction who have done so much out of Germany. What are they, in this respect, to our painters—to Fuseli, with his quaint brain, so prodigal of unearthly shapes—to John Martin, who has created over his head a whole dark, frowning, but magnificent *world*—or to David Scott, our own most cherished friend, in whose studio, while standing surrounded by pictured poems of such startling originality, such austere selection of theme, and such solemn dignity of treatment, (forgetting not himself, the grave, mild, quiet, shadowy enthusiast, with his slow, deep, sepulchral tones,) you are almost tempted to exclaim, "How dreadful is this place!"

—George Gilfillan, from "Mrs. Shelley," 1848,
A Second Gallery of Literary Portraits, 1850

Thornton Hunt "Shelley" (1863)

There can be no doubt that he had profited greatly in his moral condition, as well as in his bodily health, by the greater tranquillity which he enjoyed in the society of Mary, and also by the sympathy which gave full play to his ideas, instead of diverting and disappointing them. She was, indeed, herself a woman of extraordinary power, of heart as well as head. Many circumstances conspired to conceal some of her natural faculties. She lost her mother very young; her father—speaking with great diffidence, from a very slight and imperfect knowledge—appeared to me a harsh and ungenial man. She inherited from him her thin voice, but not the steel-edged sharpness of his own; and she inherited, not from him, but from her mother, a largeness of heart that entered proportionately into the working of her mind. She had a masculine capacity for study; for, though I suspect her early schooling was irregular, she remained a student all her life, and by painstaking industry made herself acquainted with any subject that she had to handle. Her command of history and her imaginative power are shown in such books as *Valperga* and *Castruccio;* but the daring originality of her mind comes out most distinctly in her earliest published work, *Frankenstein.* Its leading idea has been ascribed to her husband, but, I am sure, unduly; and the vividness with which she has brought out the monstrous tale in all its horror, but without coarse or revolting incidents, is a proof of the genius which she inherited alike from both her parents. It is clear, also, that the society of Shelley was to her a great school, which she did not appreciate to the full until most calamitously it was taken away; and yet, of course, she could not fail to learn the greater part of what it had become to her. This again showed itself even in her appearance, after she had spent some years in Italy; for, while she had grown far more comely than she was in her mere youth, she had acquired a deeper insight into many subjects that interested Shelley, and some others; and she had learned to express the force of natural affection, which she was born to feel, but which had somehow been stunted and suppressed in her youth. In the preface to the collected edition of his works, she says: "I have the liveliest recollection of all that was done and said during the period of my knowing him. Every impression is as clear as if stamped yesterday, and I have no apprehension of any mistake in my statements, as far as they go. In other respects I am, indeed, incompetent; but I feel the importance of the task, and regard it as my most sacred duty. I endeavor to fulfil it in a manner he would himself approve; and hope in this publication to lay the first stone of a monument due to Shelley's genius, his sufferings, and his virtues." And in the postscript, written in November, 1839, she says: "At my request, the publisher has restored the omitted passages of *Queen Mab.* I now present this edition as a complete collection of my husband's poetical works, and I do not foresee that I can hereafter add to or take away a word or line." So writes the wife-editor; and then *The Poetical Works of Percy Bysshe Shelley* begin with a dedication to Harriet, restored to its place by Mary. While the biographers of Shelley are chargeable with suppression, the most straightforward and frank of all of them is Mary, who, although not insensible to the passion of jealousy, and carrying with her the painful sense of a life-opportunity not fully used, thus writes the name of Harriet the first on her husband's monument, while she has nobly abstained from telling those things that other persons should have supplied to the narrative. I have heard her accused of an over-anxiety to be admired; and something of the sort was discernible in society: it was a weakness as venial as it was purely superficial. Away from society, she was as truthful and simple a woman as I have ever met,—was as faithful a friend as the world has produced,—using that unreserved directness towards those whom she regarded with affection which is the very crowning glory of friendly intercourse. I suspect that these qualities came out in their greatest force after her calamity; for many things which she said in her regret, and passages in Shelley's own poetry, make me doubt whether little habits of temper, and possibly of a refined and exacting coquettishness, had not prevented him from acquiring so full a knowledge of her as she had of him.

—Thornton Hunt, "Shelley," *Atlantic*,
February 1863, pp. 198–199

Helen Moore "*Frankenstein*, and Other Writings" (1886)

The published books of an author bear no necessary relation to his literary work, still less are they a gauge of his intellectual life. The faculty for literary production is something apart, often possessed by those who have little worth producing, denied to those who die—as galleons sink—carrying their golden wealth with them. Of no one is this more true than of Mrs. Shelley. Her literary productions were few and disproportionate to her intellectual force; disappointing when viewed side by side with her peculiar gift of evoking the most artistic literary work in others. Her published writings comprise, *Frankenstein*, in 1818; *Valperga*, 1823; *The Last Man, 1824*; *Perkin Warbeck*, 1830; *Lodore*, 1835; and *Falkner*, 1837; the Italian and Spanish lives in *Lardner's Encyclopedia*, with the exception of "Tasso" and "Galileo." She published also Shelley's prose works, his poems, with valuable notes, two volumes of travels, *Rambles in Germany and Italy*, besides contributing to the magazines.

Of Mrs. Shelley's writings, *Frankenstein* is without question the most noteworthy. From the day of its first appearance in print down to the present, it has had accorded to it a position as a unique and remarkable production. This reputation, gained equally from two classes who rarely agree in reading the same book, still less in praising it—thoughtful *litterateurs* and mere readers of stories,—it has steadily maintained. This fact of itself is doubtless due to, and in a measure significant of, the dual character of the romance. It is one of the few books that can be called *sui generis*. The advent of such books into the literary world is always a subject of interest. And the wonder is not lessened when we are told that this book was the production of a girl of eighteen, and her first attempt at sustained literary work. Allusion has already been made to the period of Mrs. Shelley's life in which *Frankenstein* was written, but in order to gain a critical comprehension of the work, the details of its production are of the highest interest.

During the summer of 1816, while the Shelleys were neighbors of Lord Byron, on the borders of Lake Geneva, the intercourse between the two poets and their households was daily and intimate. Byron was at that time composing the third canto of "Childe Harold," and as each successive scene was finished he brought his work to his poet neighbor, who thus partook of the first fruits of a genius he was so well adapted to recognize and value. Moreover, the prolonged rains keeping them in-doors, they chanced to find some volumes of fiction,—principally ghost stories and fantastic fairy tales translated from the French and German. The drift of much of their talk tended into the atmosphere of the supernatural and horrible.

It is worthy of passing note that many of these stories were of a strictly allegorical type. Thus one was the history of the inconstant lover, who having deserted his betrothed when most he should have befriended her, chose a bride, and clasped her to his arms only to find himself embracing the pale ghost of his deserted. Another story was of a parent who by crime bestowed life upon a race and was doomed to give the kiss of death to all the sons of his ill-fated house, just as they in turn reached the age of promise.

While under the influence of these fantastic tales and the impromptu ones which they told each other, the agreement was made that each should write a ghost story. The proposition was Byron's; it was accorded to and entered upon by all. The poets themselves failed, and it is more than probable that the persistence of Mrs. Shelley was due rather to the wishes and urgency of Shelley than to any innate energy or will of her own in the matter. He, from the time of their first acquaintance, had been anxious that she should attempt literary work of some kind, partly because of his faith in the theory of heredity, and partly from a confidence in his own estimate of her mental qualities. He believed that the daughter of William Godwin and Mary Wollstonecraft, the woman whose mental brightness and spirit had for himself a never-failing endurance, could not but be remarkable in any literary work to which she might turn her mind.

Mrs. Shelley herself, in the preface of the last London edition of *Frankenstein,* published during her life, has told how she tried day after day to think of a plot; to invent something uncanny or horribly fantastic, and how each morning, to the question, "Have you thought of a story?" she was obliged to answer "No," until a train of thought supplied by conversation of a metaphysical tone which she had listened to between Shelley and Byron, entered into her state of reverie in semi-sleep, and suggested the essential outlines of the plot of *Frankenstein.*

What was thus suggested was probably nothing more than the central figures of the weird conception. Nothing could be simpler than the plot, nothing more horrible than the situations and the details. Frankenstein is a student who, by the study of occult sciences, acquires the power of imparting life to a figure which he had made. Graves and charnel-house had furnished the needed material from which he had constructed this colossal human form. To the thing thus prepared he is able to impart life. It lives and possesses human attributes. The rest of the tale is occupied in depicting the nameless horrors which visited Frankenstein as the result of his creation. The thing becomes the bane of his life. He tries to fly from it, but there is no final escape. One by one, the monster that he had created slays the brother, friend, sister, and bride of the luckless student, who himself finally falls a victim to his own wretched and untoward creation. The monster, upon its part, strives to adapt itself to life, but fails; finds no possibility of companionship, no admission into any human fellowship.

Such in brief outline is the plot, if it can be so called, of the tale which, with eager hands, the youthful romancer penned before the first horror of the idea had faded from her brain. At Shelley's suggestion the story was amplified. The introductory letters were inserted and the pastoral episode and other incidents were added to the later part of the narrative. As originally written the story began with the words, "It was on a dreary night of November that I beheld the accomplishment of my toils." In the work as published these words introduce Chapter IV.

Regarded as a mere tale, it is difficult to account for the hold this story has always had upon the minds of the reading world. As a story it does not justify its own success. To say that it is remarkable as a work of imagination does not meet the difficulty. By a work of the imagination, as used in the current criticism of *Frankenstein,* is simply meant that it is a fantastic romance, such as we find in the *Arabian Nights,* or in the prose tales of Poe. But a position utterly different from these is accorded to *Frankenstein.*

We have intimated that there was a dual quality in it, to which it owed its singular power and place in literature. One element is doubtless the horror of the tale and the weird fancy of the author's imagination in the ordinary acceptation of the word. But it is to an entirely different department of mental conception that we must look for the secret of its peculiar influence. The faculty of imagination is something more than the recalling and rearrangements of past impressions. Profoundly considered, it is that function of the mind which formulates, as though real, a state of things which if present would so appear. It is the power of projecting the mind into unhappened realities. It is the faculty of picturing unseen verities. There is thus in it a prophetic element, not at all miraculous, but dependent upon subtle laws of association and suggestion. It is to this element that *Frankenstein* owes its power over thoughtful minds. It is by virtue of the allegorical element in it that it holds its high position as a work of the imagination. Yet so unobtrusively is the allegory woven through the thread of the romance, that, while always felt, it can scarcely be said to have been detected. Certain it is that no one has directed attention to this phase, or carefully attempted an analysis of the work, with the view of deducing the meaning thus legible between the lines.

That Mrs. Shelley herself was conscious of this element is certain, by the double title she gave it,—*Frankenstein, or the Modern Prometheus.* Furthermore, that she should thus embody, under the apparent guise of a weird story, suggestions of moral truths, development of mental traits,—normal and abnormal,—and hints at, and solutions of, social questions, was in strict accord both with her own intellectual state and with the circumstances under which *Frankenstein* was produced. And yet nothing is more improbable than that it was written with such design, or that the youthful author was fully aware or even conscious of the extent to which the allegorical overlies largely the narrative in her work. This very unconsciousness of result, this obliviousness to hidden truths, is a distinguishing mark of genius. To take daily account of stock proclaims the small trader, not the merchant prince. Placed in a congenial atmosphere, genius in breathing the breath of life will exhale truths. The very gist of genius is embodied in this hidden relation to truth. That mind has genius which, detecting germs of truth under forms where the common eye sees them not, affords in itself the place and pabulum for their growth.

We know the circumstance under which the book was written; the stories which suggested it were all weird in form and allegorical in type; the minds of those by whom Mrs. Shelley was at that time surrounded were minds to whom the mystical was the natural mode of thought and speech. Her own inherited and acquired mental traits were markedly of this same character. Furthermore, at this time the influence of Shelley was strongest upon her. Not that of one nature mastering and overpowering a weaker, but that yet stronger bond of one mind fitted by nature and oneness of motive to gain insight into, and be in unison with, the other.

Such, in a remarkable degree, was her relation at this time to Shelley; to her his nature was revealed. They had spoken and dwelt upon his past until it was an open book to her. His aims and his failures, his aspirations and fears, his nature and philosophy were familiar and ever present to her mind. Moreover, from him she had learned much about the great world of men and things, broadening her nature and conceptions beyond the ordinary limit of feminine knowledge; indeed, with the result of attaching her own peculiar insight to the facts and ideas thus included within her extending horizon. In both of their minds the tendency to dwell on social and ethical problems was strong, and to such natures union means cubic strength. What wonder that, if, underlying her story thus produced, should lie partly concealed or vaguely hinted, social and moral ideas, awaiting but recognition, to become in turn the suggestors of their own redevelopment in the minds of us who read.

That some, nay, many, of these have an almost direct bearing upon Shelley himself, either as proceeding from him or pointing to him, is to be expected; to say that they all thus have would be perhaps straining a theory otherwise tenable. What we can safely affirm is that he who, with this idea of the allegorical substratum, will reread the story, will be richly repaid in the suggestions the mind cannot fail to receive, and which, according to the mind of each, will attach to the nature of Shelley himself, or, more widely taken, will stand as general truths, applicable alike to all.

Such a general truth is that pictured in the character and pursuit of the student Frankenstein himself. He exhibits to us the man of one idea, absorbed in but one department of science, not only abandoning other studies, but rejecting the ordinary avocations of life. Family, friend, even the voice of her who loved him, fails to recall him to action or to a sense of the proper proportion of things. We see the result not only in the loss of symmetry and balance in his character, but find it having its legitimate effect in making him the slave of his own too concentrated studies. So that finally he becomes possessed by the ruling idea he had so dearly cherished, and the reward of his infatuation is the delusion that he can accomplish that which a healthful mind would have avoided,—a delusion which had grown up in the very seclusion and isolation of life that the unhappy student had adopted; to which the fitting antidote would have been the diversion of the commonplace interests which he had carefully excluded. The power to produce the horrible creature, as the fruit of this delusion, is but the poetic justice of his sentence. The terrible result of his creation furnishes the morale and teaching of the allegory. Into this part of the story is interposed the train of thought which is suggested by the construction of the human form by Frankenstein. In its preparation the student selects the most beautiful models for each limb and feature. He spares no pains, and each separate anatomical part is, taken by itself, perfect in symmetry and adaptation. But when once the breath of life is breathed into the creation, and life quickens its being and gleams from its eyes, and function succeeds in the hitherto inanimate parts, all beauty disappears; the separate excellence of each several part is lost in the general incongruity and lack of harmony of the whole.

Can art see no suggestiveness in this? Can society, in its attempt to manufacture conglomerate masses out of dissimilar elements, learn nothing from the teaching here inculcated?

Once become a living being, Frankenstein and this monster that he had made bear to one another the sustained relation of creator and creature. Throughout the entire narrative this relationship is one long allegory with phases as diverse as a prism. Most prominent is the total failure to create that which should find place in life only by growth. In the sad, lone, utter incompatibility which environed the creature,—in the inability of others to accept or tolerate it,—in its own desperate, heart-sickening attempts to educate and train itself into harmony and communion with those who should have been its fellow-beings, and in its final despair and terrible outlawry and revenge, is shown the futility of the attempt to regulate human beings, or their concerns, except under the laws of growth and development. And *Frankenstein* contains no deeper teaching than that we cannot legislate happiness into this world; that such attempt at last, after affording a maximum of misery, returns to plague the inventor.

Another phase of this relationship between the creator and his creature is so strongly suggestive of a certain period of Shelley's religious life that the mind hesitates before denying the likeness. The creature of Frankenstein, finding itself in a world in which all happiness is denied it; to which its powers of strengthfulness, however exercised, bring it no good, but serve only to increase its misery and sense of loneliness, turns to its creator and, with alternate curses and prayers, beseeches him to either slay it or fit the world for its companionship. In this dilemma the creator does neither. He merely admits either his unwillingness or his inability to do that which simple justice to his creature, to say nothing of his love and duty, would prompt. Thus the creator is made to figure as lacking either justice or omnipotence.

How Shelleyan this idea, the closest student of him will best judge.

But the chief allegorical interest in the narrative concerns itself about that tendency in the human being to discard the established order of things and to create for itself a new and independent existence. In the simple story, Frankenstein made a being responsible to him alone for its creation,—a being not produced by the ordinary course of life, not amenable or even adaptable to the existing world of men. Right or wrong, better or worse, the creature may be, but different certainly, and this irreconcilable disparity points back ever to its origin, which had been anomalous and strange.

The whole story is but the elaboration of the embarrassment and dangers which flow from departure from the ordinary course of nature; this forced attempt to invade society from within. What strong existence in real life of this same tendency Mary Shelley had seen in those nearest and dearest to her! She has not failed to learn the lesson of her mother's history; time analyzes rather than destroys. And the life of Mary Wollstonecraft was doubtless seen by the clear-minded daughter in stronger contrast of light and shade than it had been by its contemporaries. Who knew so well the glories of that life? Its successes as well as its miseries had sprung from the self-same causes as those of Frankenstein,—from the breach of the conventional; from overstepping the limits; from creating an individuality and a sphere of existence denied it by Nomos, and consequently sure of the hostility of society.

To this same cause Shelley himself attributed justly the events and moral struggle of his own life. From earliest childhood revolt against convention, and rebellion against authority, had characterized him. His perpetual tendency, like that of Mary Wollstonecraft, like that typified in *Frankenstein,* was ever to create for himself an existence not conforming to the ways of the world.

As we read the story of the modern Prometheus, and page by page trace the evolution of this idea, the ethical aspect is oppressive in its prophetic truth. Each must do this for himself. One thing, however, we may note. The visitation of judgment, the terrible results of the exercise of the power of creation, do not begin, do not recoil upon Frankenstein, until he has actually launched his creature into the world of men about him. So long as he kept the scheme within himself; so long as the influence of the thought and work was confined to him alone, no evil came; on the contrary, after a certain point the struggle after this ideal was a stimulation and an incentive of the highest order. It was only when the overt act of introducing his new existence into the world was accomplished, that misery began to flow from it to all concerned, and even to those apparently not concerned in it. This is the saving clause in the prophetic allegory. Without this it would fail to square with the truth.

See how far-reaching are the ideas which this allegory evokes, how subtle its suggestions are. Mind after mind has felt the power of this story, so simple in its apparent construction, and has again and again returned to it, not asking itself why; feeling a power it did not recognize, much less analyze; hovering, in fact, around it as birds do when charmed, because of an attraction which was persistent and real, although unknown, even unsuspected. All attraction implies some sort of a magnet. Nothing attracts so powerfully as the true.

The world, by its acknowledgment of the coercive quality of *Frankenstein*, has given silent acceptance of its genius. The other works, novels, critiques, biographies, while they have had literary merit, feeling, even power, have not shown genius. *Frankenstein* alone was personal, it alone reflected Mrs. Shelley's true self. Her other books contain simply what she wrote in them: this alone contains what was written in her. Being, as she was, stronger in her personality than as a literary artist, the book that alone partook of that personality would alone partake of her peculiar genius. This, considered in its fullest light, *Frankenstein* does.

It is a thankless task to sit in judgment upon a novel like *Valperga,* and only the difficulty of obtaining the work and the curiosity to know Mrs. Shelley's most serious endeavor at romance, justify the extended extracts which follow. Formed upon the old-fashioned models, it, like them, essentially lacks action, incident, and dramatic expression. It is unrelieved by nicely-drawn character sketches. It so abounds in long and learned speeches, dull descriptions, lifeless records of events, that to our highly exacting modern mind, as a novel, it is a complete failure. But it is not as a novel that the book ought to be judged. As an illustration of its author's mental and moral development it has a place and a purpose. For although she has a certain sympathetic insight into the imaginative, the emotional; although she delights in the deeply tragical,— page follows page of unmitigated melancholy—it is totally without the light and shade which would make us feel the pathos of the story intensely. Indeed, one could not call it pathetic; it is simply tragical.

Not an emotion of pity visits you while you read; not a spark of enthusiasm, not an impulse of sympathy. Its people are as dead to you as they have been these hundreds of years to the world. One reads the three volumes stolidly, unmoved; interested only because of the insight which one gains of its author.

Castruccio, Prince of Lucca, the tyrant, the caustic wit of history, the first soldier and satirist of his age, moves laboriously through the book. His ambitions do not penetrate, his villanies do not touch one. He is a thing without life, without passion; the events of his career are dull-recorded facts. Mrs. Shelley has not done justice to his keen and crafty generalship, to his trenchant and powerful satire. You do not get a glimpse of the man of history, who, when he was dying in the zenith of his glory, said, "Lay me on my face in the coffin, for everything will be reversed ere long after my departure;" or who rebuked a young man whom he met coming out of a house of ill repute, and who blushed at seeing Castruccio,—"It was when you went in that you should have colored, not when you come out." Again, when in a storm Castruccio was alarmed, a stupid fool derided, saying he had no fear, as he did not value his own life at a farthing. "Everybody," said Castruccio, "makes the best estimate of his own wares." When a sage rebuked Castruccio for some extravagances at an evening revelry, he replied, "He who is held as a wise man by day, will not be taken to be a fool by night." And again, on remarking the radiant countenance of an envious man, he exclaimed, "Is it that some good hath befallen thee, or that some evil hath befallen another?"

What Mrs. Shelley tried to do—and this, I take it, to be the motive of the book—was to show how from a generous, deep-souled, guileless youth, Castruccio became a cruel, ambitious tyrant, a being deaf to all the appeals of mercy or justice. She has given us an account of his exiled youth, its innocent occupations, its gentle and ennobling influences, its dreams of power and glory for his oppressed native city, Lucca. She has told how, after an apprenticeship spent in the English Court of Edward the Second, in the wars of Flanders, and in the atmosphere of intriguing European countries, he appears as the liberator of his native city; how, after destroying the Guelphic rule by banishing three hundred Guelph families, his idea of liberty was to reinstate the Ghibellines, of which he, the last heir of the noble Antiminelli family, was the head; how, moderate in all his habits and wants, he was yet insatiable in his ambition. Liberty for his country being only the ruse to conceal his greed for power and autocracy.

She has shown how the pure and elevated nature of Euthanasia, his betrothed bride, whose ideal love for him was only equalled by her desire for peace and freedom for her distracted Italy, was as naught to hinder the evil development of his own mind; how the terrible misfortunes of the inspired and misled Beatrice brought no serious regret to him, the careless cause of her misery. It is true that she has shown us all this, but we stand as upon the outer wall, viewing the conflict through the obscurations of the dust and confusion. We fail to discern there the great soldier, the real Castruccio.

The characters of the two women, Euthanasia, Countess of Valperga, and Beatrice, Prophetess of Ferrara, are drawn with more vigor. The intimate workings of their souls are laid bare to us; the deep melancholy of their lives is portrayed with all the detail of one gifted in such analysis. We are reminded of Romola in the story of Euthanasia's life. Nearly two hundred years earlier, in an old library in the same city of Florence, Euthanasia, like Romola, spent her young life reading dull, musty parchments to her blind father, and her after life was not unlike Romola's in its moral conflicts.

In the young Euthanasia, as she sat at her father's feet and drank eagerly his eloquent rhapsodies on the Latin poets, Mrs. Shelley unconsciously describes herself. She says of her heroine, "Her soul was adapted for the reception of all good." Her own education under Shelley's guidance was not unlike that of the child Euthanasia, who from love mastered with amazing skill the difficult Latin transcriptions on the old parchments, that she might read them to her father, for Shelley writes of Mary's progress in Latin shortly after their marriage,—"She has satisfied my best expectations." Many qualities of heart and mind attributed to Euthanasia or Beatrice, one recognizes as but the unconscious portrayal of her own nature. Euthanasia grows up as a Guelph and a Florentine, holding sacred the friendship of the noble-hearted Castruccio, who had been her knight and playmate before his exile. One by one, her father, mother, brothers die, and she is left the last survivor of her family. After Castruccio's return to Italy they renew their vows and are betrothed; but it is now that she sees with despair the seeds of evil in her lover's character which finally divide them. The conflict between Euthanasia's love for Castruccio and her hatred of tyranny and bloodshed is perhaps the chief interest of the romance.

But it is the character of Beatrice—a character fraught with passion and madness—which displays the peculiar power of Mrs. Shelley's imagination; the power of realizing and dealing with the terrible. Like Frankenstein, Beatrice is the result of an abnormal and one-sided development. Like him, she creates for herself a strange and unnatural state of existence. Like him, she suffers the fatal consequence of an intense absorption to one idea,—the idea of her divine inspiration. Here again does the dual tendency of Mrs. Shelley's mind show itself. Beatrice is the outgrowth of all the religious frenzies and persecutions of the age; her prophetic dreams and enthusiasms are the wild and morbid development of a highly overstrung and unbalanced mind, encouraged by the superstitious reverence of her countrymen and friends and *her* own credulous belief in her divine inspirations. Her final awakening, her realization of the deception under which she has lived, her love for Castruccio, her pilgrimage to Rome, her abhorrence of the religion in which she had been nurtured, and which had made her fanaticism possible, her despair of truth or humanity, her final madness, are all highly dramatic possibilities, had Mrs. Shelley but let the simple truths speak for themselves; but she so dissipates the strength of her situations by long and tedious sentences and dull narrations that you feel like one who, walking over endless stretch of plain, longs for broken country.

The tone of the book is pure and high. There is in it the intense earnestness that actuated Mary Shelley throughout her life. There are careful and laborious details of manners and customs; long and erudite speeches, religious and political; a conscientious study of Italy and her internal strife. The flowing eloquence and rhapsodies of the imaginative Beatrice are well sustained; the unswerving truth and nobility of Euthanasia's character are drawn with tenderness and appreciation. But the book will not stand the test of a good novel; its characters do not remain in your mind like the memories of real people. They are passionless and lifeless.

—Helen Moore, from *"Frankenstein,* and Other Writings," *Mary Wollstonecraft Shelley,* 1886, pp. 244–264

FLORENCE ASHTON MARSHALL (1889)

Lodore, Mrs. Shelley's fifth novel, came out in 1835. It differs from the others in being a novel of society, and has been stigmatised, rather unjustly, as weak and colourless, although at the time of its publication it had a great success. It is written in a style which is now out of date, and undoubtedly fails to fulfil the promise of power held out by *Frankenstein* and to some extent by *Valperga,* but it bears on every page the impress of the refinement and sensibility of the author, and has, moreover, a special interest of its own, due to the fact that some of the incidents are taken from actual occurrences in her early life, and some of the characters sketched from people she had known.

—Florence Ashton Marshall, *The Life and Letters of Mary Wollstonecraft Shelley,* 1889, vol. 2, p. 264

Lucy Madox Rossetti "Literary Work" (1890)

This highly imaginative work of Mary Shelley's twenty-sixth year contains some of the author's most powerful ideas; but is marred in the commencement by some of her most stilted writing.

The account of the events recorded professes to be found in the cave of the Cumasan Sibyl, near Naples, where they had remained for centuries, outlasting the changes of nature and, when found, being still two hundred and fifty years in advance of the time foretold. The accounts are all written on the sibylline leaves; they are in all languages, ancient and modern; and those concerning this story are in English.

We find ourselves in England, in 2073, in the midst of a Republic, the last king of England having abdicated at the quietly expressed wish of his subjects. This book, like all Mrs. Shelley's, is full of biographical reminiscences; the introduction gives the date of her own visit to Naples with Shelley, in 1818; the places they visited are there indicated; the poetry, romance, the pleasures and pains of her own existence, are worked into her subjects; while her imagination carries her out of her own surroundings. We clearly recognise in the ideal character of the son of the abdicated king an imaginary portrait of Shelley as Mary would have him known, not as she knew him as a living person. To give an adequate idea of genius with all its charm, and yet with its human imperfections, was beyond Mary's power. Adrian, the son of kings, the aristocratic republican, is the weakest part, and one cannot help being struck by Mary Shelley's preference for the aristocrat over the plebeian. In fact, Mary's idea of a republic still needed kings' sons by their good manners to grace it, while, at the same time, the king's son had to be transmuted into an ideal Shelley. This strange confusion of ideas allowed for, and the fact that over half a century of perhaps the earth's most rapid period of progress has passed, the imaginative qualities are still remarkable in Mary. Balloons, then dreamed of, were attained; but naturally the steam-engine and other wonders of science, now achieved, were unknown to Mary. When the plague breaks out she has scope for her fancy, and she certainly adds vivid pictures of horror and pathos to a subject which has been handled by masters of thought at different periods. In this time of horror it is amusing to note how the people's candidate, Ryland, represented as a vulgar specimen of humanity, succumbs to abject fear. The description of the deserted towns and grass-grown streets of London is impressive. The fortunes of the family, to whom the last man, Lionel Verney, belongs, are traced through their varying phases, as one by one the dire plague assails them, and Verney, the only man who recovers from the disease, becomes the leader of the remnant of the English nation. This small handful of humanity leaves England, and wanders through France on its way to the favoured southern countries where human aid, now so scarce, was less needed. On this journey Mrs. Shelley avails herself of reminiscences of her own travelling with Shelley some few years before; and we pass the places noted in her diary; but strange grotesque figures cross the path of the wanderers, who are decimated each day. At one moment a dying acrobat, deserted by his companions, is seen bounding in the air behind a hedge in the dusk of evening. At another, a black figure mounted on a horse, which only shows itself after dark, to cause apprehensions soon calmed by the death of the poor wanderer, who wished only for distant companionship through dread of contagion. Dijon is reached and passed, and here the old Countess of Windsor, the ex-Queen of England, dies: she had only been reconciled to her changed position by the destruction of humanity. Once, near Geneva, they come upon the sound of divine music in a church, and find a dying girl playing to her blind father to keep up the delusion to the last. The small party, reduced by this time to five, reach Chamouni, and the grand scenes so familiar to Mary contrast with the final tragedy of the human race; yet one more dies, and only four of one family remain; they bury the dead man in an ice cavern, and with this last victim find the pestilence has ended, after a seven years' reign over the earth. A weight is lifted from the atmosphere, and the world is before them; but now alone they must visit her ruins; and the beauty of the earth and the love of each other, bear them up till none but the last man remains to complete the Cumasan Sibyl's prophecy.

Various stories of minor importance followed from Mrs. Shelley's pen, and preparations were made for the lives of eminent literary men. But it was not till the year preceding her father's death that we have *Lodore*, published in 1835. Of this novel we have already spoken in relation to the separation of Shelley and Harriet. Mary had too much feeling of art in her work to make an imaginary character a mere portrait, and we are constantly reminded in her novels of the different wonderful and interesting personages whom she knew intimately, though most of their characters were far too subtle and complex to be unravelled by her, even with her intimate knowledge. Indeed, the very fact of having known some of the greatest people of her age, or of almost any age, gives an appearance of affectation to her novels, as it fills them with characters so far from the common run that their place in life cannot be reduced to an ordinary fashionable level. Romantic episodes there may be, but their true place is in the theatre of time of which they are the movers, not the Lilliputians of life who are slowly worked on and moulder by them, and whose small doings are the material of most novels. We know of few novelists who have touched at all successfully on the less known characters. This accomplishment seems to need the great poet himself.

The manner in which Lady Lodore is influenced seems to point to Harriet; but the unyielding and revengeful side of her character has certainly more of Lady Byron. She is charmingly described, and shows a great deal of insight on Mary's part into the life of fashionable people of her time, which then, perhaps more than now, was the favourite theme with novelists. This must be owing to a certain innate Tory propensity in the English classes or masses for whom Mary Shelley had to work hard, and for whose tendencies in this respect she certainly had a sympathy. Mary's own life, at the point we have now reached, is also here touched on in the character of Ethel, Lord and Lady Lodore's daughter, who is brought up in America by her father, and on his death entrusted to an aunt, with injunctions in his will that she is not to be allowed to be brought in contact with her mother. Her character is sweetly feminine and trusting, and in her fortunate love and marriage (in all but early money matters) might be considered quite unlike Mary's own less fortunate experiences; but in her perfect love and confidence in her husband, her devotion and unselfishness through the trials of poverty in London, the descriptions of which were evidently taken from Mary's own experiences, there is no doubt of the resemblance, as also in her love and reverence for all connected with her father. There are also passages undoubtedly expressive of her own inner feelings—such as this when describing the young husband and wife at a *tete-a-tete* supper:—

> Mutual esteem and gratitude sanctified the unreserved sympathy which made each so happy in the other. Did they love the less for not loving "in sin and fear"? Far from it. The certainty of being the cause of good to each other tended to foster the most delicate of all passions, more than the rough ministrations of terror and the knowledge that each was the occasion of injury. A woman's heart is peculiarly unfitted to sustain this conflict. Her sensibility gives keenness to her imagination and she magnifies every peril, and writhes beneath every sacrifice which tends to humiliate her in her own eyes. The natural pride of her sex struggles with her desire to confer happiness, and her peace is wrecked.

What stronger expression of feeling could be needed than this, of a woman speaking from her heart and her own experiences? Does it not remind one of the moral on this subject in all George Eliot's writing, where she shows that the outcome of what by some might be considered minor transgressions against morality leads even in modern times to the Nemesis of the most terrible Greek Dramas?

The complicated money transactions carried on with the aid of lawyers were clearly a reminiscence of Shelley's troubles, and of her own incapacity to feel all the distress contingent so long as she was with him, and there was evidently money somewhere in the family, and it would come some time. In this novel we also perceive that Mary works off her pent-up feelings with regard to Emilia Viviani. It cannot be supposed that the corporeal part of Shelley's creation of *Epipsychidion* (so exquisite in appearance and touching in manner and story as to give rise, when transmitted through the poet's brain, to the most perfect of love ideals) really ultimately became the fiery-tempered worldly-minded virago that Mary Shelley indulges herself in depicting, after first, in spite of altering some relations and circumstances, clearly showing whom the character was intended for. It is true that Shelley himself, after investing her with divinity to serve the purposes of art, speaks later of her as a very commonplace worldly-minded woman; but poets, like artists, seem at times to need lay figures to attire with their thoughts. Enough has been shown to prove that there is genuine subject of interest in this work of Mary's thirty-seventh year.

The next work, *Falkner,* published in 1837, is the last novel we have by Mary Shelley; and as we see from her letter she had been passing through a period of ill-health and depression while writing it, this may account for less spontaneity in the style, which is decidedly more stilted; but, here again, we feel that we are admitted to some of the circle which Mary had encountered in the stirring times of her life, and there is undoubted imagination with some fine descriptive passages.

The opening chapter introduces a little deserted child in a picturesque Cornish village. Her parents had died there in apartments, one after the other, the husband having married a governess against the wishes of his relations; consequently, the wife was first neglected on her husband's death; and on her own sudden death, a few months later, the child was simply left to the care of the poor people of the village—a dreamy, poetic little thing, whose one pleasure was to stroll in the twilight to the village churchyard and be with her mamma. Here she was found by Falkner, the principal character of the romance, who had selected this very spot to end a ruined existence; in which attempt he was frustrated by the child jogging his arm to move him from her mother's grave. His life being thus saved by the child's instrumentality, he naturally became interested in her. He is allowed to look through the few remaining papers of the parents. Among these he finds an unfinished letter of the wife, evidently addressed to a lady he had known, and also indications who the parents were. He was much moved, and offered to relieve the poor people of the child and to restore her to her relations.

The mother's unfinished letter to her friend contains the following passage, surely autobiographical:—

> When I lost Edwin (the husband), I wrote to Mr. Raby (the husband's father) acquainting him with the sad intelligence, and asking for a maintenance for myself and my child. The family solicitor answered my letter. Edwin's conduct had, I was told, estranged his family from him, and they could only regard me as one encouraging his disobedience and apostasy. I had no claim on them. If my child were sent to them, and I would promise to abstain from all intercourse with her, she should be brought up with her cousins, and treated in all respects like one of the family. I declined their barbarous offer, and haughtily and in few words relinquished every claim on their bounty, declaring my intention to support and bring up my child myself. This was foolishly done, I fear; but I cannot regret it, even now.
>
> I cannot regret the impulse that made me disdain these unnatural and cruel relatives, or that led me to take my poor orphan to my heart with pride as being all my own. What had they done to merit such a treasure? And did they show themselves capable of replacing a fond and anxious mother?

This reminds the reader of the correspondence between Mary and her father on Shelley's death.

It suffices to say that Falkner became so attached to the small child, that by the time he discovered her relations he had not the heart to confide her to their hard guardianship, and as he was compelled to leave England shortly, he took her with him, and through all difficulties he contrived that she should be well guarded and brought up. There is much in the character of Falkner that reminds the reader of Trelawny, the gallant and generous friend of Byron and Shelley in their last years, the brave and romantic traveller. The description of Falkner's face and figure must have much resembled that of Trelawny when young, though, of course, the incidents of the story have no connection with him. In the meantime the little girl is growing up, and the nurses are replaced by an English governess, whom Falkner engages abroad, and whose praises and qualifications he hears from everyone at Odessa. The story progresses through various incidents foreshadowing the cause of Falkner's mystery. Elizabeth, the child, now grown up, passes under his surname. While travelling in Germany they come across a youth of great personal attraction, who appears, however, to be of a singularly reckless and misanthropical disposition for one so young. Elizabeth seeming attracted by his daring and beauty, Falkner suddenly finds it necessary to return to England. Shortly afterwards, he is moved to go to Greece during the War of Independence, and wishes to leave Elizabeth with her relations in England; but this she strenuously opposes so far as to induce Falkner to let her accompany him to Greece, where he places her with a family while he rushes into the thick of the danger, only hoping to end his life in a good cause. In this he nearly succeeds, but Elizabeth, hearing of his danger, hastens to his side, and nurses him assiduously through the fever brought on from his wounds and the malarious climate. By short stages and the utmost care, she succeeds in reaching Malta on their homeward journey, and Falkner, a second time rescued from death by his beloved adopted child, determines not again to endanger recklessly the life more dear to her than that of many fathers. Again, at Malta, during a fortnight's quarantine, the smallness of the world of fashionable people brings them in contact with an English party, a Lord and Lady Cecil, who are travelling with their family. Falkner is too ill to see anyone, and when Elizabeth finally gets him on board a vessel to proceed to Genoa, he seems rapidly sinking. In his despair and loneliness, feeling unable to cope with all the difficulties of burning sun and cold winds, help unexpectedly comes: a gentleman whom Elizabeth has not before perceived, and whom now she is too much preoccupied to observe, quietly arranges the sail to shelter the dying man from sun and wind, places pillows, and does all that is possible; he even induces the poor girl to go below and rest on a couch for a time while he watches. Falkner becomes easier in the course of the night; he sleeps and gains in strength, and from this he progresses till, while at Marseilles, he hears the name, Neville, of the unknown friend who had helped to restore him to life. He becomes extremely agitated and faints. On being restored to consciousness he begs Elizabeth to continue the journey with him alone, as he can bear no one but her near him. The mystery of Falkner's life seems to be forcing itself to the surface.

The travellers reach England, and Elizabeth is sought out by Lady Cecil, who had been much struck by her devotion to her father. Elizabeth is invited to stay with Lady Cecil, as she much needs rest in her turn. During a pleasant time of repose near Hastings, Elizabeth hears Lady Cecil talk much of her brother Gerard; but it is not till he, too, arrives on a visit, that she acknowledges to herself that he is really the same Mr. Neville whom she had met, and from whom she had received such kindness. Nor had Gerard spoken of Elizabeth; he had been too much drawn towards her, as his life also is darkened by *a* mystery. They spend a short tranquil time together, when a letter announces the approaching arrival of Sir Boyvill Neville, the young man's father (although Lady Cecil called Gerard her brother, they were not really related; Sir Boyvill had married the mother of Lady Cecil, who was the offspring of a previous marriage).

Gerard Neville at once determines to leave the house, but before going refers Elizabeth to his sister, Lady Cecil, to hear the particulars of the tragedy which surrounds him. The story told is this. Sir Boyvill Neville was a man of the world with all the too frequent disbelief in women and selfishness. This led to his becoming very tyrannical when he married, at the age of 45, Alethea, a charming young woman who had recently lost her mother, and whose father, a retired naval officer of limited means, would not hear of her refusing so good an offer as Sir Boyvill's. After their marriage Sir Boyvill, feeling himself too fortunate in having secured so charming and beautiful a wife, kept out of all society, and after living abroad for some years took her to an estate he possessed in Cumberland. They lived there shut out from all the world, except for trips which he took himself to London, or elsewhere, whenever *ennui* assailed him. They had, at the time we are approaching, two charming children, a beautiful boy of some ten years and a little girl of two. At this time while Alethea was perfectly happy with her children, and quite contented with her retirement, which she perceived took away the jealous tortures of her husband, he left home for a week, drawn out to two months, on one of his periodical visits to the capital. Lady Neville's frequent letters concerning her home and her children were always cheerful and placid, and the time for her husband's return was fixed. He arrived at the appointed hour in the evening. The servants were at the door to receive him, but in an instant alarm prevailed; Lady Neville and her son Gerard were not with him. They had left the house some hours before to walk in the park, and had not since been seen or heard of, an unprecedented occurrence. The alarm was raised; the country searched in all directions, but ineffectually, during a fearful tempest. Ultimately the poor boy was found unconscious on the ground, drenched to the skin. On his being taken home, and his father questioning him, all that could be heard were his cries "Come back, mamma; stop, stop for me!" Nothing else but the tossings of fever. Once again, "Then she has come back," he cried, "that man did not take her quite away; the carriage drove here at last." The story slowly elicited from the child on his gaining strength was this. On his going for a walk with his mother in the park, she took the key of a gate which led into a lane. A gentleman was waiting outside. Gerard had never seen him before, but he heard his mother call him Rupert. They walked together through the lane accompanied by the child, and talked earnestly. She wept, and the boy was indignant. When they reached a cross-road, a carriage was waiting. On approaching it the gentleman pulled the child's hands from hers, lifted her in, sprang in after, and the coachman drove like the wind, leaving the child to hear his mother shriek in agony, "My child—my son!" Nothing more could be discovered; the country was ransacked in vain. The servants only stated that ten days ago a gentleman called, asked for Lady Neville and was shown in to her; he remained some two hours, and on his leaving it was remarked that she had been weeping. He had called again but was not admitted. One letter was found, signed "Rupert," begging for one more meeting, and if that were granted he would leave her and his just revenge for ever; otherwise, he could not tell what the consequences might be on her husband's return that night. In answer to this letter she went, but with her child, which clearly proved her innocent intention. Months passed with no fresh result, till her husband, beside himself with wounded pride, determined to be avenged by obtaining a Bill of Divorce in the House of Lords, and producing his son Gerard as evidence against his lost mother, whom he so dearly loved. The poor child by this time, by dint of thinking and weighing every word he could remember, such as "I grieve deeply for you, Rupert: my good wishes are all I have to give you," became more and more convinced that his mother was taken forcibly away, and would return at any moment if she were able. He only longed for the time when he should be old enough to go and seek her through the world. His father was relentless, and the child was brought before the House of Lords to repeat the evidence he had innocently given against her; but when called on to speak in that awful position, no word could be drawn from him except "She is innocent." The House was moved by the brave child's agony, and resolved to carry on the case without him, from the witnesses whom he had spoken to, and finally they pronounced a decree of divorce in Sir Boyvill's favour. The struggle and agony of the poor child are admirably described, as also his subsequent flight from his father's house, and wanderings round his old home in Cumberland. In his fruitless search for his mother he reached a deserted sea-coast. After wandering about for two months barefoot, and almost starving but for the ewe's milk and bread given him by the cottagers, he was recognized. His father, being informed, had him seized and brought home, where he was confined and treated as a criminal. His state became so helpless that even his father was at length moved to some feeling of self-restraint, and finally took Gerard with him abroad, where he was first seen at Baden by Elizabeth and Falkner. There also he first met his sister by affinity, Lady Cecil. With her he lost somewhat his defiant tone, and felt that for his mother's sake he must not appear to others as lost in sullenness and despair. He now talked of his mother, and reasoned about her; but although he much interested Lady Cecil, he did not convince her really of his mother's innocence, so much did all circumstances weigh against her. But now, during Elizabeth's visit to Lady Cecil, a letter is received by Gerard and his father informing them that one Gregory Hoskins believed he could give some information; he was at Lancaster. Sir Boyvill, only anxious to hush up the matter by which his pride had suffered, hastened to prevent his son from taking steps to re-open the subject. This Hoksins was originally a native of the district round Dromoor, Neville's home, and had emigrated to America at the time of Sir Boyvill's marriage. At one time—years ago—he met a man named Osborne, who confided to him how he had gained money before coming to America by helping a gentleman to carry off a lady, and how terribly the affair ended, as the lady got drowned in a river near which they had placed her while nearly dead from fright, on the dangerous coast of Cumberland. On returning to England, and hearing the talk about the Nevilles in his native village, this old story came to his mind, and he wrote his letter. Neville, on hearing this, instantly determined to proceed to Mexico, trace out Osborne, and bring him to accuse his mother's murderer.

All these details were written by Elizabeth to her beloved father. After some delay, one line entreated her to come to him instantly for one day.

Falkner could not ignore the present state of things—the mutual attraction of his Elizabeth and of Gerard. Yet how, with all he knew, could that be suffered to proceed? Never, except by eternal separation from his adored child; but this should be done. He would now tell her his story. He could not speak, but he wrote it, and now she must come and receive it from him. He told of all his solitary, unloved youth, the miseries and tyranny of school to the unprotected—a reminiscence of Shelley; how, on emerging from childhood, one gleam of happiness entered his life in the friendship of a lady, an old friend of his mother's, who had one lovely daughter; of the happy, innocent time spent in their cottage during holidays; of the dear lady's death; of her daughter's despair; then how he was sent off to India; of letters he wrote to the daughter Alethea, letters unanswered, as the father, the naval officer, intercepted all; of his return, after years, to England, his one hope that which had buoyed him up through years of constancy, to meet and marry his only love, for that he felt she was and must remain. He recounted his return, and the news he received; his one rash visit to her to judge for himself whether she was happy—this, from her manner, he could not feel, in spite of her delight in her children; his mad request to see her; mad plot, and still madder execution of it, till he had her in his arms, dashing through the country, through storm and thunder, unable to tell whether she lived or died; the first moment of pause; the efforts to save the ebbing life in a ruined hut; the few minutes' absence to seek materials for fire; the return, to find her a floating corpse in the wild little river flowing to the sea; the rescue of her body from the waves; her burial on the sea-shore; and his own subsequent life of despair, saved twice by Elizabeth. All this was told to the son, to whom Falkner denounced himself as his mother's destroyer. He named the spot where the remains would be found. And now what was left to be done? Only to wait a little, while Sir Boyvill and Gerard Neville proved his words, and traced out the grave. An inquest was held, and Falkner apprehended. A few days passed, and then Elizabeth found her father gone; and by degrees it was broken to her that he was in Carlisle gaol on the charge of murder. She, who had not feared the dangers in Greece of war and fever, was not to be deterred now; she, who believed in his innocence. No minutes were needed to decide her to go straight to Carlisle, and remain as near as she could to the dear father who had rescued and cared for her when deserted. Gerard, who was with his father when the bones were exhumed at the spot indicated, soon realised the new situation. His passion for justice to his mother did not deaden his feeling for others. He felt that Falkner's story was true, and though nothing could restore his mother's life, her honour was intact. Sir Boyvill would leave no stone unturned to be revenged, rightly or wrongly, on the man who had assailed his domestic peace; but Gerard saw Elizabeth, gave what consolation he could, and determined to set off at once to America to seek Osborne, as the only witness who could exculpate Falkner from the charge of murder. After various difficulties Osborne was found in England, where he had returned in terror of being taken in America as accomplice in the murder. With great difficulty he is brought to give evidence, for all his thoughts and fears are for himself; but at length, when all hopes seem failing, he is induced by Elizabeth to give his evidence, which fully confirms Falkner's statement.

At length the day of trial came. The news of liberty arrived. "Not Guilty!" Who can imagine the effect but those who have passed innocently through the ordeal? Once more all are united. Gerard has to remain for the funeral of his father, who had died affirming his belief, which in fact he had always entertained, in Falkner's innocence. Lady Cecil had secured for Elizabeth the companionship of Mrs. Raby, her relation on the father's side. She takes Falkner and Elizabeth home to the beautiful ancestral Belleforest. Here a time of rest and happiness ensues. Those so much tried by adversity would not let real happiness escape for a chimera; honour being restored, love and friendship remained, and Gerard, Elizabeth, and Falkner felt that now they ought to remain together, death not having disunited them.

Too much space may appear to be here given to one romance; but it seems just to show the scope of Mary's imaginative conception. There are certainly both imagination and power in carrying it out. It is true that the idea seems founded, to some extent, on Godwin's Caleb Williams, the man passing through life with a mystery; the similar names of Falkner and Falkland may even be meant to call attention to this fact. The three-volume form, in this as in many novels, seems to detract from the strength of the work in parts, the second volume being noticeably drawn out here and there. It may be questioned, also, whether the form adopted in this as in many romances of giving the early history by way of narrative told by one of the *dramatis persona* to another, is the desirable one—a point to which we have already adverted in relation to *Frankenstein*. Can it be true to nature to make one character give a description, over a hundred pages long, repeating at length, word for word, long conversations which he has never heard, marking the changes of colour which he has not seen—and all this with a minuteness which even the firmest memory and the most loquacious tongue could not recall? Does not this give an unreality to the style incompatible with art, which ought to be the mainspring of all imaginative work? This, however, is not Mrs. Shelley's error alone, but is traceable through many masterpieces. The author, the creator, who sees the workings of the souls of his characters, has, naturally, memory and perception for all. Yet Mary Shelley, in this as in most of her work, has great insight into character. Elizabeth's grandfather in his dotage is quite a photograph from life; old Oswig Raby, who was more shrivelled with narrowness of mind than with age, but who felt himself and his house, the oldest in England, of more importance than aught else he knew of. His daughter-in-law, the widow of his eldest son, is also well drawn; a woman of upright nature who can acknowledge the faults of the family, and try to retrieve them, and who finally does her best to atone for the past.

—Lucy Madox Rossetti,
"Literary Work," 1890

Richard Garnett "Introduction" (1891)

It is customary to regard Mary Shelley's claims to literary distinction as so entirely rooted and grounded in her husband's as to constitute a merely parasitic growth upon his fame. It may be unreservedly admitted that her association with Shelley, and her care of his writings and memory after his death, are the strongest of her titles to remembrance. It is further undeniable that the most original of her works is also that which betrays the strongest traces of his influence. *Frankenstein* was written when her brain, magnetized by his companionship, was capable of an effort never to be repeated. But if the frame of mind which engendered and sustained the work was created by Shelley, the conception was not his, and the diction is dissimilar to his. Both derive from Godwin, but neither is Godwin's. The same observation, except for an occasional phrase caught from Shelley, applies to all her subsequent work. The frequent exaltation of spirit, the ideality and romance, may well have been Shelley's—the general style of execution neither repeats nor resembles him.

Mary Shelley's voice, then, is not to die away as a mere echo of her illustrious husband's. She has the *prima facie* claim to a hearing due to every writer who can assert the possession of a distinctive individuality; and if originality be once conceded to *Frankenstein,* as in all equity it must, none will dispute the validity of a title to fame grounded on such a work. It has solved the question itself—it is famous. It is full of faults venial in an author of nineteen; but, apart from the wild grandeur of the conception, it has that which even the maturity of mere talent never attains—the insight of genius which looks below the appearances of things, and perhaps even reverses its own first conception by the discovery of some underlying truth. Mary Shelley's original intention was probably that which would alone have occurred to most writers in her place. She meant to paint Frankenstein's monstrous creation as an object of unmitigated horror. The perception that he was an object of intense compassion as well imparted a moral value to what otherwise would have remained a daring flight of imagination. It has done more: it has helped to create, if it did not itself beget, a type of personage unknown to ancient fiction. The conception of a character at once justly execrable and truly pitiable is altogether modern. Richard the Third and Caliban make some approach towards it; but the former is too self-sufficing in his valour and his villainy to be deeply pitied, and the latter too senseless and brutal. Victor Hugo has made himself the laureate of pathetic deformity, but much of his work is a conscious or unconscious variation on the original theme of *Frankenstein.*

None of Mary Shelley's subsequent romances approached *Frankenstein* in power and popularity. The reason may be summed up in a word—Languor. After the death of her infant son in 1819, she could never again command the energy which had carried her so vigorously through *Frankenstein*. Except in one instance, her work did not really interest her. Her heart is not in it. *Valperga* contains many passages of exquisite beauty; but it was, as the authoress herself says, "a child of mighty slow growth;" "laboriously dug," Shelley adds, "out of a hundred old chronicles," and wants the fire of imagination which alone could have interpenetrated the mass and fused its diverse ingredients into a satisfying whole. Of the later novels, *The Last Man* excepted, it is needless to speak, save for the autobiographic interest with which Professor Dowden's fortunate discovery has informed the hitherto slighted pages of *Lodore*. But *The Last Man* demands great attention, for it is not only a work of far higher merit than commonly admitted, but of all her works the most characteristic of the authoress, the most representative of Mary Shelley in the character of pining widowhood which it was her destiny to support for the remainder of her life. It is an idealized version of her sorrows and sufferings, made to contribute a note to the strain which celebrates the final dissolution of the world. The languor which mars her other writings is a beauty here, harmonizing with the general tone of sublime melancholy. Most pictures of the end of the world, painted or penned, have an apocalyptic character. Men's imaginations are powerfully impressed by great convulsions of nature; fire, tempest, and earthquake are summoned to effect the dissolution of the expiring earth. In *The Last Man* pestilence is the sole agent, and the tragedy is purely human. The tale consequently lacks the magnificence which the subject might have seemed to invite, but, on the other hand, gains in pathos—a pathos greatly increased when the authoress's identity is recollected, and it is observed how vividly actual experience traverses her web of fiction. None can have been affected by Mary Shelley's work so deeply as Mary Shelley herself; for the scenery is that of her familiar haunts, the personages are her intimates under thin disguises, the universal catastrophe is but the magnified image of the overthrow of her own fortunes; and there are pages on pages where every word must have come to her fraught with some unutterably sweet or bitter association. Yet, though her romance could never be to the public what it was to the author, it is surprising that criticism should have hitherto done so little justice either to its pervading nobility of thought or to the eloquence and beauty of very many inspired passages.

When *The Last Man* is reprinted it will come before the world as a new work. The same is the case with the short tales in this collection, the very existence of which is probably unknown to those most deeply interested in Mary Shelley. The entire class of literature to which they belong has long ago gone into Time's wallet as "alms for oblivion." They are exclusively contributions to a form of publication utterly superseded in this hasty age—the Annual, whose very name seemed to prophesy that it would not be perennial. For the creations of the intellect, however, there is a way back from Avernus. Every new generation convicts the last of undue precipitation in discarding the work of its own immediate predecessor. The special literary form may be incapable of revival; but the substance of that which has pleased or profited its age, be it Crashaw's verse, or Etherege's comedies, or Hoadly's pamphlets, or what it may, always repays a fresh examination, and is always found to contribute some element useful or acceptable to the literature of a later day. The day of the "splendid annual" was certainly not a vigorous or healthy one in the history of English *belles-lettres*. It came in at the ebb of the great tide of poetry which followed on the French Revolution, and before the insetting of the great tide of Victorian prose. A pretentious feebleness characterizes the majority of its productions, half of which are hardly above the level of the album. Yet it had its good points, worthy to be taken into account. The necessary brevity of contributions to an annual operated as a powerful check on the loquacity so unfortunately encouraged by the three-volume novel. There was no room for tiresome descriptions of minutiae, or interminable talk about uninteresting people. Being, moreover, largely intended for the perusal of high-born maidens in palace towers, the annuals frequently affected an exalted order of sentiment, which, if intolerable in insincere or merely mechanical hands, encouraged the emotion of a really passionate writer as much as the present taste for minute delineation represses it. This perfectly suited Mary Shelley. No writer felt less call to reproduce the society around her. It did not interest her in the smallest degree. The bent of her soul was entirely towards the ideal. This ideal was by no means buried in the grave of Shelley. She aspired passionately towards an imaginary perfection all her life, and solaced disappointment with what, in actual existence, too often proved the parent of fresh disillusion. In fiction it was otherwise; the fashionable style of publication, with all its faults, encouraged the enthusiasm, rapturous or melancholy, with which she adored the present or lamented the lost. She could fully indulge her taste for exalted sentiment in the Annual, and the necessary limitations of space afforded less scope for that creeping languor which relaxed the nerve of her more ambitious productions.

In these little tales she is her perfect self, and the reader will find not only the entertainment of interesting fiction, but a fair picture of the mind, repressed in its energies by circumstances, but naturally enthusiastic and aspiring, of a lonely, thwarted, misunderstood woman, who could seldom do herself justice, and whose precise place in the contemporary constellation of genius remains to be determined.

The merit of a collection of stories, casually written at different periods and under different influences, must necessarily be various. As a rule, it may be said that Mary Shelley is best when most ideal, and excels in proportion to the exaltation of the sentiment embodied in her tale. Virtue, patriotism, disinterested affection, are very real things to her; and her heroes and heroines, if generally above the ordinary plane of humanity, never transgress the limits of humanity itself. Her fault is the other way, and arises from a positive incapacity for painting the ugly and the commonplace. She does her best, but her villains do not impress us. Minute delineation of character is never attempted; it lay entirely out of her sphere. Her tales are consequently executed in the free, broad style of the eighteenth century, towards which a reaction is now fortunately observable. As stories, they are very good. The theme is always interesting, and the sequence of events natural. No person and no incident, perhaps, takes a very strong hold upon the imagination; but the general impression is one of a sphere of exalted feeling into which it is good to enter, and which ennobles as much as the photography of ugliness degrades. The diction, as usual in the imaginative literature of the period, is frequently too ornate, and could spare a good many adjectives. But its native strength is revealed in passages of impassioned feeling; and remarkable command over the resources of the language is displayed in descriptions of scenes of natural beauty. The microscopic touch of a Browning or a Meredith, bringing the scene vividly before the mind's eye, is indeed absolutely wanting; but the landscape is suffused with the poetical atmosphere of a Claude or a Danby. The description at the beginning of "The Sisters of Albano" is a characteristic and beautiful instance.

The biographical element is deeply interwoven with these as with all Mary Shelley's writings. It is of especial interest to search out the traces of her own history, and the sources from which her descriptions and ideas may have been derived. "The Mourner" has evident vestiges of her residence near Windsor when *Alastor* was written, and probably reflects the general impression derived from Shelley's recollections of Eton. The visit to Passtum in "The Pole" recalls one of the most beautiful of Shelley's letters, which Mary, however, probably never saw. Claire Clairmont's fortunes seem glanced at in one or two places; and the story of "The Pole" may be partly founded on some experience of hers in Russia. Trelawny probably suggested the subjects of the two Greek tales, "The Evil Eye," and "Euphrasia." "The Mortal Immortal" is a variation on the theme of *St. Leon,* and "Transformation" on that of *Frankenstein.* These are the only tales in the collection which betray the influence of Godwin, and neither is so fully worked out as it might have been. Mary Shelley was evidently more at home with a human than with a superhuman ideal; her enthusiasm soars high, but does not transcend the possibilities of human nature. The artistic merit of her tales will be diversely estimated, but no reader will refuse the authoress facility of invention, or command of language, or elevation of soul.

—Richard Garnett, "Introduction,"
*Tales and Stories of Mary Wollstonecraft
Shelley,* 1891, pp. v–xii

C.H. HERFORD (1897)

The wife of Shelley and daughter of Godwin and Mary Wollstonecraft shines a good deal by reflected light, but she has one well-grounded title to literary remembrance in her romance of *Frankenstein.* It originated in the speculative discussions of the memorable summer of 1816, when the Shelleys and Byron were daily companions at the Villa Diodati. Though doubtless a tale of wonder, *Frankenstein* belongs in reality less to the school of Lewis, than to that of Godwin's *St. Leon.* Its invention betrays a vein of eager philosophic and scientific curiosity of which Lewis's purely literary mind was quite innocent. The problem of creating life had fascinated the daring brains of the Revolution as it had done those of the Renascence. To suppose it solved was merely to prolong and expand tendencies already vigorous in experience, while the wonders of Lewis and his tribe were wilful negations of experience, 'shot from a pistol' with a boyish delight in the impossible. The vivid drawing of the discomforts of supernatural or quasi-supernatural knowledge, in particular, shows the influence of *St. Leon.* She subsequently attempted historical romance (*Valperga, or the Life and Adventures of Castruccio, Prince of Lucca,* written at Pisa in 1821, published 1823, the *Perkin Warbeck,* 1830) with estimable success. In spite of much descriptive and analytic talent she shared the inaptitude for history which marked the Godwinian and Radcliffian schools alike. *The Last Man* (1826) which so deeply impressed the not very susceptible Jefferson Hogg, has a pathetic significance as shadowing her own tragic loneliness,—the 'loneliness of Crusoe'—as she herself long afterwards declared it to have been.

—C.H. Herford, *The Age of Wordsworth*, 1897, pp. 97–98

CLARA HELEN WHITMORE (1910)

It is impossible to comprehend the Byronic craze which swept cool-headed England off her feet during the regency. *Childe Harold* was the fashion, and many a hero of romance, even down to the time of *Pendennis*, aped his fashions. Disraeli and Bulwer were among his disciples. Bulwer's early novels, *Falkland* and *Pelham*, were influenced by him; and *Vivian Grey* and *Venetia* might have been the offspring of Byron's prose brain, so completely was Disraeli under his influence at the time.

The poorest of the novels of this class, but the one which gives the most intimate picture of Byron, is *Glenarvon*, by Lady Caroline Lamb. Its hero is Byron. The plot follows the outlines of her own life, and all the characters were counterparts of living people whom she knew. Calantha, the heroine, representing Lady Caroline, is married to Lord Avondale, or William Lamb, better known as Lord Melbourne, at one time Premier of England. Lord and Lady Avondale are very happy, until Glenarvon, "the spirit of evil," appears and dazzles Calantha. Twice she is about to elope with him, but the thought of her husband and children keeps her back. They part, and for a time tender *billets-doux* pass between them, until Calantha receives a cruel letter from Glenarvon, in which he bids her leave him in peace. Other well-known people appeared in the book. Lord Holland was the Great Nabob, Lady Holland was the Princess of Madagascar, and Samuel Rogers was the Yellow Hyena or the Pale Poet. The novel had also a moral purpose; it was intended to show the danger of a life devoted to pleasure and fashion.

Of course the book made a sensation. Lady Caroline Lamb, the daughter of Earl Bessborough, the granddaughter of Earl Spencer, related to nearly all the great houses of England, had all her life followed every impulse of a too susceptible imagination. Her infatuation for Lord Byron had long been a theme for gossip throughout London. She invited him constantly to her home; went to assemblies in his carriage; and, if he were invited to parties to which she was not, walked the streets to meet him; she confided to every chance acquaintance that she was dying of love for him. Yet, as one reads of this affair, one suspects that this devotion was nothing more than the infatuation of a high-strung nature for the hero of a romance. In writing to a friend about her husband, she says, "He was privy to my affair with Lord Byron and laughed at it." On her death-bed she said of her husband, "But remember, the only noble fellow I ever met with was William Lamb."

A month after her death, Lord Melbourne wrote a sketch of her life for the *Literary Gazette*. In this he said:

"Her character it is difficult to analyse, because, owing to the extreme susceptibility of her imagination, and the unhesitating and rapid manner in which she followed its impulses, her conduct was one perpetual kaleidoscope of changes. . . . To the poor she was invariably charitable—he was more: in spite of her ordinary thoughtlessness of self, for them she had consideration as well as generosity, and delicacy no less than relief. For her friends she had a ready and active love; for her enemies no hatred: never perhaps was there a human being who had less malevolence; as all her errors hurt only herself, so against herself only were levelled her accusation and reproach."

How far Byron was in earnest in this tragicomedy is more difficult to determine. In one letter to her he writes: "I was and am yours, freely and entirely, to obey, to honour, to love, and fly with you, where, when, and how yourself might and may determine." That Byron was piqued when he read the book, his letter to Moore proves: "By the way, I suppose you have seen *Glenarvon*. It seems to me if the authoress had written the truth—the whole truth—the romance would not only have been more romantic, but more entertaining. As for the likeness, the picture can't be good; I did not sit long enough." It was not pleasing to Lord Byron's vanity to appear in her book as the spirit of evil, beside her husband, a high-minded gentleman, ready to sacrifice for his friends everything "but his honour and integrity."

Notwithstanding the humorous elements in the connection of Lord Byron and Lady Caroline Lamb, the story is pathetic. His poetic personality attracted her as the light does the poor moth. Disraeli caricatured her in the character of Mrs. Felix Lorraine in *Vivian Grey*, and introduced her into *Venetia* under the title of Lady Monteagle, where he made much of her love for the poet Cadurcis, otherwise Lord Byron.

Lady Caroline Lamb wrote two other novels, but they are of no value. In her third, *Ada Reis*, considered her best, she introduced Bulwer as the good spirit.

The little poem written by Lady Caroline Lamb on the day fixed for her departure from Brocket Hall, after it had been decided that she was to live in retirement away from her husband and son, shows tenderness and poetic feeling:

> They dance—they sing—they bless the day.
> I weep the while—and well I may:
> Husband, nor child, to greet me come.
> Without a friend—without a home:
> I sit beneath my favourite tree,
> Sing then, my little birds, to me,
> In music, love, and liberty.

At the time that the British public was smiling graciously, even if a little humorously, upon Lady Caroline Lamb, and was lionising Lord Byron, it spurned from its presence with the greatest disdain Percy and Mary Shelley. Even after the death of Shelley, when Mary returned to London with herself and son to support, it received her as the prodigal daughter for whom the crumbs from the rich man's table must suffice.

Mary Shelley had inherited from her mother the world's frown. Mary Wollstonecraft Godwin had been, the greater part of her life, at variance with society. She was the author, as has been said, of the *Vindication of the Rights of Woman*, and had for a long time been an opponent of marriage, chiefly because the civil laws pertaining to it deprived both husband and wife of their proper liberty. Her bitter experience with Imlay had, however, so modified her views on this latter subject that she became the wife of William Godwin a short time before the birth of their daughter Mary, who in after years became Mrs. Shelley. Although her mother died at her birth, Mary Godwin was deeply imbued with her theories of life. She had read her books, and had often heard her father express the same views concerning the bondage of marriage and its uselessness. Her elopement with Shelley while his wife Harriet was still living gains a certain sanction from the fact that she plighted her troth to him at her mother's grave. After the sad death of Harriet, however, Shelley and Mary Godwin conceded to the world's opinion, and were legally married. But the anger of society was not appeased, and, even after both had become famous, it continued to ignore the poet Shelley and his gifted wife.

At the age of nineteen Mrs. Shelley was led to write her first novel. Mr. and Mrs. Shelley and Byron were spending the summer of 1816 in the mountains of Switzerland. Continuous rain kept them in-doors, where they passed the time in reading ghost stories. At the suggestion of Byron, each one agreed to write a blood-curdling tale. It is one of the strange freaks of invention that this young girl succeeded where Shelley and Byron failed. Byron wrote

a fragment of a story which was printed with *Mazeppa*. Shelley also began a
story, but when he had reduced his characters to a most pitiable condition,
he wearied of them and could devise no way to bring the tale to a fitting
conclusion. After listening to a conversation between the two poets upon
the possibilities of science discovering the secrets of life, the story known as
Frankenstein, or the Modern Prometheus shaped itself in Mary's mind.

Frankenstein is one of those novels that defy the critic. Everyone
recognises that the letters written by Captain Walton to his sister in which
he tells of his meeting with Frankenstein, and repeats to her the story he
has just heard from his guest, makes an awkward introduction to the real
narrative. Yet all this part about Captain Walton and his crew was added
at the suggestion of Shelley after the rest of the story had been written.
But the narrative of *Frankenstein* is so powerful, so real, that, once read,
it can never be forgotten. Mrs. Shelley wrote in the introduction of the
edition of 1839 that, before writing it, she was trying to think of a story,
"one that would speak to the mysterious fears of our nature, and awaken
thrilling horror—one to make the reader dread to look round, to curdle
the blood and quicken the beatings of the heart." That she has done this the
experience of every reader will prove.

But the story has a greater hold on the imagination than this alone
would give it. The monster created by Frankenstein is closely related to our
own human nature. "My heart was fashioned to be susceptible of love and
sympathy," he says, "and, when wrenched by misery to vice and hatred, it did
not endure the violence of the change without torture, such as you cannot
even imagine." There is a wonderful blending of good and evil in this demon,
and, while the magnitude of his crimes makes us shudder, his wrongs and his
loneliness awaken our pity. "The fallen angel becomes a malignant devil. Yet
even that enemy of God and man had friends and associates in his desolation;
I am quite alone," the monster complains to his creator. Who can forget the
scene where he watches Frankenstein at work making for him the companion
that he had promised? Perhaps sadder than the story of the monster is that of
Frankenstein, who, led by a desire to widen human knowledge, finds that the
fulfilment of his lofty ambition has brought only a curse to mankind.

In 1823, Mary Shelley published a second novel, *Valperga*, so named from
a castle and small independent territory near Lucca. Castruccio Castracani,
whose life Machiavelli has told, is the hero of the story. The greatest soldier
and satirist of his times, the man of the novel is considered inferior to the
man of history. Mrs. Shelley had read broadly before beginning the book,
and she has described minutely the customs of the age about which she is

writing. Shelley pronounced it "a living and moving picture of an age almost forgotten."

The interest centres in the two heroines, Euthanasia, Countess of Valperga, and Beatrice, Prophetess of Ferrara. Strong, intellectual, and passionate, not until the time of George Eliot did women of this type become prominent in fiction. Euthanasia, a Guelph and a Florentine, with a soul "adapted for the reception of all good, "was betrothed to the youth Castruccio, whom she at that time loved. Later, when his character deteriorated under the influence of selfish ambition, she ceased to love him, and said, "He cast off humanity, honesty, honourable feeling, all that I prize." Castruccio belonged to the Ghibelines, so that the story of their love is intertwined with the struggle between these two parties in Italy.

But more beautiful than the intellectual character of Euthanasia, is the spiritual one of Beatrice, the adopted daughter of the bishop of Ferrara, who is regarded with feelings of reverence by her countrymen, because of her prophetic powers. Pure and deeply religious, she accepted all the suggestions of her mind as a message from God. When Castruccio came to Ferrara and was entertained by the bishop as the prince and liberator of his country, she believed that together they could accomplish much for her beloved country: "She prayed to the Virgin to inspire her; and, again giving herself up to reverie, she wove a subtle web, whose materials she believed heavenly, but which were indeed stolen from the glowing wings of love." No wonder she believed the dictates of her own heart, she whose words the superstition of the age had so often declared miraculous. She was barely seventeen and she loved for the first time. How pathetic is her disillusionment when Castruccio bade her farewell for a season, as he was about to leave Ferrara. She had believed that the Holy Spirit had brought Castruccio to her that by the union of his manly qualities and her divine attributes some great work might be fulfilled. But as he left her, he spoke only of earthly happiness:

"It was her heart, her whole soul she had given; her understanding, her prophetic powers, all the little universe that with her ardent spirit she grasped and possessed, she had surrendered, fully, and without reserve; but, alas! the most worthless part alone had been accepted, and the rest cast as dust upon the winds."

Afterwards, when she wandered forth a beggar, and was rescued by Euthanasia, she exclaimed to her:

"You either worship a useless shadow, or a fiend in the clothing of a God."

The daughter of Mary Wollstonecraft could fully sympathise with Beatrice. In the grief, almost madness, with which Beatrice realises her self-deception, there are traces of Frankenstein. Perhaps no problem plucked from the tree of good and evil was so ever-present to Mary Shelley as why misery so often follows an obedience to the highest dictates of the soul. Both her father and mother had experienced this; and she and Shelley had tasted of the same bitter fruit. In the analysis of Beatrice's emotions Mrs. Shelley shows herself akin to Charlotte Brontë.

Three years after the death of Shelley, she published *The Last Man*. It relates to England in the year 2073 when, the king having abdicated his throne, England had become a republic. Soon after this, however a pestilence fell upon the people, which drove them upon the continent, where they travelled southward, until only one man remained. The plot is clumsy; the characters are abstractions.

But the feelings of the author, written in clear letters on every page, are a valuable addition to the history of the poet Shelley and his wife. Besides her fresh sorrow for her husband, Byron had died only the year before. Her mind was brooding on the days the three had spent together. Her grief was too recent to be shaken from her mind or lost sight of in her imaginative work. Shelley, and the scenes she had looked on with him, the conversations between him and his friends, creep in on every page. Lionel Verney, the Last Man, is the supposed narrator of the story. He thus describes Adrian, the son of the king: "A tall, slim, fair boy, with a physiognomy expressive of the excess of sensibility and refinement, stood before me; the morning sunbeams tinged with gold his silken hair, and spread light and glory over his beaming countenance ... he seemed like an inspired musician, who struck, with unerring skill, the 'lyre of mind,' and produced thence divinest harmony. . . . His slight frame was over informed by the soul that dwelt within. . . . He was gay as a lark carrolling from its skiey tower. . . . The young and inexperienced did not understand the lofty severity of his moral views, and disliked him as a being different from themselves." Shelley, of course, was the original of this picture. Lord Byron suggested the character of Lord Raymond: "The earth was spread out as a highway for him; the heavens built up as a canopy for him." "Every trait spoke predominate self-will; his smile was pleasing, though disdain too often curled his lips—lips which to female eyes were the very throne of beauty and love. . . . Thus full of contradictions, unbending yet haughty, gentle yet fierce, tender and again neglectful, he by some strange art found easy entrance to the admiration and affection of women; now caressing and now tyrannising over them according to his mood, but in every change a despot."

A large part of the three volumes is taken up with a characterisation of Adrian and Lord Raymond, the latter of whom falls when fighting for the Greeks. How impossible it was for her to rid her mind of her own sorrow is shown at the end of the third volume, where Adrian is drowned, and Lionel Verney is left alone. He thus says of his friend:

"All I had possessed of this world's goods, of happiness, knowledge, or virtue—I owed to him. He had, in his person, his intellect, and rare qualities, given a glory to my life, which without him it had never known. Beyond all other beings he had taught me that goodness, pure and simple, can be an attribute of man."

Mrs. Shelley made the great mistake of writing this novel in the first person. *The Last Man*, who is telling the story, although he has the name of Lionel, is most assuredly of the female sex. The friendship between him and Adrian is not the friendship of man for man, but rather the love of man and woman.

Mrs. Shelley's next novel, *Lodore*, written in 1835, thirteen years after the death of her husband, had a better outlined plot and more definite characters. But again it echoes the past. Lord Byron's unhappy married relations and Shelley's troubles with Harriet are blended in the story, Lord Byron furnishing the character in some respects of Lord Lodore, while his wife, Cornelia Santerre, resembles both Harriet and Lady Byron. Lady Santerre, the mother of Cornelia, augments the trouble between Lord and Lady Lodore, and, contrary to the evident intentions of the writer, the reader's sympathies are largely with Cornelia and Lady Santerre. When Lodore wishes Cornelia to go to America to save him from disgrace, Lady Santerre objects to her daughter's accompanying him:

"He will soon grow tired of playing the tragic hero on a stage surrounded by no spectators; he will discover the folly of his conduct; he will return, and plead for forgiveness, and feel that he is too fortunate in a wife who has preserved her own conduct free from censure and remark while he has made himself a laughing-stock to all."

These words strangely bring to mind Lord Byron as having evoked them.

Again Lady Lodore's letter to her husband at the time of his departure to America reminds one of Lady Byron:

"If heaven have blessings for the coldly egotistical, the unfeeling despot, may those blessings be yours; but do not dare to interfere with emotions too pure, too disinterested for you ever to understand. Give me my child, and fear neither my interference nor resentment."

Lady Lodore's character changes in the book, and becomes more like that of Harriet Shelley. As Mrs. Shelley wrote, fragments of the past evidently came into her mind and influenced her pen, and her original conception of the characters was forgotten. Clorinda, the beautiful, eloquent, and passionate Neapolitan, was drawn from Emilia Viviani, who had suggested to Shelley his poem *Epipsychidion*, while both Horatio Saville, who had "no thought but for the nobler creations of the soul, and the discernment of the sublime laws of God and nature," and his cousin Villiers, also an enthusiastic worshipper of nature, possessed many of Shelley's qualities.

Besides two other novels of no value, *Perkin Warbeck* and *Falkner*, Mrs. Shelley wrote numerous short stories for the annuals, at that time so much in vogue. In 1891, these were collected and edited with an appreciative criticism by Sir Richard Garnett. Many of them have the intensity and sustained interest of *Frankenstein*.

After the death of her husband, grief and trouble dimmed Mrs. Shelley's imagination.

But the pale student Frankenstein, the Monster he created, and the beautiful priestess, Beatrice, three strong conceptions, testify to the genius of Mary Shelley.

—Clara Helen Whitmore, from
Lady Caroline Lamb. Mrs. Shelley, 1910

WORKS

FRANKENSTEIN

John Wilson Crocker presents us with a scathing review of *Frankenstein*, referring to the novel as "a horrible and disgusting absurdity." Crocker takes issue with Mary Shelley's use of language, equating it with the speech heard from the mentally ill, which in turn leads to Crocker's suspicion as to the sanity of the author, born to such a strange family. "Mr. Godwin is the patriarch of a literary family, whose chief skill is in delineating the wanderings of the intellect, and which strangely delights in the most afflicting and humiliating of human miseries." In sum, *Frankenstein* is held to be an offensive work, devoid of any allegorical subplot or ethical lessons that many other critics have so strongly elucidated. "Our taste and our judgment alike revolt at this kind of writing, and the greater the ability with which it may be executed the worse it is—it inculcates, no lesson of conduct, manners, or morality; it cannot mend, and will not even amuse its readers. . . ."

In his praise of *Frankenstein* as a masterpiece in a class by itself, Sir Walter Scott provides a brilliant and thoroughgoing analysis of the generic elements that make this a classic *sui generis*. In an effort to classify Mary Shelley's novel, Scott spends considerable effort in cataloguing literary works that bear some resemblance to the novel. Within the subgenres of romantic fiction, Scott outlines the varying degrees of credibility to be found in their treatment of nature and human behavior. At the first level of romance, there are tales of the marvelous, which he sees as implicit forays into the fantastic, accompanied by rich and lavishly embellished landscapes, while the characters are ferried through a wondrous and supernatural terrain. At the next level, Scott identifies a more sophisticated subgenre that is more philosophically oriented. In this second subgenre, the fantastic is concerned with transforming nature in order to probe the psychological effect on human beings rather than merely being an exercise into the wealth of the imagination as in the first group.

> To make more clear the distinction we have endeavoured to draw between the marvellous and the effects of the marvellous, ... Gulliver stuck into a marrow bone, and Master Thomas Thumb's disastrous fall into the bowl of hasty-pudding, are, in the general outline, kindred incidents; but the jest is exhausted in the latter case, when the accident is told; whereas in the former, it lies not so much in the comparatively pigmy size which subjected Gulliver to such a ludicrous misfortune, as in the tone of grave and dignified feeling with which he resents the disgrace of the incident.

At the third level of romance, however, is *Frankenstein*, which Scott sees directly linked to Godwin's *St. Leon*, where an alchemical principle is at work. Victor Frankenstein is in pursuit of the elixir of life and realizes his goal with the creation of his hideous monster. The dire consequences that result, visited on Victor Frankenstein for dabbling in forbidden knowledge, serve as a classic example of the fate that befalls all alchemists (who are invariably subversive characters in literature), as they try to defy the boundaries of human understanding. However, what makes *Frankenstein* unique for Scott is the fact that Erasmus Darwin and other scientific writers in Germany had noted the possibility of generating life in a laboratory. Indeed, Percy Bysshe Shelley had attended various medical lectures in London by such eminent doctors as John Abernathy and William Lawrence. Furthermore, in Scott's estimation, what adds to the credibility of Mary Shelley's story is the novel's plain and highly effective language.

> It is no slight merit in our eyes, that the tale, though wild in incident, is written in plain and forcible English, without exhibiting that mixture of hyperbolical Germanisms with which tales of wonder are usually told, as if it were necessary that the language should be as extravagant as the fiction. The ideas of the author are always clearly as well as forcibly expressed; and his descriptions of landscape have in them the choice requisites of truth, freshness, precision, and beauty.

Richard Henry Horne assigns *Frankenstein* to the genre of imaginative romance, a format that requires a writer to be enthusiastically motivated in the expression of an important idea. Horne pits the imaginative romance against the gothic romance, with the former providing a refreshing change from the extravagant horrors of the gothic tale, which he believes only serve to stir up the emotions with no other purpose beyond that. Specifically, Horne argues that the monster in *Frankenstein* serves a multitude of important functions. Not only an example of the sublime in its hideous and wild conception, the monster also pleads his cause to humanity against the cruelty inherent to some men, thus becoming a type of spokesperson for the oppressed. "[W]hen he finally disappears on his raft on the icy sea to build his own funeral pile, he pleads the cause of all that class who have so strong a claim on the help and sympathy of the world, yet find little else but disgust, or, at best, neglect." Furthermore, Horne makes the same case as other critics for a particular type of allegory in *Frankenstein*, namely one that represents the consequences of treading beyond the borders of permissible knowledge. In a brief comment on *Valperga*, Horne believes its merits reside in its representation of a hero who is both brave and tyrannical at the same time. "This is doing a good work, taking the false glory from the eyes and showing things as they are."

Margaret Oliphant refers to *Frankenstein* as an exceptional and powerful happenstance for Mary Shelley, a stroke of inspiration never to be duplicated in subsequent writings, which she believes are the manifestations of a widow in mourning. Discussing the author's later works, she writes, "Mary Shelley's individual appearances afterwards are only those of a romantically-desolate widow, pouring out her grief and fondness in sentimental gushes, which look somewhat overstrained and ridiculous in print, whatever they may have done in fact. . . ."

An unsigned review in *The British Critic* of April 1818 gives *Frankenstein* an unfavorable evaluation. While conceding to the presence of some instances of strong writing, "bear[ing] marks of considerable power," the critic deems the novel as a whole to be absurd and even suggests that its nightmarish quality could be hazardous to our health. "[W]e feel ourselves as much harassed, after rising from the perusal of these three spirit-wearing volumes, as if we had been over-dosed with laudanum, or hag-ridden by the night-mare." Overall, the reviewer finds few redeeming features within a ridiculous and "anomalous" text that he believes to be devoid of purpose and which, in his final analysis, is attributable to the fact that it is written by a female. "The writer of it is, we understand, a female; this is an aggravation of that which is the prevailing fault of the novel; but if our authoress can forget the gentleness of her sex, it is no reason why we should; and we shall therefore dismiss the novel without further comment."

Edith Birkhead credits Mary Shelley and the circle of friends gathered at the Villa Diodati in the summer of 1816 for having dispensed with many of the trappings of the gothic romance. In 1816, when Mary Shelley and her companions set themselves the task of composing supernatural stories, "it was wise to dispense with the shrieking chorus of malevolent abbesses, diabolical monks, intriguing marquises, Wandering Jews or bleeding specters, who had been so grievously overworked in previous performances." She praises Mary Shelley for having found a new theme in *Frankenstein*, demonstrating an originality that was independent of the influence of her predecessors. Nevertheless, while Birkhead celebrates Mary's originality, she nevertheless finds the intricate plot of framing devices extraneous and distracting, burdened by Walton's narration and ultimately weakening its most intriguing theme, the creation of life in the laboratory. Birkhead believes that Mary ultimately lost control of her story and that her novel would have been more successful as a tale. She attributes this debilitation to Percy's intervention in asking Mary to develop the idea in greater length.

> If Mrs. Shelley had abandoned the awkward contrivance of putting the narrative into the form of a dying man's confession, reported verbatim in a series of letters, and had opened her story, as she apparently intended, at the point where Frankenstein, after weary years of research, succeeds in creating a living being, her novel would have gained in force and intensity.

As to her next novel, *Valperga*, Birkhead finds that Mary's meticulous and studied research on medieval Italy impedes her imagination so that the narrative gets bogged down by the depth of her extensive learning. Birkhead does acknowledge, however, that the characterization of Castruccio bears resemblance to Milton's Satan. As to *The Last Man*, Birkhead feels the novel is weakened by its strong autobiographical elements and that it suffers from a lack of strong characterization, though she admits that Mary Shelley has demonstrated a keen psychological insight. She commends the work for its aesthetic elements, which evidence Percy Shelley's influence: "[O]ccasional passages of wonderful beauty recall Shelley's imagery; and in conveying the pathos of loneliness, personal feeling lends nobility and eloquence to her style." Finally, Birkhead mentions some of the tales that fall within the genre of terror, such as *A Tale of the Passions, or the Death of Despina*, which presents a conventional rogue who suffers from an extreme egotism and is completely given over to the imposition and realization of his own inclinations; *The Mortal Immortal*, which she finds reminiscent of Godwin's *St. Leon*; and *Transformation*, a tale replete with the same pathos of unsightliness as Frankenstein's creature, though that story is treated more as a fairy tale rather than one focused on terror.

John Wilson Crocker "Frankenstein, or the Modern Prometheus" (1818)

Frankenstein, a Swiss student at the university of Ingolstadt, is led by a peculiar enthusiasm to study the structure of the human frame, and to attempt to follow to its recondite sources 'the stream of animal being.' In examining the causes of *life,* he informs us, antithetically, that he had first recourse to *death.*—He became acquainted with anatomy; but that was not all; he traced through vaults and charnel-houses the decay and corruption of the human body, and whilst engaged in this agreeable pursuit, examining and analyzing the minutias of mortality, and the phenomena of the change from life to death and from death to life, a sudden light broke in upon him—

> A light so brilliant and wondrous, yet so simple, that while I became dizzy with the immensity of the prospect which it illustrated, I was surprized that among so many men of genius, who had directed their inquiries toward the same science, I alone should be reserved to discover so astonishing a secret.
>
> Remember, I am NOT recording the vision of a madman. The sun does not more certainly shine in the heavens, than that which I now affirm is true. Some miracle might have produced it, yet the stages of the discovery were distinct and probable. After days and nights of incredible labour and fatigue, I succeeded in discovering the cause of generation and life; nay; more, I became myself capable of bestowing animation upon lifeless matter.

Having made this wonderful discovery, he hastened to put it in practice; by plundering graves and stealing, not bodies, but parts of bodies, from the church-yard: by dabbling (as he delicately expresses it) with the unhallowed damps of the grave, and torturing the living animal to animate lifeless clay, our modern Prometheus formed a filthy image to which the last step of his art was to communicate being:—for the convenience of the process of his animal manufacture, he had chosen to form his figure about eight feet high, and he endeavoured to make it as handsome as he could—he succeeded in the first object and failed in the second; he made and animated his giant; but by some little mistake in the artist's calculation, the intended beauty turned out the ugliest monster that ever deformed the day. The creator, terrified at his own work, flies into one wood, and the work, terrified at itself, flies into another. Here the monster, by the easy process of listening at the window of a cottage, acquires a complete education: he learns to think, to talk, to read prose and verse; he becomes acquainted with geography, history, and natural philosophy, in short, 'a most delicate monster.' This credible course of study, and its very natural success, are brought about by a combination of circumstances almost as natural. In the aforesaid cottage, a young *Frenchman* employed his time in teaching an *Arabian* girl all these fine things, utterly unconscious that while he was whispering soft lessons in his fair one's ear, he was also tutoring Frankenstein's hopeful son. The monster, however, by due diligence, becomes highly accomplished: he reads Plutarch's *Lives, Paradise Lost,* Volney's *Ruin of Empires,* and the *Sorrows of Werter.* Such were the works which constituted the Greco-Anglico-Germanico-Gallico-Arabic library of a Swabian hut, which, if not numerous, was at least miscellaneous, and reminds us, in this particular, of Lingo's famous combination of historic characters—'Mahomet, Heliogabalus, Wat Tyler, and Jack the Painter.' He learns also to decypher some writings which he carried off from the laboratory in which he was manufactured; by these papers he becomes acquainted with the name and residence of Frankenstein and his family, and as his education has given him so good a taste as to detest himself, he has also the good sense to detest his creator for imposing upon him such a horrible burden as conscious existence, and he therefore commences a series of bloody persecutions against the unhappy Frankenstein—he murders his infant brother, his young bride, his bosom friend; even the very nursery maids of the family are not safe from his vengeance, for he contrives that they shall be hanged for robbery and murder which he himself commits.

The monster, however, has some method in his madness: he meets his Prometheus in the valley of Chamouny, and, in a long conversation, tells him the whole story of his adventures and his crimes, and declares, that he will 'spill much more blood and become worse,' unless Frankenstein will *make* (we should perhaps say *build)* a wife for him; the *Sorrows of Werter* had, it seems, given him a strange longing to find a Charlotte, of a suitable size, and it is plain that none of Eve's daughters, not even the enormous Charlotte[1] of the Variétés herself, would have suited this stupendous fantoccino. A compliance with this natural desire his kind-hearted parent most reasonably promises; but, on further consideration, he becomes alarmed at the thoughts of reviving the race of Anak, and he therefore resolves to break his engagement, and to defeat the procreative propensities of his ungracious child—hence great wrath and new horrors—parental unkindness and filial ingratitude. The monster hastens to execute his promised course of atrocity, and the monster-maker hurries after to stab or shoot him, and so put an end to his proceedings. This chase leads Frankenstein through Germany and France, to England, Scotland, and Ireland, in which latter country, he is taken up by a constable called Daniel Nugent, and carried before Squire Kirwan a magistrate, and very nearly hanged for a murder committed by the monster. We were greatly edified with the laudable minuteness which induces the author to give us the names of these officers of justice; it would, however, have been but fair to have given us also those of the impartial judge and enlightened jury who acquitted him, for acquitted, as our readers will be glad to hear, honourably acquitted, he was at the assizes of Donegal.—Escaped from this peril, he renews the chase, and the monster, finding himself hard pressed, resolves to fly to the most inaccessible point of the earth; and, as our Review had not yet enlightened mankind upon the real state of the North Pole, he directs his course thither as a sure place of solitude and security; but Frankenstein, who probably had read Mr. Daines Barrington and Colonel Beaufoy on the subject, was not discouraged, and follows him with redoubled vigour, the monster flying on a sledge drawn by dogs, according to the Colonel's proposition, and Prometheus following in another—the former, however, had either more skill or better luck than the latter, whose dogs died, and who must have been drowned on the breaking up of the ice, had he not been fortunately picked up in the nick of time by Mr. Walton, the master of an English whaler, employed on a voyage of discovery towards the North Pole. On board this ship poor Frankenstein, after telling his story to Mr. Walton, who has been so kind as to write it down for our use, dies of cold, fatigue and horror; and soon after, the monster, who had borrowed (we presume from the flourishing colony of East Greenland) a kind of raft, comes alongside the ship, and notwithstanding his huge bulk, jumps in at Mr. Walton's cabin window, and is surprized by that gentleman pronouncing a funeral oration over the departed Frankenstein; after which, declaring that he will go back to the Pole, and there *burn* himself on a funeral pyre (of ice, we conjecture) of his own collecting, he jumps again out of the window into his raft, and is out of sight in a moment.

Our readers will guess from this summary, what a tissue of horrible and disgusting absurdity this work presents.—It is piously dedicated to Mr. Godwin, and is written in the spirit of his school. The dreams of insanity are embodied in the strong and striking language of the insane, and the author, notwithstanding the rationality of his preface, often leaves us in doubt whether he is not as mad as his hero. Mr. Godwin is the patriarch of a literary family, whose chief skill is in delineating the wanderings of the intellect, and which strangely delights in the most afflicting and humiliating of human miseries. His disciples are a kind of *out-pensioners of Bedlam,* and, like 'Mad Bess' or 'Mad

Tom,' are occasionally visited with paroxysms of genius, and fits of expression, which make sober-minded people wonder and shudder. . . .

But when we have thus admitted that *Frankenstein* has passages which appal the mind, and make the flesh creep we have given it all the praise (if praise it can be called) which we dare to bestow. Our taste and our judgment alike revolt at this kind of writing, and the greater the ability with which it may be executed the worse it is—it inculcates, no lesson of conduct, manners, or morality; it cannot mend, and will not even amuse its readers, unless their taste have been deplorably vitiated—it fatigues the feelings without interesting the understanding; it gratuitously harasses the heart, and wantonly adds to the store, already too great, of painful sensations. The author has powers, both of conception and language, which employed in a happier direction might, perhaps, (we speak dubiously,) give him a name among those whose writings amuse or amend their fellow-creatures; but we take the liberty of assuring him, and hope that he may be in a temper to listen to us, that the style which he has adopted in the present publication merely tends to defeat his own purpose, if he really had any other object in view than that of leaving the wearied reader, after a struggle between laughter and loathing, in doubt whether the head or the heart of the author be the most diseased.

Notes

1. In the parody of Werter, at the Variétés in Paris, the Charlotte is ludicrously corpulent.

—John Wilson Crocker, from "Frankenstein, or the Modern Prometheus," *Quarterly Review,* January 1818, pp. 379–385

SIR WALTER SCOTT "REMARKS ON *FRANKENSTEIN*" (1818)

Did I request thee, Maker, from my clay
To mould me man? Did I solicit thee
From darkness to promote me?—
(Paradise Lost)

This is a novel, or more properly a romantic fiction, of a nature so peculiar, that we ought to describe the species before attempting any account of the individual production.

The first general division of works of fiction, into such as bound the events they narrate by the actual laws of nature, and such as, passing these limits, are managed by marvellous and supernatural machinery, is sufficiently obvious and decided. But the class of marvellous romances admits of several subdivisions. In the earlier productions of imagination, the poet, or tale-teller does not, in his own opinion, transgress the laws of credibility, when he introduces into his narration the witches, goblins, and magicians, in the existence of which he himself, as well as his hearers, is a firm believer. This good faith, however, passes away, and works turning upon the marvellous are written and read merely on account of the exercise which they afford to the imagination of those who, like the poet Collins, love to riot in the luxuriance of Oriental fiction, to rove through the meanders of enchantment, to gaze on the magnificence of golden palaces, and to repose by the water-falls of Elysian gardens. In this species of composition, the marvellous is itself the principal and most important object both to the author and reader. To describe its effect upon the mind of the human personages engaged in its wonders, and dragged along by its machinery, is comparatively an inferior object. The hero and heroine, partakers of the supernatural character which belongs to their adventures, walk the maze of enchantment with a firm and undaunted step, and appear as much at their ease, amid the wonders around them, as the young fellow described by the *Spectator*, who was discovered taking a snuff with great composure in the midst of a stormy ocean, represented on the stage of the Opera.

A more philosophical and refined use of the supernatural in works of fiction, is proper to that class in which the laws of nature are represented as altered, not for the purpose of pampering the imagination with wonders, but in order to show the probable effect which the supposed miracles would produce on those who witnessed them. In this case, the pleasure ordinarily derived from the marvellous incidents is secondary to that which we extract from observing how mortals like ourselves would be affected,

By scenes like these which, daring to depart
From sober truth, are still to nature true.

Even in the description of his marvels, however, the author who manages this style of composition with address, gives them an indirect importance with the reader, when he is able to describe with nature, and with truth, the effects which they are calculated to produce upon his *dramatis personae*. It will be remembered, that the sapient Partridge was too wise to be terrified at the mere appearance of the ghost of Hamlet, whom he knew to be a man dressed up in pasteboard armour for the nonce—it was when he saw the "little man," as he called Garrick, so frightened, that a sympathetic horror took hold of him. Of this we shall presently produce some examples from the narrative before us. But success in this point is still subordinate to the author's principal object, which is less to produce an effect by means of the marvels of the narrations, than to open new trains and channels of thought, by placing men in supposed situations of an extraordinary and preternatural character, and then describing the mode of feeling and conduct which they are most likely to adopt.

To make more clear the distinction we have endeavoured to draw between the marvellous and the effects of the marvellous, considered as separate objects, we may briefly invite our readers to compare the common tale of *Tom Thumb* with *Gulliver's Voyage to Brobdingnag*; one of the most childish fictions, with one which is pregnant with wit and satire, yet both turning upon the same assumed possibility of the existence of a pigmy among a race of giants. In the former case, when the imagination of the story-teller has exhausted itself in every species of hyperbole, in order to describe the diminutive size of his hero, the interest of the tale is at an end; but in the romance of the Dean of St Patrick's, the exquisite humour with which the natural consequences of so strange and unusual a situation is detailed, has a canvass on which to expand itself, as broad as the luxuriance even of the author's talents could desire. Gulliver stuck into a marrow bone, and Master Thomas Thumb's disastrous fall into the bowl of hasty-pudding, are, in the general outline, kindred incidents; but the jest is exhausted in the latter case, when the accident is told; whereas in the former, it lies not so much in the comparatively pigmy size which subjected Gulliver to such a ludicrous misfortune, as in the tone of grave and dignified feeling with which he resents the disgrace of the incident.

In the class of fictitious narrations to which we allude, the author opens a sort of account-current with the reader; drawing upon him, in the first place, for credit to that degree of the marvellous which he proposes to employ; and becoming virtually bound, in consequence of this indulgence, that his personages shall conduct themselves, in the extraordinary circumstances in which they are placed, according to the rules of probability, and the nature of the human heart. In this view, the *probable* is far from being laid out of sight even amid the wildest freaks of imagination; on the contrary, we grant the extraordinary postulates which the author demands as the foundation of his narrative, only on condition of his deducing the consequences with logical precision.

We have only to add, that this class of fiction has been sometimes applied to the purposes of political satire, and sometimes to the general illustration of the powers and workings of the human mind. Swift, Bergerac, and others, have employed it for the former purpose, and a good illustration of the latter is the well known *Saint Leon* of William Godwin. In this latter work, assuming the possibility of the transmutation of metals, and of the *elixir vitce,* the author has deduced, in the course of his narrative, the probable consequences of the possession of such secrets upon the fortunes and mind of him who might enjoy them. *Frankenstein* is a novel upon the same plan with *Saint Leon;* it is said to be written by Mr. Percy Bysshe Shelley, who, if we are rightly informed, is son-in-law to Mr. Godwin; and it is inscribed to that ingenious author.

In the preface, the author lays claim to rank his work among the class which we have endeavoured to describe.

> The event on which this fiction is founded has been supposed by Dr Darwin, and some of the physiological writers of Germany, as not of impossible occurrence. I shall not be supposed as according the remotest degree of serious faith to such an imagination; yet, in assuming it as the basis of a work of fancy, I have not considered myself as merely weaving a series of supernatural terrors. The event on which the interest of the story depends is exempt from the disadvantages of a mere tale of spectres or enchantment. It was recommended by the novelty of the situations which it develops; and, however impossible as a physical fact, affords a point of view to the imagination for the delineating of human passions more comprehensive and commanding than any which the ordinary relations of existing events can yield.
>
> I have thus endeavoured to preserve the truth of the elementary principles of human nature, while I have not scrupled to innovate upon their combinations. The *Iliad,* the tragic poetry of Greece,—Shakespeare, in the *Tempest* and *Midsummer Night's Dream,*—and most especially Milton, in *Paradise Lost,* conform to this rule; and the most humble novellist, who seeks to confer or receive amusement from his labours, may, without presumption, apply to prose fiction a license, or rather a rule, from the adoption of which so many exquisite combinations of human feeling have resulted in the highest specimens of poetry.

We shall, without farther preface, detail the particulars of the singular story, which is thus introduced.

A vessel, engaged in a voyage of discovery to the North Pole, having become embayed among the ice at a very high latitude, the crew, and particularly the captain or owner of the ship, are surprised at perceiving a gigantic form pass at some distance from them, on a car drawn by dogs, in a place where they conceived no mortal could exist. While they are speculating on this singular apparition, a thaw commences, and disengages them from their precarious situation. On the next morning they pick up, upon a floating fragment of the broken ice, a sledge like that they had before seen, with a human being in the act of perishing. He is with difficulty recalled to life, and proves to be a young man of the most amiable manners and extended acquirements, but, extenuated by fatigue, wrapped in dejection and gloom of the darkest kind. The captain of the ship, a gentleman whose ardent love of science had engaged him on an expedition so dangerous, becomes attached to the stranger, and at length extorts from him the wonderful tale of his misery, which he thus attains the means of preserving from oblivion.

Frankenstein describes himself as a native of Geneva, born and bred up in the bosom of domestic love and affection. His father—his friend Henry Clerval—Elizabeth, an orphan of extreme beauty and talent, bred up in the same house with him, are possessed of all the qualifications which could render him happy as a son, a friend, and a lover. In the course of his studies he becomes acquainted with the works of Cornelius Agrippa, and other authors treating of occult philosophy, on whose venerable tomes modern neglect has scattered no slight portion of dust. Frankenstein remains ignorant of the contempt in which his favourites are held, until he is separated from his family to pursue his studies at the university of Ingolstadt. Here he is introduced to the wonders of modern chemistry, as well as of natural philosophy in all its branches. Prosecuting these sciences into their innermost and most abstruse recesses, with unusual talent and unexampled success, he at length makes that discovery on which the marvellous part of the work is grounded. His attention had been especially bound to the structure of the human frame and of the principle of life. He engaged in physiological researches of the most recondite and abstruse nature, searching among charnel vaults and in dissection rooms, and the objects most insupportable to the delicacy of human feelings, in order to trace the minute chain of causation which takes place in the change from life to death, and from death to life. In the midst of this darkness a light broke in upon him.

"Remember," says his narrative, "I am not recording the vision of a madman. The sun does not more certainly shine in the heavens than that which I now affirm is true. Some miracle might have produced it, yet the stages of the discovery were distinct and probable. After days and nights of incredible labour and fatigue, I succeeded in discovering the cause of generation and life; nay, more, I became my self capable of bestowing animation upon lifeless matter."

This wonderful discovery impelled Frankenstein to avail himself of his art by the creation (if we dare to call it so), or formation of a living and sentient being. As the minuteness of the parts formed a great difficulty, he constructed the figure which he proposed to animate of a gigantic size, that is, about eight feet high, and strong and large in proportion. The feverish anxiety with which the young philosopher toils through the horrors of his secret task, now dabbling among the unhallowed reliques of the grave, and now torturing the living animal to animate the lifeless clay, are described generally, but with great vigour of language. Although supported by the hope of producing a new species that should bless him as his creator and source, he nearly sinks under the protracted labour, and loathsome details, of the work he had undertaken, and scarcely is his fatal enthusiasm sufficient to support his nerves, or animate his resolution. The result of this extraordinary discovery it would be unjust to give in any words save those of the author. We shall give it at length as an excellent specimen of the style and manner of the work.

> It was on a dreary night of November that I beheld the accomplishment of my toils. With an anxiety that almost amounted to agony, I collected the instruments of life around me, that I might infuse a spark of being into the lifeless thing that lay at my feet. It was already one in the morning; the rain pattered dismally against the panes, and my candle was nearly burnt out, when, by the glimmer of the half-extinguished light, I saw the dull yellow eye of the creature open; it breathed hard, and a convulsive motion agitated its limbs.
>
> How can I describe my emotions at this catastrophe, or how delineate the wretch whom with such infinite pains and care I had endeavoured to form? His limbs were in proportion, and I had selected his features as beautiful. Beautiful!—Great God! His yellow skin scarcely covered the work of muscles and arteries beneath; his hair was of a lustrous black, and flowing; his teeth of a pearly whiteness; but these luxuriances only formed a more horrid contrast with his watery eyes, that seemed almost of the same colour as the dun

white sockets in which they were set—his shrivelled complexion, and straight black lips.

The different accidents of life are not so changeable as the feelings of human nature. I had worked hard for nearly two years, for the sole purpose of infusing life into an inanimate body. For this I had deprived myself of rest and health. I had desired it with an ardour that far exceeded moderation; but now that I had finished, the beauty of the dream vanished, and breathless horror and disgust filled my heart. Unable to endure the aspect of the being I had created, I rushed out of the room, and continued a long time traversing my bedchamber, unable to compose my mind to sleep. At length lassitude succeeded to the tumult I had before endured; and I threw myself on the bed in my clothes, endeavouring to seek a few moments of forgetfulness. But it was in vain: I slept indeed, but I was disturbed by the wildest dreams. I thought I saw Elizabeth, in the bloom of health, walking in the streets of Ingolstadt. Delighted and surprised, I embraced her; but as I imprinted the first kiss on her lips, they became livid with the hue of death; her features appeared to change, and I thought that I held the corpse of my dead mother in my arms; a shroud enveloped her form, and I saw the grave-worms crawling in the folds of the flannel. I started from my sleep with horror; a cold dew covered my forehead, my teeth chattered, and every limb became convulsed; when, by the dim and yellow light of the moon, as it forced its way through the window-shutters, I beheld the wretch—the miserable monster whom I had created. He held up the curtain of the bed; and his eyes, if eyes they may be called, were fixed on me. His jaws opened, and he muttered some inarticulate sounds, while a grin wrinkled his cheeks. He might have spoken, but I did not hear; one hand was stretched out, seemingly to detain me, but I escaped, and rushed down stairs. I took refuge in the court-yard belonging to the house which I inhabited; where I remained during the rest of the night, walking up and down in the greatest agitation, listening attentively, catching and fearing each sound as if it were to announce the approach of the demoniacal corpse to which I had so miserably given life.

Oh! no mortal could support the horror of that countenance. A mummy again endued with animation could not be so hideous as that wretch. I had gazed on him while unfinished; he was ugly then; but when those muscles and joints were rendered capable of motion, it became a thing such as even Dante could not have conceived.

I passed the night wretchedly. Sometimes my pulse beat so quickly and hardly, that I felt the palpitation of every artery; at others, I nearly sank to the ground through languor and extreme weakness. Mingled with this horror, I felt the bitterness of disappointment: dreams, that had been my food and pleasant rest for so long a space, were now become a hell to me; and the change was so rapid, the overthrow so complete!

Morning, dismal and wet, at length dawned, and discovered, to my sleepless and aching eyes, the church of Ingolstadt, its white steeple and clock, which indicated the sixth hour. The porter opened the gates of the court, which had that night been my asylum, and I issued into the streets, pacing them with quick steps, as if I sought to avoid the wretch whom I feared every turning of the street would present to my view. I did not dare return to the apartment which I inhabited, but felt impelled to hurry on, although wetted by the rain, which poured from a black and comfortless sky.

I continued walking in this manner for some time, endeavouring, by bodily exercise, to ease the load that weighed upon my mind. I traversed the streets without any clear conception of where I was or what I was doing. My heart palpitated in the sickness of fear; and I hurried on with irregular steps, not daring to look about me:

> Like one who, on a lonely road
>   Doth walk in fear and dread,
> And, having once turn'd round, walks on,
>   And turns no more his head;
> Because he knows a frightful fiend
>   Doth close behind him tread.[1]

He is relieved by the arrival of the diligence from Geneva, out of which jumps his friend Henry Clerval, who had come to spend a season at the college. Compelled to carry Clerval to his lodgings, which, he supposed, must still contain the prodigious and hideous specimen of his Promethean art, his feelings are again admirably described, allowing always for the extraordinary cause supposed to give them birth.

I trembled excessively; I could not endure to think of, and far less to allude to, the occurrences of the preceding night. I walked with a quick pace, and we soon arrived at my college. I then reflected, and the thought made me shiver, that the creature whom I had left in my apartment might still be there, alive, and walking about. I dreaded to behold this monster; but I feared still more that Henry should see him. Entreating him therefore to remain a few minutes at the bottom of the stairs, I darted up towards my own room. My hand was already on the lock of the door before I recollected myself. I then paused; and a cold shivering came over me. I threw the door forcibly open, as children are accustomed to do when they expect a spectre to stand in waiting for them on the other side; but nothing appeared. I stepped fearfully in: the apartment was empty; and my bed-room was also freed from its hideous guest. I could hardly believe that so great a good fortune could have befallen me; but when I became assured that my enemy had indeed fled, I clapped my hands for joy, and ran down to Clerval.

The animated monster is heard of no more for a season. Frankenstein pays the penalty of his rash researches into the *arcana* of human nature, in a long illness, after which the two friends prosecute their studies for two years in uninterrupted quiet. Frankenstein, as may be supposed, abstaining, with a sort of abhorrence, from those in which he had once so greatly delighted. At the lapse of this period, he is made acquainted with a dreadful misfortune which has befallen his family, by the violent death of his youngest brother, an interesting child, who, while straying from his keeper, had been murdered by some villain in the walks of Plainpalais. The marks of strangling were distinct on the neck of the unfortunate infant, and a gold ornament which it wore, and which was amissing, was supposed to have been the murderer's motive for perpetrating the crime.

At this dismal intelligence Frankenstein flies to Geneva, and impelled by fraternal affection, visits the spot where this horrid accident had happened. In the midst of a thunderstorm, with which the evening had closed, and just as he had attained the fatal spot on which Victor had been murdered, a flash of lightning displays to him the hideous demon to which he had given life, gliding towards a neighbouring precipice. Another flash shows him hanging among the cliffs, up which he scrambles with far more than mortal agility, and is seen no more. The inference, that this being was the murderer of his brother, flashed on Frankenstein's mind as irresistibly as the lightning itself, and he was tempted to consider the creature whom he had cast among mankind to work, it would seem, acts of horror and depravity, nearly in the light of his own vampire let loose from the grave, and destined to destroy all that was dear to him.

Frankenstein was right in his apprehensions. Justine, the maid to whom the youthful Victor had been intrusted, is found to be in possession of the golden trinket which had been taken from the child's person; and by a variety of combining circumstances of combined evidence, she is concluded to be the murtheress, and, as such, condemned to death and executed. It does not appear that Frankenstein attempted to avert her fate, by communicating his horrible secret; but, indeed, who would have given him credit, or in what manner could he have supported his tale?

In a solitary expedition to the top of Mount Aveyron, undertaken to dispel the melancholy which clouded his mind, Frankenstein unexpectedly meets with the monster he had animated, who compels him to a conference and a parley. The material demon gives an account, at great length, of his history since his animation, of the mode in which he acquired various points of knowledge, and of the disasters which befell him, when, full of benevolence and philanthropy, he endeavoured to introduce himself into human society. The most material part of his education was acquired in a ruinous pig-stye—a Lyceum which this strange student occupied, he assures us, for a good many months undiscovered, and in constant observance of the motions of an amiable family, from imitating whom he learns the use of language, and other accomplishments, much more successfully than Caliban, though the latter had a conjuror to his tutor. This detail is not only highly improbable, but it is injudicious, as its unnecessary minuteness tends rather too much to familiarize us with the being whom it regards, and who loses, by this *lengthy* oration, some part of the mysterious sublimity annexed to his first appearance. The result is, this monster, who was at first, according to his own account, but a harmless monster, becomes ferocious and malignant, in consequence of finding all his approaches to human society repelled with injurious violence and offensive marks of disgust. Some papers concealed in his dress acquainted him with the circumstances and person to whom he owed his origin; and the hate which he felt towards the whole human race was now concentrated in resentment against Frankenstein. In this humour he murdered the child, and disposed the picture so as to induce a belief of Justine's guilt. The last is an inartificial circumstance: this indirect mode of mischief was not likely to occur to the being the narrative presents to us. The conclusion of this strange narrative is a peremptory demand on the part of the demon, as he is usually termed, that Frankenstein should renew his fearful experiment, and create for him an helpmate hideous as himself, who should have no pretence for shunning his society. On this condition he promises to withdraw to some distant desert, and shun the human race for ever. If his creator shall refuse him this consolation, he vows the prosecution of the most frightful vengeance. Frankenstein, after a long pause of reflection, imagines he sees that the justice due to the miserable being, as well as to mankind, who might be exposed to so much misery, from the power and evil dispositions of a creature who could climb perpendicular cliffs and exist among glaciers, demanded that he should comply with the request; and granted his promise accordingly.

Frankenstein retreats to one of the distant islands of the Orcades, that in secrecy and solitude he might resume his detestable and ill-omened labours, which now were doubly hideous, since he was deprived of the enthusiasm with which he formerly prosecuted them. As he is sitting one night in his laboratory, and recollecting the consequences of his first essay in the Promethean art, he begins to hesitate concerning the right he had to form another being as malignant and bloodthirsty as that he had unfortunately already animated. It is evident that he would thereby give the demon the means of propagating a hideous race, superior to mankind in strength and hardihood, who might render the very existence of the present human race a condition precarious and full of terror, just as these reflections lead him to the conclusion that his promise was criminal, and ought not to be kept, he looks up, and sees, by the light of the moon, the demon at the casement.

> A ghastly grin wrinkled his lips as he gazed on me, where I sat fulfilling the task which he allotted to me. Yes, he had followed me in my travels; he had loitered in forests, hid himself in caves, or taken refuge in wide and desert heaths; and he now came to mark my progress, and claim the fulfilment of my promise.
>
> As I looked on him, his countenance expressed the utmost extent of malice and treachery. I thought with a sensation of madness on my promise of creating another like to him, and, trembling with passion, tore to pieces the thing on which I was engaged. The wretch saw me destroy the creature on whose future existence he depended for happiness, and, with a howl of devilish despair and revenge, withdrew.

At a subsequent interview, described with the same wild energy, all treaty is broken off betwixt Frankenstein and the work of his hands, and they part on terms of open and declared hatred and defiance. Our limits do not allow us to trace in detail the progress of the demon's vengeance. Clerval falls its first victim, and under circumstances which had very nearly conducted the new Prometheus to the gallows as his supposed murderer. Elizabeth, his bride, is next strangled on her wedding-night; his father dies of grief; and at length Frankenstein, driven to despair and distraction, sees nothing left for him in life but vengeance on the singular cause of his misery. With this purpose he pursues the monster from clime to clime, receiving only such intimations of his being on the right scent, as served to show that the demon delighted in thus protracting his fury and his sufferings. At length, after the flight and pursuit had terminated among the frost-fogs, and icy islands of the northern ocean, and just when he had a glimpse of his adversary, the ground sea was heard, the ice gave way, and Frankenstein was placed in the perilous situation in which he is first introduced to the reader.

Exhausted by his sufferings, but still breathing vengeance against the being which was at once his creature and his persecutor, this unhappy victim to physiological discovery expires just as the clearing away of the ice permits Captain Walton's vessel to hoist sail for their return to Britain. At midnight, the daemon, who had been his destroyer, is discovered in the cabin, lamenting over the corpse of the person who gave him being. To Walton he attempts to justify his resentment towards the human race, while, at the same time, he acknowledges himself a wretch who had murdered the lovely and the helpless, and pursued to irremediable ruin his creator, the select specimen of all that was worthy of love and admiration.

> "Fear not," he continues, addressing the astonished Walton, "that I shall be the instrument of future mischief. My work is nearly complete. Neither yours nor any man's death is needed to consummate the series of my being, and accomplish that which must be done; but it requires my own. Do not think that I shall be slow to perform this sacrifice. I shall quit your vessel on the ice-raft which brought me hither, and shall seek the most northern extremity of the globe; I shall collect my funeral pile, and consume to ashes this miserable frame, that its remains may afford no light to any curious and unhallowed wretch, who would create such another as I have been.—"
>
> He sprung from the cabin-window, as he said this, upon the ice-raft which lay close to the vessel.
>
> He was soon borne away by the waves, and lost in darkness and distance.

Whether this singular being executed his purpose or no must necessarily remain an uncertainty, unless the voyage of discovery to the north pole should throw any light on the subject.

So concludes this extraordinary tale, in which the author seems to us to disclose uncommon powers of poetic imagination. The feeling with which we perused the unexpected and fearful, yet, allowing the possibility of the event, very natural conclusion of Frankenstein's experiment, shook a little even our firm nerves; although such and so numerous have been the expedients for exciting terror employed by the romantic writers of the age, that the reader may adopt Macbeth's words with a slight alteration:

We have supp'd full with horrors:
Direness, familiar to our "callous" thoughts,
Cannot once startle us.

It is no slight merit in our eyes, that the tale, though wild in incident, is written in plain and forcible English, without exhibiting that mixture of hyperbolical Germanisms with which tales of wonder are usually told, as if it were necessary that the language should be as extravagant as the fiction. The ideas of the author are always clearly as well as forcibly expressed; and his descriptions of landscape have in them the choice requisites of truth, freshness, precision, and beauty. The self-education of the monster, considering the slender opportunities of acquiring knowledge that he possessed, we have already noticed as improbable and overstrained. That he should have not only learned to speak, but to read, and, for aught we know, to write—that he should have become acquainted with *Werter*, with *Plutarch's Lives*, and with *Paradise Lost*, by listening through a hole in a wall, seems as unlikely as that he should have acquired, in the same way, the problems of *Euclid*, or the art of book-keeping by single and double entry. The author has however two apologies—the first, the necessity that his monster should acquire those endowments, and the other, that his neighbours were engaged in teaching the language of the country to a young foreigner. His progress in self-knowledge, and the acquisition of information, is, after all, more wonderful than that of *Hai Eben Yokhdan*, or *Automathes*, or the hero of the little romance called *The Child of Nature*, one of which works might perhaps suggest the train of ideas followed by the author of *Frankenstein*. We should also be disposed, in support of the principles with which we set out, to question whether the monster, how tall, agile, and strong however, could have perpetrated so much mischief undiscovered, or passed through so many countries without being secured, either on account of his crimes, or for the benefit of some such speculator as Mr Polito, who would have been happy to have added to his museum so curious a specimen of natural history. But as we have consented to admit the leading incident of the work, perhaps some of our readers may be of opinion, that to stickle upon lesser improbabilities, is to incur the censure bestowed by the Scottish proverb on those who start at straws after swallowing *windlings*.

The following lines, which occur in the second volume, mark, we think, that the author possesses the same facility in expressing himself in verse as in prose.

> We rest; a dream has power to poison sleep.
>> We rise; one wand'ring thought pollutes the day.
> We feel, conceive, or reason; laugh, or weep,
>> Embrace fond woe, or cast our cares away;
> It is the same: for, be it joy or sorrow,
>> The path of its departure still is free.
> Man's yesterday may ne'er belike his morrow;
>> Nought may endure but mutability!

Upon the whole, the work impresses us with a high idea of the author's original genius and happy power of expression. We shall be delighted to hear that he has aspired to the *paullo majora;* and in the meantime, congratulate our readers upon a novel which excites new reflections and untried sources of emotion. If Gray's definition of Paradise, to lie on a couch, namely, and read new novels, come any thing near truth, no small praise is due to him, who, like the author of Frankenstein, has enlarged the sphere of that fascinating enjoyment.

Notes

1. Coleridge's *Ancient Mariner.*

—Sir Walter Scott, "Remarks on
*Frankenstein," Blackwood's Edinburgh
Magazine,* March 1818, pp. 613–620

Unsigned Review from
The Edinburgh [Scots] Magazine (1818)

Here is one of the productions of the modern school in its highest style of caricature and exaggeration. It is formed on the Godwinian manner, and has all the faults, but many likewise of the beauties of that model. In dark and gloomy views of nature and of man, bordering too closely on impiety,—in the most outrageous improbability,—in sacrificing every thing to effect,—it even goes beyond its great prototype; but in return, it possesses a similar power of fascination, something of the same mastery in harsh and savage delineations of passion, relieved in like manner by the gentler features of domestic and simple feelings. There never was a wilder story imagined, yet, like most of the fictions of this age, it has an air of reality attached to it, by being connected with the favourite projects and passions of the times. The real events of the world have, in our day, too, been of so wondrous and gigantic a kind,—the shiftings of the scenes in our stupendous drama have been so rapid and various, that Shakespeare himself, in his wildest flights, has been completely distanced by the eccentricities of actual existence. Even he would scarcely have dared to have raised, in one act, a private adventurer to the greatest of European thrones,—to have concluded him, in the next, victorious over the necks of emperors and kings, and then, in a third, to have shewn him an exile, in a remote speck of an island, some thousands of miles from the scene of his triumphs; and the chariot which bore him along covered with glory, quietly exhibited to a gaping mechanical rabble under the roof of one of the beautiful buildings on the North Bridge of Edinburgh;—(which buildings we heartily pray may be brought as low as the mighty potentate whose Eagles are now to be seen looking out of their windows, like the fox from the ruins of Balclutha.) Our appetite, we say, for every sort of wonder and vehement interest, has in this way become so desperately inflamed, that especially as the world around us has again settled into its old dull state of happiness and legitimacy, we can be satisfied with nothing in fiction that is not highly coloured and exaggerated; we even like a story the better that it is disjointed and irregular, and our greatest inventors, accordingly, have obliged to accommodate themselves to the tests of the age, more, we believe, than their own judgment can, at all times, have approved of. The very extravagance of the present production will now, therefore, be, perhaps, in its favour, since the events which have actually passed before our eyes have made the atmosphere of miracles that in which we most readily breathe.

The story opens with a voyage of discovery to the North Pole. A young Englishman, whose mind had long been inflamed with this project, sets sail from Archangel, soon gets inclosed, as usual, among ice mountains, and is beginning to despair of success, when all his interest and thoughts are diverted suddenly into another channel, in consequence of a very singular adventure. One day a gigantic figure was seen moving northwards on a sledge, drawn by dogs, and a short time afterwards a poor emaciated wretch was picked up from a sledge that drifted close to the vessel. The Englishman soon formed a violent friendship for this stranger, and discovers him to be a person of the greatest virtues, talents, and acquirements, which are only rendered the more admirable and interesting, from the deep cloud of melancholy which frequently overshadowed them. After a time, he gets so far into his confidence, as to obtain from him the story of his life and misfortunes. His name was Frankenstein, son of a Syndic of Geneva, and of an amiable mother, who very properly dies at the beginning of the book, to leave her son and a young female cousin, who resided in the family, so disconsolate, that they could find no comfort except by falling in love. Frankenstein had been left much to his own disposal in the conduct of his studies, and, at a very early period, he had become quite *en-tête* with some of the writings of the alchemists, on which he accidentally lighted; and we were at first in expectation that, like St Leon, he was to become possessed of the philosopher's stone, or of the *elixir vitae*. He is destined, however, to obtain a still more extraordinary power, but not from the alchemists, of the futility of whose speculations he soon became convinced, but whose wild conceptions continued to give to his mind a strong and peculiar bias.

At the university, stimulated by the encouragement of some distinguished philosophers, be applied himself, with the utmost perseverance and ability, to every department of natural science, and soon became the general object of envy and admiration. His researches led him to investigate the principle of life, which he did in the old and approved manner by dissecting living animals, into all the repositories of the dead, and making himself acquainted with life and death in all their forms. The result was a most wonderful discovery,—quite simple, he says, when it was made, but yet one which he very wisely does not communicate to his English acquaintance, and which, of course, must remain a secret to the world,—no less than the discovery of the means of communicating life to an organized form. With this our young philosopher sets himself to make a man, and that he might make no blunder from taking too small a scale, unfortunately, as it turns out, his man is a giant. In a garret of his apartments, to which none but himself was ever admitted, he employs few months on this wonderful production. Many of the ingredients seem to have been of a very disgusting description, since he passed whole nights in sepulchres raking them out; he thought, however, that be had succeeded in making a giant, as gainly in appearance at last as O'Brien, or the Yorkshire Boy, and every thing was now ready for the last touch at the master, the infusion of life into the inanimate mass. In breathless expectation, in the dead of night, he performed this last momentous act of creation; and the creature opened upon him two immense ghastly yellow eyes, which struck him with instant horror. He immediately hated himself and his work, and flew, in a state of feverish agony, to his room below; but, finding himself followed thither by the monster, he rushed out into the streets, where he walked about in fearful agitation, till the morning dawned, and they began to be frequented by their inhabitants. Passing along, he saw step from a coach an intimate friend of his from Geneva. For the moment he forgot every thing that had happened, was delighted to find that his friend had come to pursue his studies along with him, and was conducting him to his apartments, when on a sudden he recollected the dreadful inmate who would probably be found in them. He ran up and examined them, and, on finding that the monster had disappeared, his joy became quite foolish and outrageous; he danced about like a madman, and his friend was not surprised when immediately after he was seized by a delirious fever, which confined him for some weeks, alleviated, however, by all the attentions which friendship could bestow.

Scarcely had he recovered, when a sad piece of intelligence arrives from home. His father writes him that his little brother had strayed from them in an evening walk, and was at last found dead, and apparently strangled. He flies home to comfort his family, but it is night ere he reaches Geneva, and the gates being shut, he remains in the neighbourhood, and walks out in the dark towards the hills. The monster on a sudden stalks past him, and moving with inconceivable rapidity, is seen by him perched on one of the highest cliffs. The thought instantly strikes him, that this fiend, the creation of his own hand, must have been the murderer of his brother, and he feels all the bitterness of despair. Very ill able to comfort others, he next morning went to his father's house, and learns, as an additional misery, that a young servant girl, who had been beloved as a friend in the family, was taken up on suspicion of the murder, and was to be tried for her life. A picture, which the child had worn on the fatal night, was found in her pocket. Though, in his own mind, he could not doubt of the real author of the murder, and his beloved Elizabeth was equally convinced that it could not be her favourite Justine, still circumstances were so strong against her, that the poor girl was condemned and executed. No wonder that Frankenstein now fell into a deep melancholy; to relieve him from which, his father took him and Elizabeth on a tour to the valley of Chamounix. This part of the book is very beautifully written; the description of the mountain scenery, and of its effect on Frankenstein's mind, is finely given. One rainy day they did not proceed on their journey, but Frankenstein, in a state of more than common depression, left them early in the inn, for the purpose of scaling the summit of Montarvet.

"It was nearly noon (he says) when I arrived at the top of the ascent. For some time I sat upon the rock that overlooks the sea of ice. A mist covered both that and the surrounding mountains. Presently a breeze dissipated the cloud, and I descended upon the glacier. The surface is very uneven, rising like the waves of a troubled sea, descending low, and interspersed by rifts that sink deep. The field of ice is about a league in width, but I spent nearly two hours in crossing it. The opposite mountain is a bare perpendicular rock. From the side where I now stood Montarvet was exactly opposite, at the distance of a league; and above it rose Mont Blanc, in awful majesty. I remained in a recess of the rock gazing on this wonderful and stupendous scene. The sea, or rather the vast river of ice, wound among its dependent mountains, whose aërial summits hung over its recess. Their icy and glittering peaks shone in the sunlight over the clouds. My heart, which was before sorrowful, was swelled with something like joy; I exclaimed, 'Wandering spirits, if indeed ye wander, and do not rest in your narrow beds, allow me this faint happiness, or take me, as your companion, away from the joys of life.' As I said this, I suddenly beheld the figure of a man at some distance advancing towards me with superhuman speed. He bounded over the crevices in the ice, among which I had walked with caution; his stature also, as he approached, seemed to exceed that of man. I was troubled: a mist came over my eyes, and I felt a faintness seize me, but I was quickly restored by the cold gale of the mountains. I perceived, as the shape came nearer, (sight tremendous and abhorred,) that it was the wretch whom I had created. I trembled with rage and horror, resolving to wait his approach, and then close with him in mortal combat. He approached; his countenance bespoke bitter anguish, combined with disdain and malignity, while its unearthly ugliness rendered it almost too horrible for human eyes."

Frankenstein at first addresses him in words of violent rage,—the monster, however, endeavours to soften him.

"Will no entreaties cause thee to turn a favourable eye upon thy creature who implores thy goodness and compassion? Believe me, Frankenstein, I was benevolent, my soul glowed with love and humanity, but am I not alone, miserably alone? You, my creator, abhor me; what hope can I gather from your fellow-creatures who owe me nothing? They spurn and hate me. The desert mountains and dreary glaciers are my refuge. I have wandered here many days; the caves of ice, which I only do not fear, are a dwelling to me, and the only one which man does not grudge. These black skies I hail, for they are kinder to me than your fellow beings. If the multitude of mankind knew of my existence, they would do as you do, and arm themselves for my destruction. Shall I not then hate them who abhor me?—Hear my tale; it is long and strange, and the temperature of this place is not fitting to your fine sensations; come to the hut upon the mountain. The sun is yet high in the heavens; before it descends to hide itself behind yon snowy precipices, and illuminate another world, you will have heard my story and can decide. On you it rests whether I quit for ever the neighbourhood of man and lead a harmless life, or become the scourge of your fellow creatures, and the author of your own speedy ruin."

The monster now begins his story, and a very amiable personage he makes himself to be. The story is well fancied and told. Immediately on his creation he wandered out into the forest of Ingoldstadt, where he remained for some days, till his different senses learnt to perform their appropriate functions, and he discovered the use of fire and various other rudiments of knowledge; and thus accomplished, he ventured forth into the great world. But in the first village that he reached he was hooted and stoned, and was obliged to take shelter in a hovel at the back of a cottage. Through a crevice in the wall, he soon became intimate with all the operations in the cottage, the inhabitants of which were an old blind man, his son and daughter. After the reception he had met with in the village, be kept himself very snug in his hole through the day, but really a good-natured monster, and finding the young man was much overwrought in cutting fuel for the family, what does he, but betake him to the wood in the night time, and collect quantities of fuel, which he piles up beside the door? The good people think themselves the favourites of some kind spirit or *brownie*. In the mean time, he learns how to apply their language, which he found he could imitate tolerably well. He gradually, too, becomes acquainted with more of their circumstances and feelings; and there was so much affection between the venerable blind man (who moreover played beautifully on a musical instrument) and his children, and they were so loving to each other,—and they were so interesting withal from their poverty, that the worthy monster took a vehement passion for them, and had the greatest inclination to make himself agreeable to them. By close study, and the occurrence of favourable opportunities, he also acquires a knowledge of written language; and one day on his rambles, lighting on a portmanteau, which contained the Sorrows of Werter, a volume of Plutarch, and Milton's Paradise Lost,—he becomes quite an adept in German sentiment, ancient heroism, and Satanic sturdiness. He now thought himself qualified to make himself acquainted with the family,—though aware of his hideous appearance, he very wisely began with the blind gentleman, on whom he ventured to make a call when the rest of the family were out of doors. He had just begun to interest the old man in his favour, when their tête-à-tête is unluckily interrupted, and the poor monster is abused and maltreated as heretofore by the villagers. He flies to the woods, furious with rage, and disappointed affection; and, finding on his return that the cottagers had forsaken the place, scared by his portentous visit, be amuses himself in his rage with setting it on fire, and then sets out in search of his creator. Other circumstances occur in his journey to give him a greater antipathy to the human race. He confesses the murder of the boy, whom, lighting upon, he wished to carry off, in the hope that he might find in him an object to attach himself to;—the murder was partly accidental,—but the slipping the picture into Justine's pocket was a piece of devilish malice. He includes with denouncing vengeance against Frankenstein and all his race, if he does not agree to one request, to create a female companion for him like himself, with whom he proposes to retire to the wilds of North America, and never again to come into contact with man.

It is needless to go minutely through the remainder of this wild fiction. After some demurring, Frankenstein at last accedes to the demand, and begins a second time the abhorred creation of a human being,—but again repents, and defies the demon; who thenceforth recommences his diabolical warfare against the unhappy philosopher,—destroys his friends and relations one by one, and finally murders his beloved Elizabeth, on the very evening of their marriage. Frankenstein, alive only to vengeance, now pursues the fiend over the world,—and it was in this chase that he had got into the neighbourhood of the North Pole, where he was but a little way behind him, but quite spent himself in the pursuit. So ends the narrative of Frankenstein, and worn out nature soon after yields to the bitterness of his thoughts and his exhausted frame. He dies, and, to the astonishment of our Englishman and the crew, the monster makes his appearance,—laments the fate of his creator,—says that his feelings of vengeance are for ever at an end,—departs, and is heard of no more.

Such is a sketch of this singular performance, in which there is much power and beauty, both of thought and expression, though, in many parts, the execution is imperfect, and bearing the marks of an unpractised hand. It is one of those works, however, which, when we have read, we do not well see why it should have been written;—for a *jeu d'esprit* it is somewhat too long, grave, and laborious,—and some of our highest and most reverential feelings receive a shock from the conception on which it turns, so as to produce a painful and bewildered state of mind while we peruse it. We are accustomed, happily, to look upon the creation of a living and intelligent being as a work that is fitted only to inspire a religious emotion, and here is an impropriety, to say no worse, in placing it in any other light. It might, indeed, be the author's view to shew that the powers of man have been wisely limited, and that misery would follow their extension,—but still the expression "Creator," applied to a mere human being, gives us the same sort of shock with the phrase, "the Man Almighty," and others of the same kind, in Mr Southey's "Curse of Kehama." All these monstrous conceptions are the consequences of the wild and irregular theories of the age; though we do not at all mean to infer that the authors who give into such freedoms have done so with any bad intentions. This incongruity, however, with our established and most sacred notions, is the chief fault in such fictions, regarding them merely is a critical point of view. Shakespeare's Caliban (though his simplicity and suitableness to the place where he is found are very delightful) is, perhaps, a more *hateful* being than our good friend in this book. But Caliban comes into existence in the received way which common superstition had pointed out; we should not have endured him if Prospero had created him. Getting over this original absurdity, the character of our monster is in good keeping;—there is a grandeur, too, in the scenery in which he makes his appearances,—the ice-mountains of the Pole, or the glaciers of the Alps; his natural tendency to kind feelings, and the manner in which they were blighted,—and all the domestic picture of the cottage, are very interesting and beautiful. We hope yet to have more productions, both from this author and his great model, Mr Godwin; but they would make a great improvement in their writings, if they would rather study the established order of nature as it appears, both in the world of matter and of mind, than continue to revolt our feelings by hazardous innovations in either of these departments.

—Unsigned, from *The Edinburgh [Scots]*
Magazine, second series, 11, March 1818,
pp. 249–253

Unsigned Review from
The British Critic (1818)

This is another anomalous story of the same race and family as Mandeville; and, if we are not misinformed, it is intimately connected with that strange performance, by more ties than one. In the present instance, it is true, we are presented with the mysteries of equivocal generation, instead of the metaphysics of a bedlamite; but he who runs as he reads, might pronounce both novels to be *similis farinae*. We are in doubt to what class we shall refer writings of this extravagant character; that they bear marks of considerable power, it is impossible to deny; but this power is so abused and perverted, that we should almost prefer imbecility; however much, of late years, we have been wearied and ennuied by the languid whispers of gentle sentimentality, they at least had the comfortable property of provoking no uneasy slumber; but we must protest against the waking dreams of horror excited by the unnatural stimulants of this later school; and we feel ourselves as much harassed, after rising from the perusal of these three spirit-wearing volumes, as if we had been over-dosed with laudanum, or hag-ridden by the night-mare.

No one can love a real good ghost story more heartily than we do; and we will toil through many a tedious duodecimo to get half a dozen pages of rational terror, provided always, that we keep company with spectres and skeletons, no longer than they maintain the just dignity of their spiritual character. Now and then too, we can tolerate a goule, so it be not at his dinner-time; and altogether, we profess to entertain a very due respect for the whole anierarchy of the daemoniacal establishment. Our prejudices in favour of legitimacy, of course, are proportionably shocked by the pretensions of any pseudo-diabolism; and all our best feelings of ghostly loyalty are excited by the usurpation of an unauthorized hobgoblin, or a nondescript fee-fa-fum.

It will be better, however, to say what little we mean to add on this point, by and by, when our readers are fairly put in possession of the subject, and enabled to form their own estimate of our opinions. In a sort of introduction, which precedes the main story of the novel, and has nothing else to do with it, we are introduced to a Mr. Walton, the Christopher Sly of the piece, with whose credulity the hero of the tale is afterwards to amuse himself. This gentleman, it seems, has had his imagination fired by an anticipation of the last number of the Quarterly Review, and is gone out to the North Pole, in quest of lost Greenland, magnetism, and the parliamentary reward. In justice to our author, we must admit that this part is well done, and we doubt whether Mr. Barrow, in plain prose, or Miss Porden herself, in more ambitious rhyme, can exceed our novelist in the description of frozen desarts and colliding ice-bergs. While employed in this pursuit, and advancing into a very high latitude, one day,

"About two o'clock the mist cleared away, and we beheld, stretched out in every direction, vast and irregular plains of ice, which seemed to have no end. Some of my comrades groaned, and my own mind began to grow watchful with anxious thoughts, when a strange sight suddenly attracted our attention, and diverted our solicitude from our own situation. We perceived a low carriage, fixed on a sledge and drawn by dogs, pass on towards the north, at the distance of half a mile: a being which had the shape of a man, but apparently of gigantic stature, sat in the sledge, and guided the dogs. We watched the rapid progress of the traveller with our telescopes, until he was lost among the distant inequalities of the ice.

"This appearance excited our unqualified wonder. We were, as we believed, many hundred miles from any land; but this apparition seemed to denote that it was not, in reality, so distant as we had supposed. Shut in, however, by ice, it was impossible to follow his track, which we had observed with the greatest attention.

"About two hours after this occurrence, we heard the ground sea; and before night the ice broke and freed our ship. We, however, lay to until the morning, fearing to encounter in the dark those large loose masses which float about after the breaking up of the ice. I profited of this time to rest for a few hours.

"In the morning, however, as soon as it was light, I went upon deck, and found all the sailors busy on one side of the vessel, apparently talking to someone in the sea. It was, in fact, a sledge, like that we had seen before, which had drifted towards us in the night on a large fragment of ice. Only one dog remained alive; but there was a human being within it whom the sailors were persuading to enter the vessel. He was not, as the other traveller seemed to be, a savage inhabitant of some undiscovered island, but a European. When I appeared on deck the master said, Here is our captain, and he will not allow you to perish on the open sea.

"On perceiving me, the stranger addressed me in English, although with a foreign accent. 'Before I come on board your vessel,' said he, 'will you have the kindness to inform me whither you are bound?'

"You may conceive my astonishment on hearing such a question addressed to me from a man on the brink of destruction and to whom I should have supposed that my vessel would have been a resource which he would not have exchanged for the most precious wealth the earth can afford. I replied, however, that we were on a voyage of discovery towards the northern pole.

"Upon hearing this he appeared satisfied and consented to come on board." Vol. I. p. 22.

After proper applications, the stranger is recovered, and of course a strong attachment, takes place between him and his preserver; and, in due season, after much struggling with melancholy and sullenness, he prevails upon himself to tell his own story.

Frankenstein was a Genevese by birth, of honorable parentage, and betrothed, from his earliest years, to an orphan cousin, with whom he had been brought up, Elizabeth Lavenza. In his youth, he manifested a strong bent for natural philosophy, at first, indeed, a little perverted by an accidental acquaintance with the early masters of this science, and an initiation into the mystical fancies of Cornelius Agrippa, Albertus Magnus, and Paracelsus; a short residence at the University of Ingolstadt, however corrected this bias, and he soon distinguished himself among the students, by his extraordinary proficiency in the various branches of chemical knowledge. One of the phaenomena which particularly engrossed his attention, was no less than "the principle of life;" to examine this, he had recourse to death, he studied anatomy, and watched the progress of decay and corruption in the human body, in dissecting rooms and charnel-houses; at length, "after days and nights of incredible labour and fatigue, I succeeded in discovering the cause of generation of life: nay, more, I became myself capable of bestowing animation upon lifeless matter."

When once in possession of this power, it is not to be supposed that he could long leave it unemployed; and, as the minuteness of parts formed a great hindrance to the speedy execution of his design, he determined to make the being which he was to endow with life, of a gigantic stature, "that is to say, about eight feet in height, and proportionably large." We pass over the months which he employed in this horrible process, and hasten to the grand period of consummation.

"It was on a dreary night of November that I beheld the accomplishment of my toils. With an anxiety that almost amounted to agony, I collected the instruments of life around me, that I might infuse a spark of being into the lifeless thing that lay at my feet. It was already one in the morning; the rain pattered dismally against the panes, and my candle was nearly burnt out, when, by the glimmer of the half-extinguished light, I saw the dull yellow eye of the creature open; it breathed hard, and a convulsive motion agitated its limbs.

"How can I describe my emotions at this catastrophe, or how delineate the wretch whom with such infinite pains and care I had endeavoured to form? His limbs were in proportion, and I had selected his features as beautiful. Beautiful!—Great God! His yellow skin scarcely covered the work of muscles and arteries beneath; his hair was of a lustrous black, and flowing; his teeth of a pearly whiteness; but these luxuriances only formed a more horrid contrast with his watery eyes, that seemed almost of the same colour as the dun white sockets in which they were set, his shrivelled complexion and straight black lips.

"The different accidents of life are not so changeable as the feelings of human nature. I had worked hard for nearly two years, for the sole purpose of infusing life into an inanimate body. For this I had deprived myself of rest and health. I had desired it with an ardour that far exceeded moderation; but now that I had finished, the beauty of the dream vanished, and breathless horror and disgust filled my heart. Unable to endure the aspect of the being I had created, I rushed out of the room, continued a long time traversing my bed chamber, unable to compose my mind to sleep. At length lassitude succeeded to the tumult I had before endured; and I threw myself on the bed in my clothes, endeavouring to seek a few moments of forgetfulness. But it was in vain: I slept, indeed, but I was disturbed by the wildest dreams. I thought I saw Elizabeth, in the bloom of health, walking in the streets of Ingolstadt. Delighted and surprised, I embraced her; but as I imprinted the first kiss on her lips, they became livid with the hue of death; her features appeared to change, and I thought that I held the corpse of my dead mother in my arms; a shroud enveloped her form, and I saw the grave-worms crawling in the folds of the flannel. I started from my sleep with horror; a cold dew covered my forehead, my teeth chattered, and every limb became convulsed: when, by the dim and yellow light of the moon, as it forced its way through the window shutters, I beheld the wretch—the miserable monster whom I had created. He held up the curtain of the bed and his eyes, if eyes they may be called, were fixed on me. His jaws opened, and he muttered some inarticulate sounds, while a grin wrinkled his cheeks. He might have spoken, but I did not hear; one hand was stretched out, seemingly to detain me, but I escaped, and rushed down stairs. I took refuge in the courtyard belonging to the house which I inhabited; where I remained during the rest of the night, walking up and down in the greatest agitation, listening attentively, catching and fearing each sound as if it were to announce the approach of the demoniacal corpse to which I had so miserably given life." Vol. I. p. 97.

While in this state of horror, he is agreeably surprized by the arrival of the friend of his youth, Henry Clerval, who had been dispatched by his family, under some alarm at the long silence which his genethliacal studies had occasioned. We shall not pretend to trace this story through the remainder of its course, suffice it to say, that the being whom he has created, pursues his steps, and operates, like his evil genius, upon every subsequent event of his life. His infant brother is murdered by the hands of this anonymous androdaemon; the servant girl, who attended the child, is executed upon circumstantial evidence; and Frankenstein himself, suspecting the real author of this foul deed, and stung with remorse, that he should have been its primary cause, commences a life of wandering, to throw off, if possible, the agony which haunts him. In the glacier of Montauvert, he has an interview with his persecutor, who succeeds, by threats, promises, and intreaties, in obtaining a hearing. The narrative which he relates, has some ingenuity in it; it is the account of a being springing at one bound into the full maturity of physical power, but whose understanding is yet to be awakened by degrees; this manhood of body, and infancy of mind, is occasionally well contrasted. Some of the steps in his intellectual progress, we confess, made us smile. He learns to read by accidentally finding *Paradise Lost*, a volume of *Plutarch's Lives*, *The Sorrows of Werter*, and *Volney's Ruins*; and his code of ethics is formed on this extraordinary stock of poetical theology, pagan biography, adulterous sentimentality, and atheistical jacobinism: yet, in spite of all his enormities, we think the monster, a very pitiable and ill-used monster, and are much inclined to join in his request, and ask Frankenstein to make him a wife; it is on the promise of this alone, that he consents to quit Europe for ever, and relieve his undutiful father from the horrors of an interminable pursuit.

In order to perform this promise, our hero is under the necessity of making a journey to England, for he "has heard of some discoveries made by an English philosopher," (and we wish he had revealed his name,) "the knowledge of which was material;" accordingly, in company with Harry Clerval, he sets off for London. By the way, they saw Tilbury Fort and remembered the Spanish Armada," (how came they to forget Whiskerandos?) "Gravesend, Woolwich, and Greenwich, places which they had heard of, even in their own country." After collecting such information as could be obtained at Surgeon's Hall, the Royal Institution, and the new drop, on the subject of his enquiry, he determines to fix his workshop of vivification in the Orkneys, picking up all the medical skill that was to be learnt at Edinburgh, *en passant*. Here he labours many months, not very agreeably it seems, on what he tells us is but, at best, a "filthy work;" the woman is almost completed, and wants only the last Promethean spark to enliven her, when, one evening, as he is moulding the body to its final shape, he is suddenly struck by the thought, that he may be assisting in the propagation of a race of daemons; and, shuddering at his own fiendish work, he destroys the creature upon which he is employed. The monster is at hand, and, fired by this unexpected breach of promise of marriage, "wrinkles his lip with a ghastly grin," and "howls devilish despair and revenge," bidding him remember that he will be with him on his wedding-night.

Henry Clerval is found dead on the coast of Ireland, to which we are next conveyed, with marks of violence. Frankenstein is thrown into prison on suspicion of the murder, and his knowledge of the perpetrator, joined to the inability of clearing himself, produces a paroxysm of lunacy. His father succeeds in proving his innocence; and they return in peace to Geneva, with no farther mishap by the way, than a fit of the night-mare at Holyhead. He is married to Elizabeth Lavenza; the monster is true to his promise, and murders her on their wedding-night; in his despair, Frankenstein devotes himself to revenge, and resolves to track the steps of the destroyer of his peace, for the remainder of his days; he pursues him successively through Germany, the Mediterranean, the Black Sea, Tartary, and Russia, and appears to have been gaining upon his flight, at the time the ground sea split the island of ice upon which both were travelling, and separated them for ever.

In a few days after he has finished his tale, Frankenstein dies, and Mr. Walton is surprized by a visit from the monster, who most unceremoniously climbs in at his cabin window. We fear it is too late to give our arctic explorers the benefit of his description; *mais le voila.*

> "I entered the cabin where lay the remains of my ill-fated and admirable friend. Over him hung a form which I cannot find words to describe; gigantic in stature, yet uncouth and distorted in its proportions. As he hung over the coffin his face was concealed by long locks of ragged hair; but one vast hand was extended, in colour and apparent texture like that of a mummy. When he heard the sound of my approach he ceased to utter exclamations of grief and horror and sprung towards the window. Never did I behold a vision so horrible as his face, of such loathsome yet appalling hideousness. I shut my eyes involuntarily and endeavoured to recollect what were my duties with regard to this destroyer. I called on him to stay." p. 179

After a short conversation, which Mr. Walton was not very anxious to protract, he takes his leave, with the very laudable resolution of seeking the northern extremity of the globe, where he means to collect his funeral pile, and consume his frame to ashes, that its remains may afford no light to any curious and unhallowed wretch who would create such another. We cannot help wishing, that our ships of discovery had carried out the whole impression of his history, for a similar purpose. We need scarcely say, that these volumes have neither principle, object, nor moral; the horror which abounds in them is too grotesque and *bizarre* ever to approach near the sublime, and when we did not hurry over the pages in disgust, we sometimes paused to laugh outright; and yet we suspect, that the diseased and wandering imagination, which has stepped out of all legitimate bounds, to frame these disjointed combinations and unnatural adventures, might be disciplined into something better. We heartily wish it were so, for there are occasional symptoms of no common powers of mind, struggling through a mass of absurdity, which well nigh overwhelms them; but it is a sort of absurdity that approaches so often the confines of what is wicked and immoral, that we dare hardly trust ourselves to bestow even this qualified praise. The writer of it is, we understand, a female; this is an aggravation of that which is the prevailing fault of the novel; but if our authoress can forget the gentleness of her sex, it is no reason why we should; and we shall therefore dismiss the novel without further comment.

—Unsigned, from *The British Critic*,
April 1818, pp. 432–438

HESTER LYNCH PIOZZI (1820)

How changed is the taste of verse, prose, and painting! since *le bon vieux temps*, dear Madam! Nothing attracts us but what terrifies, and is within—*if within*—a hair's-breadth of positive disgust. The picture of Death on his Pale Horse, however, is very grand certainly—and some of the strange things they *write* remind me of Squire Richard's visit to the Tower Menagerie, when he says "They are *pure* grim devils,"—particularly a wild and hideous tale called *Frankenstein*.

—Hester Lynch Piozzi, letter to F
anny Burney, October 20, 1820

RICHARD HENRY HORNE "MRS. SHELLEY" (1844)

The imaginative romance as distinguished from the historical romance, and the actual or social life fiction, is of very rare occurrence in the literature of the present day. Whether the cause lies with the writers or the public, or the character of events and influence now operating on society, certain it is that the imaginative romance is almost extinct among us.

We had outgrown the curdling horrors and breathless apprehensions of Mrs. Ratcliffe, and the roseate pomps of Miss Jane Porter. But why have we no Frankensteins, for that fine work is in advance of the age? Perhaps we ought to seek the cause of the scarcity in the difficulty of the production. A mere fruitless, purposeless excitement of the imagination will not do *now*. The imaginative romance is required to be a sort of epic—a power to advance—a something to propel the frame of things. Such is Bulwer's *Zanoni,* a profound and beautiful work of fiction, which has been reviewed in its place, and in which Godwin's *St. Leon* found a worthy successor. With this single exception, the first place among the romances of our day belongs to the *Frankenstein* of Mrs. Shelley.

The solitary student with whom the longing desire to pry into the secrets of nature ends in the discovery of the vital principle itself, and the means of communicating it, thus describes the consummation of his toils. We quote the passage as illustrative of the genius by which the extravagance of the conception is rendered subservient to artistical effect:—

> It was on a dreary night of November, that I beheld the accomplishment of my toils. With an anxiety that almost amounted to agony, I collected the instruments of life around me, that I might infuse a spark of being into the lifeless thing that lay at my feet. It was already one in the morning; the rain pattered dismally against the panes, and my candle was nearly burnt out, when, by the glimmer of the half-extinguished light, I saw the dull yellow eye of the creature open; it breathed hard, and a convulsive motion agitated its limbs.
>
> How can I describe my emotions at this catastrophe, or how delineate the wretch whom with such infinite pains and care I had endeavoured to form? His limbs were in proportion, and I had selected his features as beautiful. Beautiful!—Great God! His yellow skin scarcely covered the work of muscles and arteries beneath; his hair was of a lustrous black, and flowing; his teeth of a pearly whiteness; but these luxuriances only formed a more horrid contrast with his watery eyes, that seemed almost of the same colour as the dun white sockets in which they were set, his shrivelled complexion, and straight black lips.

The Monster in *Frankenstein,* sublime in his ugliness, his simplicity, his passions, his wrongs and his strength, physical and mental, embodies in the wild narrative more than one distinct and important moral theory or proposition. In himself he is the type of a class deeply and cruelly aggrieved by nature—the Deformed or hideous in figure or countenance, whose sympathies and passions are as strong as their bodily deformity renders them repulsive. An amount of human woe, great beyond reckoning, have such experienced. When the Monster pleads his cause against cruel man, and when he finally disappears on his raft on the icy sea to build his own funeral pile, he pleads the cause of all that class who have so strong a claim on the help and sympathy of the world, yet find little else but disgust, or, at best, neglect.

The Monster created by Frankenstein is also an illustration of the embodied consequences of our actions. As he, when formed and endowed with life, became to his imaginary creator an everlasting ever-present curse, so may one single action, nay a word, or it may be a thought, thrown upon the tide of time become to its originator a curse, never to be recovered, never to be shaken off.

Frankenstein suggests yet another analogy. It teaches the tragic results of attainment when an impetuous irresistible passion hurries on the soul to its doom. Such tragic results are the sacrificial fires out of which humanity rises purified. They constitute one form of the great ministry of Pain. The conception of *Frankenstein* is the converse of that of the delightful German fiction of Peter Schlemil, in which the *loss* of his shadow (reputation or honour) leads on the hero through several griefs and troubles to the great simplicity of nature and truth; while in *Frankenstein* the *attainment* of a gigantic reality leads through crime and desolation to the same goal, but it is only reached in the moment of death. . . .

Mrs. Shelley has published, besides *Frankenstein,* a romance entitled *Valperga,* which is less known than the former, but is of high merit. She exhibits in her hero, a brave and successful warrior, arriving at the height of his ambition, endowed with uncommon beauty and strength, and with many good qualities, yet causes him to excite emotions of reprobation and pity, because he is cruel and a tyrant, and because in the truth of things he is unhappy. This is doing a good work, taking the false glory from the eyes and showing things as they are. There are two female characters of wonderful power and beauty. The heroine is a lovely and noble creation. The work taken as a whole, if below *Frankenstein* in genius, is yet worthy of its author and of her high rank in the aristocracy of genius, as the daughter of Godwin and Mary Wolstonecraft, and the widow of Shelley.

—Richard Henry Horne, "Mrs. Shelley,"
A New Spirit of the Age, 1844, pp. 317–321

Margaret Oliphant (1882)

Lewis, popularly known as Monk Lewis, paid Byron a visit at his villa, and became one of the little society, which was often confined within four walls by the rain, and eager after every new excitement, as people imprisoned in a country house so universally are. They told each other ghost stories, and tales of mystery and wonder under the inspiration of the kind little inoffensive romancer, who was then master of that branch of the arts; and he or some one else suggested that they should all write for their mutual diversion tales of this character. The only one who carried out the suggestion was Mary, the youngest of the party, a girl not yet eighteen, notwithstanding the turmoil of life into which she had been plunged. That a young creature of this age should have produced anything at once so horrible and so original as the hideous romance of *Frankenstein,* is one of the most extraordinary accidents in literature; and that she should never, having made such a beginning, have done anything more, is almost equally wonderful. Byron is said to have begun a similar sketch, entitled "The Vampyre," which his physician-attendant, Polidori, afterwards added to and printed; but none of the detailed records of the time inform us what were the feelings of excitement and terror with which the little company, thrilled by the tales of Lewis, listened to the portentous and extraordinary production with which the fair small girl, with her big forehead and her sedate aspect, out-Heroded Herod. Mary Shelley's individual appearances afterwards are only those of a romantically-desolate widow, pouring out her grief and fondness in sentimental gushes, which look somewhat overstrained and ridiculous in print, whatever they may have done in fact; but to hear her read, with her girlish lips, this most extraordinary and terrible of imaginations, must have been a sensation unparalleled. It is one of the books adopted into the universal memory, which everybody alludes to, and thousands who can never have read it understand the main incidents of—which is a wonderful instance of actual fame. That this should be merely stated as a fact in the history, and no one pause to wonder at it, is another odd instance of the insensibility of contemporaries.

—Margaret Oliphant, *The Literary History
of England, 1790–1825,* 1882, vol. 3,
pp. 69–70

EDITH BIRKHEAD (1921)

As the novel of terror passes from the hands of Mrs. Radcliffe to those of "Monk" Lewis, Maturin and their imitators, there is a crashing crescendo of emotion. The villain's sardonic smile is replaced by wild outbursts of diabolical laughter, his scowl grows darker and darker, and as his designs become more bloody and more dangerous, his victims no longer sigh plaintively, but give utterance to piercing shrieks and despairing yells; tearful Amandas are unceremoniously thrust into the background by vindictive Matildas, whose passions rage in all their primitive savagery; the fearful ghost "fresh courage takes," and stands forth audaciously in the light of day; the very devil stalks shamelessly abroad in manifold disguises. We are caught up from first to last in the very tempest, torrent and whirlwind of passion. When the novel of terror thus throws restraint to the winds, outrageously o'ersteps the modesty of nature and indulges in a farrago of frightfulness, it begins to defeat its own purposes and to fail in its object of freezing the blood. The limit of human endurance has been reached—and passed. Emphasis and exaggeration have done their worst. Battle, murder, and sudden death—even spectres and fiends—can appal no more. If the old thrill is to be evoked again, the application of more ingenious methods is needed.

Such novels as Maturin's *Family of Montorio*, though "full of sound and fury," fail piteously to vibrate the chords of terror, which had trembled beneath Mrs. Radcliffe's gentle fingers. The instrument, smitten forcibly, repeatedly, desperately, resounds not with the answering note expected, but with an ugly, metallic jangle. *Melmoth the Wanderer*, Maturin's extraordinary masterpiece, was to prove—as late as 1820—that there were chords in the orchestra of horror as yet unsounded; but in 1816, when Mary Shelley and her companions set themselves to compose supernatural stories, it was wise to dispense with the shrieking chorus of malevolent abbesses, diabolical monks, intriguing marquises, Wandering Jews or bleeding spectres, who had been so grievously overworked in previous performances. Dr. Polidori's skull-headed lady, Byron's vampire-gentleman, Mrs. Shelley's man-created monster—a grotesque and gruesome trio—had at least the attraction of novelty. It is indeed remarkable that so young and inexperienced a writer as Mary Shelley, who was only nineteen when she wrote *Frankenstein*, should betray so slight a dependence on her predecessors. It is evident from the records of her reading that the novel of terror in all its guises was familiar to her. She had beheld the majestic horror of the halls of Eblis; she had threaded her way through Mrs. Radcliffe's artfully constructed Gothic castles; she had braved the terrors of the German Ritter-, Räuber und Schauer-Romane; she had assisted, fearful, at Lewis's midnight diablerie; she had patiently unravelled the "mystery" novels of Godwin and of Charles Brockden Brown.[1] Yet, despite this intimate knowledge of the terrible and supernatural in fiction, Mrs. Shelley's theme and her way of handling it are completely her own. In an "acute mental vision," as real as the visions of Blake and of Shelley, she beheld her monster and the "pale student of unhallowed arts" who had created him, and then set herself to reproduce the thrill of horror inspired by her waking dream. *Frankenstein* has, indeed, been compared to Godwin's *St. Leon*, but the resemblance is so vague and superficial, and *Frankenstein* so immeasurably superior, that Mrs. Shelley's debt to her father is negligible. St. Leon accepts the gift of immortality, Frankenstein creates a new life, and in both novels the main interest lies in tracing the effect of the experiment on the soul of the man, who has pursued scientific inquiry beyond legitimate limits. But apart from this, there is little resemblance. Godwin chose the supernatural, because it chanced to be popular, and laboriously built up a cumbrous edifice, completing it by a sheer effort of will-power. His daughter, with an imagination naturally more attuned to the gruesome and fantastic, writes, when once she has wound her way into the heart of the story, in a mood of breathless excitement that drives the reader forward with feverish apprehension.

The name of Mrs. Shelley's *Frankenstein* is far-famed; but the book itself, overshadowed perhaps by its literary associations, seems to have withdrawn into the vast library of famous works that are more often mentioned than read. The very fact that the name is often bestowed on the monster instead of his creator seems to suggest that many are content to accept Mrs. Shelley's "hideous phantom" on hearsay evidence rather than encounter for themselves the terrors of his presence. The story deserves a happier fate, for, if it be read in the spirit of willing surrender that a theme so impossible demands, it has still power momentarily "to make the reader dread to look round, to curdle the blood and to quicken the beatings of the heart." The record of the composition of *Frankenstein* has been so often reiterated that it is probably better known than the tale itself. In the summer of 1816—when the Shelleys were the neighbours of Byron near Lake Geneva—Byron, Shelley, Mary Shelley and Dr. Polidori, after reading some volumes of ghost stories[2] and discussing the supernatural and its manifestations, each agreed to write a ghost story. It has been asserted that an interest in spectres was stimulated by a visit from "Monk" Lewis, but we have evidence that Mrs. Shelley was already writing her story in June,[3] and that Lewis did not arrive at the Villa Diodati till August 14th.[4] The conversation with him about ghosts took place four days later. Shelley's story, based on the experiences of his early youth, was never completed. Byron's fragment formed the basis of Dr. Polidori's *Vampyre*. Dr. Polidori states that his supernatural novel, *Ernestus Berchtold*, was begun at this time; but the skull-headed lady, alluded to by Mary Shelley as figuring in Polidori's story, is disappointingly absent. It was an argument between Byron and Shelley about Erasmus

Darwin's theories that brought before Mary Shelley's sleepless eyes the vision of the monster miraculously infused by its creator with the spark of life. *Frankenstein* was begun immediately, completed in May, 1817, and published in 1818.

Mrs. Shelley has been censured for setting her tale in a clumsy framework, but she tells us in her preface that she began with the words: "It was on a dreary night of November." This sentence now stands at the opening of Chapter V., where the plot begins to grip our imagination; and it seems not unfair to assume that the introductory letters and the first four chapters, which contain a tedious and largely unnecessary account of Frankenstein's early life, were written in deference to Shelley's plea that the idea should be developed at greater length, and did not form part of her original plan. The uninteresting student, Robert Walton, to whom Frankenstein, discovered dying among icebergs, tells his story, is obviously an afterthought. If Mrs. Shelley had abandoned the awkward contrivance of putting the narrative into the form of a dying man's confession, reported verbatim in a series of letters, and had opened her story, as she apparently intended, at the point where Frankenstein, after weary years of research, succeeds in creating a living being, her novel would have gained in force and intensity. From that moment it holds us fascinated. It is true that the tension relaxes from time to time, that the monster's strange education and the Godwinian precepts that fall so incongruously from his lips tend to excite our mirth, but, though we are mildly amused, we are no longer merely bored. Even the protracted descriptions of domestic life assume a new and deeper meaning, for the shadow of the monster broods over them. One by one those whom Frankenstein loves fall victims to the malice of the being he has endowed with life. Unceasingly and unrelentingly the loathsome creature dogs our imagination, more awful when he lurks unseen than when he stands actually before us. With hideous malignity he slays Frankenstein's young brother, and by a fiendish device causes Justine, an innocent girl, to be executed for the crime. Yet ere long our sympathy, which has hitherto been entirely with Frankenstein, is unexpectedly diverted to the monster who, it would seem, is wicked only because he is eternally divorced from human society. Amid the magnificent scenery of the Valley of Chamounix he appears before his creator, and tells the story of his wretched life, pleading: "Everywhere I see bliss from which I alone am irrevocably excluded. I was benevolent and good; misery made me a fiend. Make me happy, and I shall again be virtuous."

He describes how his physical ugliness repels human beings, who fail to realise his benevolent intentions. A father snatches from his arms the child he has rescued from death; the virtuous family, whom he admires and would fain serve, flee affrighted from his presence. To educate the monster, so that his thoughts and emotions may become articulate, and, incidentally, to accentuate his isolation from society, Mrs. Shelley inserts a complicated story about an Arabian girl, Sofie, whose lover teaches her to read from Plutarch's *Lives*, Volney's *Ruins of Empire*, *The Sorrows of Werther*, and *Paradise Lost*. The monster overhears the lessons, and ponders on this unique library, but, as he pleads his own cause the more eloquently because he knows Satan's passionate outbursts of defiance and self-pity, who would cavil at the method by which he is made to acquire his knowledge? "The cold stars shone in mockery, and the bare trees waved their branches above me; now and then the sweet voice of a bird burst forth amidst the universal stillness. All save I were at rest or in enjoyment. I, like the arch fiend, bore a hell within me." And later, near the close of the book: "The fallen angel becomes a malignant devil. Yet even that enemy of God and man had friends and associates in his desolation; I am alone." His fate reminds us of that of *Alastor, the Spirit of Solitude*, who:

"Over the world wanders for ever
Lone as incarnate death."

After the long and moving recital of his woes, even the obdurate Frankenstein cannot resist the justice of his demand for a partner like himself. Yet when the student recoils with horror from his half-accomplished task and sees the creature maliciously peering through the window, our hatred leaps to life once more and burns fiercely as the monster adds to his crimes the murder of Clerval, Frankenstein's dearest friend, and of Elizabeth on her wedding night. We follow with shuddering anticipation the long pursuit of the monster, expectant of a last, fearful encounter which shall decide the fate of the demon and his maker. Amid the region of eternal ice, Frankenstein catches sight of him, but fails to reach him. At last, beside the body of his last victim—Frankenstein himself—the creature is filled with remorse at the "frightful catalogue" of his sins, and makes a final bid for our sympathy in the farewell speech to Walton, before climbing on an ice-raft to be "borne away by the waves and lost in darkness and distance."

Like *Alastor*, *Frankenstein* was a plea for human sympathy, and was, according to Shelley's preface, intended "to exhibit the amiableness of domestic affection and the excellence of universal virtue." The monster has the perception and desire of goodness, but, by the circumstances of his abnormal existence, is delivered over to evil. It is this dual nature that prevents him from being a mere automaton. The monster indeed is far more real than the shadowy beings whom he pursues. Frankenstein is less an individual than a type, and only interests us through the emotions which his conflict with the monster arouses. Clerval, Elizabeth and Frankenstein's relatives are passive sufferers whose psychology does not concern us. Mrs. Shelley rightly lavishes her skill on the central figure of the book, and succeeds, as effectually as Frankenstein himself, in infusing into him the spark of life. Mrs. Shelley's aim is to "awaken thrilling horror," and, incidentally, to "exhibit the excellence of domestic virtue," and for her purpose the demon is of paramount importance. The involved, complex plot of a novel seemed to pass beyond Mrs. Shelley's control. A short tale she could handle successfully, and Shelley was unwise in inciting her to expand *Frankenstein* into a long narrative. So long as she is completely carried away by her subject Mrs. Shelley writes clearly, but when she pauses to regard the progress of her story dispassionately, she seems to be overwhelmed by the wealth of her resources and to have no power of selecting the relevant details. The laborious introductory letters, the meticulous record of Frankenstein's education, the story of Felix and Sofie, the description of the tour through England before the creation of the second monster is attempted, are all connected with the main theme by very frail links and serve to distract our attention in an irritating fashion from what really interests us. In the novel of mystery a tantalising delay may be singularly effective. In a novel which depends chiefly for its effect on sheer horror, delays are merely dangerous. By resting her terrors on a pseudo-scientific basis and by placing her story in a definite locality, Mrs. Shelley waives her right to an entire suspension of disbelief. If it be reduced to its lowest terms, the plot of *Frankenstein*, with its bewildering confusion of the prosaic and the fantastic, sounds as crude, disjointed and inconsequent as that of a nightmare. Mrs. Shelley's timid hesitation between imagination and reality, her attempt to reconcile incompatible things and to place a creature who belongs to no earthly land in familiar surroundings, prevents *Frankenstein* from being a wholly satisfactory and alarming novel of terror. She loves the fantastic, but she also fears it. She is weighted down by commonsense, and so flutters instead of soaring, unwilling to trust herself far from the material world. But the fact that she was able to vivify her grotesque skeleton of a plot with some degree of success is no mean tribute to her gifts. The energy and vigour of her style, her complete and serious absorption in her subject, carry us safely over many an absurdity. It is only in the duller stretches of the narrative, when her heart is not in her work, that her language becomes vague, indeterminate and blurred, and that she muffles her thoughts

in words like "ascertain," "commencement," "peruse," "diffuse," instead of
using their simpler Saxon equivalents. Stirred by the excitement of the events
she describes, she can write forcibly in simple, direct language. She often
frames short, hurried sentences such as a man would naturally utter when
breathless with terror or with recollections of terror. The final impression
that *Frankenstein* leaves with us is not easy to define, because the book is so
uneven in quality. It is obviously the shapeless work of an immature writer
who has had no experience in evolving a plot. Sometimes it is genuinely
moving and impressive, but it continually falls abruptly and ludicrously short
of its aim. Yet when all its faults have been laid bare, the fact remains that
few readers would abandon the story half-way through. Mrs. Shelley is so
thoroughly engrossed in her theme that she impels her readers onward, even
though they may think but meanly of her story as a work of art.

Mrs. Shelley's second novel, *Valperga, or the Life and Adventures of
Castruccio, Prince of Lucca*, published in 1823, was a work on which she
bestowed much care and labour, but the result proves that she writes best
when the urgency of her imagination leaves her no leisure either to display
her learning or adorn her style. She herself calls *Valperga* a "child of mighty
slow growth," and Shelley adds that it was "raked out of fifty old books."
Mrs. Shelley, always an industrious student, made a conscientious survey
of original sources before fashioning her story of mediaeval Italy, and she is
hampered by the exuberance of her knowledge. The novel is not a romance
of terror; but Castruccio, though his character is sketched from authentic
documents, seems towards the end of the story to resemble the picturesque
villain who numbered among his ancestry Milton's Satan. He has "a majestic
figure and a countenance beautiful but sad, and tarnished by the expression
of pride that animated it." Beatrice, the gifted prophetess who falls deep
in love with Castruccio, ends her days in the dungeons of the Inquisition.
Mrs. Shelley's aim, however, is not to arouse fear, but to trace the gradual
deterioration of Castruccio's character from an openhearted youth to a crafty
tyrant. The blunt remarks of Godwin, who revised the manuscript, are not
unjust, but fall with an ill grace from the pen of the author of *St. Leon*: "It
appears in reading, that the first rule you prescribed was: 'I will let it be long.'
It contains the quantity of four volumes of *Waverley*. No hard blow was ever
hit with a woodsaw."[5]

In *The Last Man*, which appeared in 1825, Mrs. Shelley attempted a
stupendous theme, no less than a picture of the devastation of the human
race by plague and pestilence. She casts her imagination forward into
the twenty-first century, when the last king of England has abdicated the

throne and a republic is established. Very wisely, she narrows the interest by concentrating on the pathetic fate of a group of friends who are among the last survivors, and the story becomes an idealised record of her own sufferings. The description of the loneliness of the bereft has a personal note, and reminds us of her journal, where she expresses the sorrow of being herself the last survivor, and of feeling like a "cloud from which the light of sunset has passed."[6] Raymond, who dies in an attempt to place the standard of Greece in Stamboul, is a portrait of Byron; and Adrian, the late king's son, who finally becomes Protector, is clearly modelled on Shelley. Yet in spite of these personal reminiscences, their characters lack distinctness. Idris, Clara and Perdita are faintly etched, but Evadne, the Greek artist, who cherishes a passion for Raymond, and dies fighting against the Turks, has more colour and body than the other women, though she is somewhat theatrical. Mrs. Shelley conveys emotion more faithfully than character, and the overwrought sensibilities and dark forebodings of the diminished party of survivors who leave England to distract their minds by foreign travel are artfully suggested. The leaping, gesticulating figure, whom their jaded nerves and morbid fancy transform into a phantom, is a delirious ballet-dancer; and the Black Spectre, mistaken for Death Incarnate, proves only to be a plague-stricken noble, who lurks near the party for the sake of human society. These "reasonable" solutions of the apparently supernatural remind us of Mrs. Radcliffe's method, and Mrs. Shelley shows keen psychological insight in her delineation of the state of mind which readily conjures up imaginary terrors. When Lionel Verney is left alone in the universe, her power seems to flag, and instead of the final crescendo of horror, which we expect at the end of the book, we are left with an ineffective picture of the last man in Rome in 2095 deciding to explore the countries he has not yet viewed. As he wanders amid the ruins he recalls not only "the buried Caesars," but also the monk in *The Italian*, of whom he had read in childhood—a striking proof of Mrs. Shelley's faith in the permanence of Mrs. Radcliffe's fame.

Though the style of *The Last Man* is often tediously prolix and is disfigured by patches of florid rhetoric and by inappropriate similes scattered broadcast, occasional passages of wonderful beauty recall Shelley's imagery; and, in conveying the pathos of loneliness, personal feeling lends nobility and eloquence to her style. With so ambitious a subject, it was natural that she should only partially succeed in carrying her readers with her. Though there are oases, the story is a somewhat tedious and dreary stretch of narrative that can only be traversed with considerable effort.

Mrs. Shelley's later works—*Perkin Warbeck* (1830), a historical novel; *Lodore* (1835), which describes the early life of Shelley and Harriet; *Falkner* (1837), which was influenced by *Caleb Williams*—do not belong to the history of the novel of terror; but some of her short tales, contributed to periodicals and collected in 1891, have gruesome and supernatural themes. *A Tale of the Passions, or the Death of Despina*,[7] a story based on the struggles of the Guelphs and the Ghibellines, contains a perfect specimen of the traditional villain of the novel of terror:

"Every feature of his countenance spoke of the struggle of passions and the terrible egotism of one who would sacrifice himself to the establishment of his will: his black eyebrows were scattered, his grey eyes deep-set and scowling, his look at once stern and haggard. A smile seemed never to have disturbed the settled scorn which his lips expressed; his high forehead was marked by a thousand contradictory lines."

This terrific personage spends the last years of his life in orthodox fashion as an austere saint in a monastery.

The Mortal Immortal, a variation on the theme of *St. Leon*, is the record of a pupil of Cornelius Agrippa, who drank half of the elixir his master had compounded in the belief that it was a potion to destroy love. It is written on his three hundred and twenty-third birthday. *Transformation*, like *Frankenstein*, dwells on the pathos of ugliness and deformity, but the subject is treated rather in the spirit of an eastern fairy tale than in that of a novel of terror. The dwarf, in return for a chest of treasure, borrows a beautiful body, and, thus disguised, wins the love of Juliet, and all ends happily. Mrs. Shelley's short stories[8] reveal a stronger sense of proportion than her novels, and are written in a more graceful, fluent style than the books on which she expended great labour.

The literary history of Byron's fragmentary novel and of Polidori's short story, *The Vampyre*, is somewhat tangled, but the solution is to be found in the diary of Dr. John William Polidori, edited and elucidated by William Michael Rossetti. The day after that on which Polidori states that all the competitors, except himself, had begun their stories, he records the simple fact: "Began my ghost-story after tea." He gives no hint as to the subject of his tale, but Mrs. Shelley tells us that Polidori had some idea of a "skull-headed lady, who was so punished for looking through a key-hole, and who was finally buried in the tomb of the Capulets." In the introduction to *Ernestus Berchtold, or the Modern Oedipus*, he states definitely: "The tale here presented to the public is one I began at Coligny, when *Frankenstein* was planned, and when a noble author, having determined to descend from his lofty range, gave up a few hours to a tale of terror, and wrote the fragment published at the end of Mazeppa."

Notes

1. List of books read 1814–1816.
2. *Fantasmagoriana: ou Recueil d'Histoires d'Apparitions, de Spectres, de Revenans, trad. d'Allemand par un Amateur.* Paris, 1812.
3. *Diary of John William Polidori,* June 17, 1816.
4. Byron, *Letters and Journals,* 1899, iii. 446. Mary Shelley, *Life and Letters,* 1889, i. 586. Extract from Mary Shelley's *Diary,* Aug. 14, 1816.
5. Nov. 15, 1823, *Life and Letters of Mary Wollstonecraft Shelley* (Marshall), ii. 52.
6. *Life and Letters,* ii. 88.
7. *Romancist and Novelist's Library.*
8. Reprinted in *Treasure House of Tales by Great Authors,* ed. Garnett, 1891.

—Edith Birkhead, "Later Developments
of the Tale of Terror," 1921

VALPERGA

In an anonymous review in the March 1823 issue of *Blackwood's Magazine*, the critic finds *Valperga* a great disappointment and spends considerable time explaining the elements that comprise the untapped potential that resides within the extraordinary history of Castruccio. Unfortunately, for the reviewer, Mary Shelley has regrettably not recognized this potential and has instead written a story that leaves the reader with a dull and lifeless portrait of an otherwise incisive Italian wit. To make his point especially salient, the critic compares Mary Shelley's account to the brief but eminently forceful presentation found in Machiavelli (1469–1527), an Italian diplomat and political philosopher best known for his work *The Prince*. "The life of him, by Machiavel, does not cover more than twenty or thirty duodecimo pages; yet, one rises from that brief sketch with a much more lively and perfect notion of the man, than from the perusal of the three closely printed volumes now on our table. There is not one spark of wit in all this book. . . . Machiavel . . . tells stories enough to have suggested the true '*Castruccio vein.*'" The reviewer further states that the sheer length of *Valperga* serves to turn the account of Castruccio's persona into an "amusing romance" then goes on to share a prescription for writing historical fiction, elements of which are clearly lacking in *Valperga*. "The framer of an historical romance should not be reminding us at every turn, that his *principal* object is to show off his own knowledge of strange manners, or power of fine writing." As a final criticism, the reviewer takes issue with Mary Shelley giving the reader another portrait of Napoléon Bonaparte, who has already been heralded in a surfeit of prior romances. Nevertheless, he recommends *Valperga* for its skillful depiction of a complex romantic plot full of overflowing passion.

A far different opinion is rendered in another unsigned review from the August 1823 issue of *La Belle Assemblée,* in which *Valperga* is lauded as worthy of the reputation Mary Shelley established with *Frankenstein.* Though the critic admits that *Valperga* is occasionally given over to gloominess, it is nevertheless held up as exemplary for its historical acuity. The reviewer goes on to praise Mary Shelley's powerful exposition of Castruccio's character.

UNSIGNED REVIEW FROM *BLACKWOOD'S EDINBURGH MAGAZINE* (1823)

We opened the packet, which we knew to contain this book, with great expectations. *Frankenstein,* at the time of its appearance, we certainly did not suspect to be the work of a female hand; the name of Shelley was whispered, and we did not hesitate to attribute the book to *Mr* Shelley. Soon, however, we were set right. We learned that *Frankenstein* was written by *Mrs* Shelley; and then we most undoubtedly said to ourselves, "For a man it was excellent, but for a woman it is wonderful." What we chiefly admired, in that wild production, was vigour of imagination and strength of language; these were unquestionable attributes, and they redeemed the defects of an absurd groundwork and an incoherent fable; and, moreover, they tempted us, and every body else, to forgive the many long passages of feeble conception and feeble execution, with which the vigorous scenes were interwoven.

The history of Castruccio Castracani, on the other hand, had been long familiar to us in the glowing and energetic sketch of Machiavelli. Perhaps, on the whole, we should have been more rejoiced in the prospect of meeting Mrs Shelley again on the same dark territory, where she had first displayed so many striking powers; but the story of Castruccio we were willing to consider as not unlikely to furnish, in such hands, the basis and materials of a most romantic fiction. The bitter sarcasm that peeped out here and there in *Frankenstein,* will be displayed, said we, with the utmost advantage; for here the authoress has chosen for her hero, one who was not only the first soldier of his time, but the first satirist also. The marvellous rise of such a man to sovereign and tyrannic power, his preservation of all his original manners in that high estate, his deep ambition, his fiery valour, his sportive wit, his searing ironies, his untimely death, and the calm mockeries with which he prepared to meet it—here, said we, are noble materials, such as might well engage the fancy of the most gifted author. We must confess, that in much of what we looked for, we have been disappointed; but yet, even here at the outset, we do not hesitate to say, that if we have not met with what we expected, we have met with other things almost as good.

Our chief objection, indeed, may be summed up in one word—Mrs Shelley has not done justice to the character of Castruccio. The life of him, by Machiavel, does not cover more than twenty or thirty duodecimo pages; yet, one rises from that brief sketch with a much more lively and perfect notion of the man, than from the perusal of the three closely printed volumes now on our table. There is not one spark of wit in all this book, and yet the keen Italian wit of Castruccio was one of the most striking features in his real character, and ought to have been among the most prominent in a work representing him throughout, in action and conversation. Machiavel, in two or three pages, tells stories enough to have suggested the true *"Castruccio vein."* Who does not remember that famous one of his rebuking a young man, whom he met coming out of a house of ill fame, and who blushed on being recognized? "It was when you went in that you should have coloured," said Castruccio, "not when you come out." Who does not remember his behaviour in the storm at sea? Castruccio expressing some alarm, was rebuked by a stupid fool, who said, that for him he did not value his own life a farthing. "Everybody," quoth Castruccio, "makes the best estimate of his own wares." When a thick-skulled wine-bibber boasted that he could drink such and such quantities without being the worse of it—it was Castruccio who answered, "Aye, and your ox could drink still more if he had a mind." It was the sagacious Castruccio, who, when some sage friend abused him for the extravagances he had been guilty of at a debauch, made answer, "He that is held for a wise man by day, will hardly be taken for a fool at night." It was he that dumbfounded an orator, who concluded a long speech, by a wordy apology for his wordiness, with these consolatory words, "Pain not thyself, my dear sir, I was attending to my spaniel."—It was he, who, when he saw a certain envious one smiling to himself, asked, "Is it that some good hath befallen thee, or that some evil hath befallen another?" It was Castruccio, finally, who, when they came to his bedside, during his last illness, and asked his directions about his funeral, said, "Lay me on my face in the coffin—for everything will be reversed ere long after my departure."

Of all this sort of thing we have no trace in Mrs Shelley's book; and yet she appears to have contemplated a very full development of Castruccio's character. She gives us his infancy, his boyhood, his manhood, all in complete detail. The attempt, whether successful or not, certainly is made to depict the slow and gradual formation of a crafty and bloody Italian tyrant of the middle ages, out of an innocent, open-hearted and deeply-feeling youth. We suspect, that in the whole of this portraiture, far too much reliance has been laid on thoughts and feelings, not only modern, but modern and feminine at once. Perhaps we might say more; nay, perhaps we should not be saying too much, if we plainly expressed the opinion, that a very great part of Mrs Shelley's book has no inspiration, but that of a certain *school*, which is certainly a very modern, as well as a very mischievous one, and which ought never, of all things, to have numbered ladies among its disciples. But, in spite even of this, we have closed the book with no feelings but those of perfect kindness—and we shall say no more of matters that will, perhaps, suggest themselves to our readers quite strongly enough, without our giving ourselves any trouble.

Laying out of view Antelminelli's real life and character, we can have no hesitation in saying, that Mrs Shelley has given us a clever and amusing romance. Not doubting, that she will in due time make more attempts in the same way, we would fain point out, to so clever a person, faults which she might easily avoid in future, and which here, even more, perhaps, than in *Frankenstein*, neutralize much of her power. But, on further reflection, we believe the best way will be to leave all this to the working of experience. A very little consideration must be enough to show such a writer the absurdity of introducing so many pure episodes. The framer of an historical romance should not be reminding us at every turn, that his *principal* object is to show off his own knowledge of strange manners, or power of fine writing. If quaint manners are to be quaintly and strongly represented, the incidents, with which these are connected, ought to have a strict connexion with, and influence over, the progress of the fable, or at least the development of the principal characters of the fable. We cannot stand the stepping aside for ten pages, *merely* for the purpose of letting us see, that the writer knows the way in which the *Mysteries* of the middle ages were represented, either on, or off the Arno—we cannot spare four days of the life of Castruccio Castraccani to singers and tale-tellers, and so forth, with whom he and his story have nothing to do—we abhor all unnecessary prosing about religious sects, and we are mortally sick of "orange-tinted skies," "dirges," and "Dante."

Another thing we are very sick of, is this perpetual drumming at poor Buonaparte. That singular character is already the hero of fifty romances.

Wherever one turns, he is sure to be met by the same sort of lame, impotent, and abortive attempts to shadow out Napoleon under the guise and semblance of some greater or smaller usurper of ancient days. On one hand we have that shallow "gentleman of the press," M. Jouy, labouring to bring him out *en Sylla*. On the other, there is an, if possible, still greater and more frothy goose, "M. le Vicompte d'Arlincourt," hammering away at Charles Martel and his Renegade. Here we find Mrs Shelley flinging over the grey surtout and cocked hat of the great captain of France, the blazoned mantle of a fierce *Condottiere* of Lucca.—Anon, no question, we shall have this same *crambe recocta* served up *a la Cromwell, a la Caesar, a la Tamerlane!* Will nothing persuade all these rhapsodists to let a great man's ashes repose, at least until they have had time to cool in the urn? As for Jouy and the Viscount d'Arlincourt, they are apparently two perfect ninnies, so let them rave away about anything they please,—even though the Quarterly, descending from its usual high character, should puff their vile crudities and passionless rant, no human being blessed with half an eye will waste three minutes' thought upon them—But Mrs Shelley has talents which cannot be perverted with so much impunity. She is capable, and she is worthy of other things; and were it but that she is the daughter of Godwin, we should be sorry to find her persisting in the chase of such claptraps. For heaven's sake, leave all this nonsense to the "grande pensee" of little Jouy, the "Imagination haute et sublime" of the noble Viscount, and the "legs and impudence" of "Le Docteur O'Meara,"—and for heaven's sake, let us have no more puffs of such stuff from any quarter more reputable than Sir Pythagoras.

But enough of preliminaries. We have ventured, throwing a thousand defects out of view, to recommend *Valperga,* as, on the whole, a clever novel. . . .

Valperga is the name of a castle and small independent territory not far from Lucca. Euthanasia, Countess of Valperga, is in her own person a sovereign princess, but a warm lover of freedom, and much attached, by family connexions, to Florence, the capital of the Guelphic cause in Italy. She had been the companion of Castruccio's boyhood—she meets him while his manhood is opening in glory, and she loves him because she believes he is, and is to be, all that is good, as well as all that is glorious. The Ghibelline Castruccio, however, becomes in time a prince, a tyrant, the conqueror of half Tuscany, the dreadful threatener of annihilation to Florence. Euthanasia discovering this, will not marry him as she had promised.—From less to more she even becomes his enemy, in all but the heart;—he takes her castle from her—and reduces her to a private station:—in a word, the author has sought the chief materials of interest for her story, in the play of passions called into action by the various relations in which the usurper and this charming lady, the love of his youth, appear throughout the narrative.

By far the most striking part of this history, however, and indeed we may add, by far the finest part of the book, is that in which the loves of Castruccio and Euthanasia are broken and disturbed by those of Castruccio and a certain Beatrice of Ferrara.

This Beatrice is a most exquisite beauty of seventeen—invested in her own eyes, and in the superstitious eyes of all about her, with certain mysterious attributes. This beautiful maiden has the enthusiasm, and the pride, and the daring confidence of a priestess, a martyr, and a prophetess. She conceives herself to have been sent into the world and gifted by God for the accomplishment of some high and holy work. She expounds the language of the stars—her dark eyes kindle the souls of congregated men—she is worshipped, adored, reverenced—no one dreams or dares of connecting the idea of love with that of the "ANCILLA DEL."

Castruccio comes to Ferrara for the purpose of arranging a political revolution, in which Beatrice plays a distinguished part. They meet continually; he reveres her as a nun, but cannot be blind to her excessive beauty. She reveres him as the chosen warrior of what she imagines to be the cause of right—the man of the age, the hero of the world. Her soul is bathed in the flood of a new and overmastering passion, and boldly indeed does Mrs Shelley paint her feelings and her actions.

—Unsigned, from "Valperga,"
Blackwood's Edinburgh Magazine,
March 1823, pp. 283–285

UNSIGNED REVIEW FROM
LA BELLE ASSEMBLÉE (1823)

When we take up a work, announced as the novel before us is, as the production of a no less celebrated author than that of Frankenstein, we naturally expect to find it possessing extraordinary talent; and were that expectation not realized, we might perhaps, through disappointment, be induced to judge of it with unmeasured severity. In the present instance, however, the promise of talent is amply fulfilled, and the critical task is consequently commendatory. Valperga is notwithstanding occasionally tinged with a sombre hue, which some of our fair readers may not be altogether pleased with; yet it contains numerous passages of powerful interest, and displays not only an intimate acquaintance with the history and manners of the times, when Italy was convulsed with the party feuds of the Guelphs and Ghibelines, but also a perfect knowledge of the passions by which the human breast is agitated.

It would far exceed our present limits to give any thing like a detailed account of the plot and prominent incidents of 'Valperga;' suffice it therefore to observe, that they chiefly arise out of the interminable hatred that existed between the Ghibelines and Guelphs, and the loves of Castruccio and Euthanasia: the former being the son of Ruggieri del Antiminelli, head of one of the most distinguished Ghibeline families in Lucca, and the latter the daughter of a Guelph, named Antonio dei Adonari, between whose families strong ties of private affection had long subsisted. At length the parents of Euthanasia die, and she becomes Countess of Valperga, and consequently a person of considerable importance in the Florentine republic. Castruccio, who had imbibed the most ambitious notions, and who ardently sought for the reputation of a conqueror, in pursuance of his designs of aggrandizement, declared war against Florence, and in the course of events the castle of Valperga was included by him among those which must submit to his dominion. Euthanasia, who had endeavoured to unite the opposite parties, and to restore peace, had long since discovered the unworthiness of her former lover, for she could not fail to see that his ambition was to be satiated with nothing short of the total subjugation of her countrymen. His affection for Euthanasia gradually retreated before the sweeping forces of his ambition, and he thought now only how she could be best preserved from personal violence in the impending ruin. The castle was razed, and its dependents made subjects of Lucca; while the virtuous and noble-minded Euthanasia was reduced from the situation of Castellana of Valperga to that of a private citizen of Florence. The inordinate lust of power which displayed itself in every succeeding action of Castruccio's life, became at length too great for the patient endurance either of friends or enemies, and a conspiracy was formed against him, in which Euthanasia was induced to join, on the express condition that the life of Castruccio should be spared. The plot was, however, defeated, the conspirators executed, and Euthanasia sentenced to be banished to Sicily. Her sentence was, however, never completed, for the ship was wrecked, and all, on board perished. Castruccio survived the event only two years; and the history is here brought to a close.

The talents and passions of Castruccio, and his gradual departure from that line of conduct which distinguishes a generous and enterprizing youth, to a crafty and ambitious tyrant, are displayed with great fidelity—so powerfully, so naturally displayed, indeed, that for the sake of humanity we could wish it was less faithful. But, as if to dazzle the reader by the effect of the contrast, and to redeem our nature of its frailty, the character of Euthanasia is of the most exalted kind: a personification, in fact, of female excellence, exhibiting a rare union of feminine softness with disinterestedness and true nobleness of mind. All the subordinate characters in this admirable novel are well and forcibly drawn; some are miscreants of the deepest dye, particularly Benedetto Pepi and Trepalda; while others, Frances Guinigi, for instance, are replete with benevolence and philanthropy.

After what we have remarked, our readers will suppose that we could readily quote numerous passages of powerful interest: we are sorry that our limits prevent us from so far contributing to their gratification. To the work itself we must, and indeed we ought, in justice to the author, refer them; but we will not conclude our notice of Valperga without making one extract, by which we trust the style and sentiment of the greater portion of the work may be judged. The following is a description of Castruccio's visit to Euthanasia in prison, on the night previous to her embarking on that voyage which sealed her destiny:—

> A little before midnight Euthanasia's prison-chamber was unlocked, and the jailor entered, with a lamp in his hand, accompanied by one of majestic figure, and a countenance beautiful, but sad, and tarnished by the expression of pride that animated it. "She sleeps," whispered the jailor. His companion raised his finger in token of silence; and, taking the lamp from the man's hand, approached her mattress, which was spread upon the floor, and, kneeling down beside it, earnestly gazed upon that face he had known so well in happier days. She made an uneasy motion, as if the lamp which he held disturbed her; he placed it on the ground, and shaded it with his figure; while, by the soft light that fell upon her, he tried to read the images that were working in her mind.
>
> She appeared but slightly altered since he had first seen her. If thought had drawn some lines on her brow, the intellect which its beautiful form expressed, effaced them to the eye of the spectator: her golden hair fell over her face and neck: he gently drew it back, while she smiled in her sleep; her smile was ever past description lovely, and one might well exclaim with Dante:
>
> Quel, ch'ella par quando un poco sorride,
> Non si puo dicer, ne tenere a mente,

Sí è nuovo miracolo, e gentile.[1]

He gazed on her long; her white arm lay on her black dress, and he imprinted a sad kiss upon it; she awoke, and saw Castruccio gazing upon her.

She started up: "What does this mean?" she cried.

His countenance, which had softened as he looked upon her, now reassumed its severe expression. "Madonna," he replied, "I come to take you from this place."

She looked on him, endeavouring to read his purpose in his eyes; but she saw there no explanation of her doubts:—"And whither, do you intend to lead me?"

"That you will know hereafter."

She paused; and he added with a disdainful smile, "The Countess of Valperga need not fear, while I have the power to protect her, the fate she prepared for me."

"What fate?"

"Death!"

He spoke in an undertone, but with one of those modulations of voice which, bringing to her mind scenes of other days, was best fitted to make an impression upon her. She replied almost unconsciously—"I did not prepare death for you; God is my witness!"

"Well, Madonna, we will not quarrel about words; or, like lawyers, clothe our purposes in such a subtle guise, that it might deceive all, if truth did not destroy the spider's web. I come to lead you from prison."

It is some time before Castruccio is convinced of her sincerity, and then finds it difficult to persuade her to leave the prison, without assurances, which he refuses to give, of the safety of the other conspirators.

The jailor, who had hitherto stood in the shade near the door, could no longer contain himself. He knelt to Euthanasia, and earnestly and warmly intreated her to save herself, and not with wilful presumption to cast aside those means which God had brought about for her safety. "Remember," he cried, "your misfortunes will be on the prince's head; make him not answer for you also. Oh! lady, for his sake, for all our sakes, yield."

Castruccio was much moved to see the warmth of this man. He took the hand of Euthanasia, he also knelt: "Yes, my only and dearest friend, save yourself for my sake. Yield, beloved Euthanasia, to my intreaties. Indeed you will not die; for you well know that your life is dearer to me than my own. But yield to my request, by our former loves, I intreat; by the prayers which you offer up for my salvation, I conjure you as they shall be heard, so also hear me!"

The light of the solitary lamp fell full upon the countenance of Castruccio: it was softened from all severity; his eyes glistened, and a tear stole silently down his check as he prayed her to yield. They talk of the tears of women; but, when they flow most plenteously, they soften not the heart of man, as one tear from his eyes has power on a woman. Words and looks have been feigned; they say, though I believe them not, that women have feigned tears: but those of a man, which are ever as the last demonstration of a too full heart, force belief, and communicate to her who causes them that excess of tenderness, that intense depth of passion, of which they are themselves the sure indication.

Euthanasia had seen Castruccio weep but once before; it was many years ago, when he departed for the battle of Monte Catini; and he then sympathized too deeply in her sorrows, not to repay her much weeping with one most true and sacred tear. And now this scene was present before her; the gap of years remained unfilled; and she had consented to his request, before she again recalled her thoughts; and saw the dreary prison chamber, the glimmering lamp, and the rough form of the jailor who knelt beside Antelminelli. Her consent was scarcely obtained, when Castruccio leapt up, and, bidding her wrap her capuchin about her, led her by the hand down the steep prison-stairs, while the jailor went before them, and unlocked, and drew back the bolts of, the heavy, creaking doors.

Notes

1. *Vita Nuova di Dante.*

—Unsigned, *Valperga*, from *La Belle Assemblée*, August 1823, pp. 82–84

Unsigned Review from *Knight's Quarterly Magazine* (1824)

I do not think I ever was so much disappointed in any book as in Valperga; I had the very highest expectations of the maturing of the genius which could produce such a work as Frankenstein. The faults of Frankenstein were occasional extravagance and *over-writing*;—it was, therefore, natural to suppose that the interval of between four and five years would correct this, without impairing its freshness, force, and vigour. But in Valperga there is not the slightest trace of the same hand—instead of the rapidity and enthusiastic energy which hurries you forward in Frankenstein, every thing is cold, crude, inconsecutive, and wearisome;—not one flash of imagination, not one spank of passion—opening it as I did, with eager expectation, it must indeed have been bad for me after toiling a week to send the book back without having finished the first volume. This induced me to read Frankenstein again—for I thought I must have been strangely mistaken In my original judgment. So far, however, from this, a second reading has confirmed it. I think Frankenstein possesses extreme power, and display s capabilities such as I did hope would have produced far different things from Castruccio.

The circumstances under which Frankenstein was written are well known;—it is one of three tales agreed to be composed on supernatural subjects by the Shelleys, (Mr. or Mrs., of which more anon,) Dr. Polidori, and Lord Byron,—Frankenstein is the Shelley work,—the Vampyre Polidori's,— and that of Lord Byron (I conclude) the fragment published at the end of Mazeppa. I have but a faint recollection of this last—but I remember perfectly agreeing in a criticism of it which I saw somewhere at the time; namely, that it was in perfect contrariety to the rules of Aristotle, having neither beginning, middle, nor end. The Vampyre made considerable noise on its appearance, from its being announced as Lord Byron's; Polidori always denied being a party to this paltry imposition, whether truly or not I cannot say—but it certainly appears strange that his publishers could have played it off without at least his connivance. The deception, however, could do no more than sell off the first edition,—for nothing could be more evident than that it was impossible that Lord Byron could be the author of such a thing. I was abroad at the time it came out, and it was brought to me by a friend as a great curiosity, being Lord Byron's only prose composition, and he misled by the name, told me "his blood curdled as he read it." I had not, however, got beyond two pages before I saw that it was the most impudent of all impostures, being one that was sure to be found out, and that immediately. Accordingly, a few days after, arrived the copy of Lord Byron's letter in Galignani's Messenger, disavowing the work, which he said he had not seen, and adding, with his peculiar felicity of sneer—"If it be good, I would not rob any man of his laurels—if it be bad, I would not bear the burden of any one's dulness but my own."

Polidori was a man whose ruin it was to go abroad with Lord Byron as his physician; he by this means lived much with him and Shelley, and hence from being continually in the company of men of genius he imbibed the preposterous notion that he was a man of genius himself. I have heard a story, which I believe, of his saying to these two, that they had a *name*, but that he could write poetry as good, if not superior, to theirs. When Polidori became insupportable, and Lord Byron could stand it no longer, he returned to England, and then his story, in despite of his vanity and overweening presumption, becomes melancholy. He was bitterly pinched by poverty, and the gloom which he had, I believe, originally assumed as a foppish token of genius, became in a great degree real, from the misery of his circumstances. He could get no employment in his profession, and began to study the law. After the Vampyre, he wrote two or three things; a tragedy, a novel, and a poem—but they were all one worse than another—inveterately dull; and never, by any chance, English; they did not *sell*, and he became more and more distressed and desponding—fancying himself a second Otway,—another Chatterton. His end, poor fellow, was melancholy indeed; "yet marked by that self-conceit which was so peculiarly his characteristic. He fancied he had discovered what is termed in the language of gamesters *une martingale*; i.e., an infallible mode of winning at Rouge et Noir;—a notion which has misled, ruined, and destroyed as many as ever the philosophers' stone, or the elixir vitae did in the old days of alchemy. The consequence was what might be expected—he lost a sum utterly beyond what he could ever have any hope of paying, and killed himself.

To return to Frankenstein, it is, I think, the best instance of natural passions applied to supernatural events that I ever met with. Grant that it is possible for one man to create another, and the rest is perfectly natural and in course. I do not allude to the incidents, for they are thrown together with a haste and carelessness so apparent as to be almost confessed; but the sentiments—both of thought and passion—are given with a truth which is equal to their extraordinary vigour. I am surprised to see by the preface that Dr. Darwin, and some of the physiological writers of Germany supposed the creation of a human being "as not of impossible occurrence." I can understand that it might be possible to put together a human frame—though with the very greatest difficulty—both from the intricacy and minuteness of the conformation, the most trifling error in which would be fatal, and from the difficulty of preventing putrescence during the process, without drying up the form like a mummy, which would incapacitate it from all purposes of *life*. But, granting that, a frame could be so constructed, I cannot conceive how Dr. Darwin, who, however over-rated by his friends, was certainly a man of considerable powers of mind, I cannot conceive, I say, how he could contemplate the possibility of infusing the principle of life, when of such principle we are wholly ignorant. Many attempts have been made to say where life dwells—to prove that such or such a part is infallibly vital; but whoever could say what life itself was? This is one of the most strange of those mysteries which are hidden from human reason. The simplest operations of nature are, in their cause and process, equally inscrutable;—the whole progress and vegetation from the seed rotting in the earth, to the shoot, the sapling, the tree, the blossom, the fruit—is as utterly inscrutable by man as are the causes of his own production and existence.

The most unskilful thing in the book is the extreme ugliness of the being whom Frankenstein creates. It is not natural, that to save himself additional trouble from the minuteness of the parts, he should create a giant. He must have known the vast danger of forming one of such bodily power, whose mind it would take a considerable time to mould into humanity. Besides, though it is highly natural that the features which had been chosen individually as perfect, and which appeared so even when conjoined in the lifeless figure, should, on their being vivified, have an incongruous and unearthly aspect; yet, it is not at all probable that one with Frankenstein's science should have formed a creature of such "appalling hideousness." It is utterly inconceivable also, that he should have let the monster (as he is somewhat unfairly called) escape;—one of the thoughts which must, one would imagine, have been uppermost in his mind during his labours, would have been instructing his creature intellectually as he had formed him physically.

In the account which the creature gives of his instruction by means of watching the polished cottagers, the hastiness of the composition is the most apparent. Indeed, nothing would require such extreme trouble and carefulness as a correct representation of the mind of one who had (from whatever circumstances) reached maturity without any acquired knowledge. Those things which, from having been known to us before the period to which our remembrances reach, appear to be part of our innate consciousness, would be perfect novelty to such a being. Not only speech would be non-existent but even sight would be imperfect in him. In short, it would require much thought and some physical knowledge, joined (as I before said) to the greatest care, to render such a description at once full and accurate. In Frankenstein what there is of it is sufficiently interesting in itself, but it suggests so frequently how much more it might be wrought out, that it brings strongly into view its own imperfectness.

For my own part, I confess that my interest in the book is entirely on the side of the monster. His eloquence and persuasion, of which Frankenstein complains, are so because they are truth. The justice is indisputably on his side, and his sufferings are, to me, touching to the last degree. Are there are any sufferings, indeed, so severe as those which arise from the sensation of dereliction, or (as in this case) of isolation? Even the slightest tinge of those feelings, arising as they often do from trivial circumstances, as from passing a solitary evening in a lone and distant situation—even these, are bitter to a severe degree. What it must be, then,—what *is* it to feel oneself *alone in the world*! Fellow-feeling is the deepest of all the needs which Nature has implanted within us. The impulses which lead us to the physical preservation of our life are scarcely stronger than those which impel us to communion with our fellows. Alas! then to have no fellows!—to be, with feelings of kindliness and beneficence, the object of scorn and hate to every one whose eyes lighted on us!—to be repaid with blows and wounds for the very benefits we confer!—The poor monster always, for these reasons, touched me to the heart. Frankenstein ought to have reflected on the means of giving happiness to the being of his creation, before he *did* create him. Instead of that, he heaps on him all sorts of abuse and contumely for his *ugliness*, which was directly *his* work, and for his crimes to which his neglect gave rise.

But whence arises the extreme inferiority of Valperga? I can account for it only by supposing that Shelley wrote the first, though it was attributed to his wife,—and that she really wrote the last. Still I should not, from internal evidence, suppose Frankenstein to be the work of Shelley. It has much of his poetry and vigour—but it is wholly free from those philosophical opinions from which scarcely any of his works *are* free, and for which there are many fair openings in Frankenstein. It is equally to be observed that there are no religious reflections—and that there are many circumstances in which a mind at all religiously inclined would not have failed to have expressed some sentiments of that nature. It may be, that Mrs. Shelley wrote Frankenstein—but, knowing that its fault was extravagance, determined to be careful and correct in her next work; and, thence, as so many do from the same cause, became cold and common-place. At all events, the difference of the two books is very remarkable.

—Unsigned, from *Knight's Quarterly Magazine*,
vol. III, August–November 1824, pp. 195–199

THE LAST MAN

In an unsigned critique from the *Monthly Review* of March 1826, the reviewer maintains that the shadow of *Frankenstein* lurks in the background of *The Last Man* and is another rendition of an imaginative world bearing no resemblance to the human character or "the living drama of life." Among other things, the critic sees the project of *The Last Man* as a waste of imaginative time, while leveling a familiar complaint, the preposterous scenario in which Lionel Verney manages to survive a shipwreck and live a few months in order that he may record the story. In sum, the critic finds no redeeming elements in Mary Shelley's second work of science fiction, declaring it a "decided failure" that suffers from a surfeit of graphic details regarding the plague.

Another unfavorable and unsigned review of *The Last Man* appeared in March 1826, the overall objection being that Mary Shelley simply did not know how to manage a theme full of great imaginative potential and instead produced an uninspired work in which the sublime is replaced by the silly and inconsequential. "We were agaze for the wonders of imaginative delineation, and we wondered indeed to find nothing before our eyes by fancies, 'neither new nor rare' decked out in frippery and tinsel." As to the often voiced complaint about Lionel Verney surviving long enough to record his story, the critic suggests that the Cumaean Sibyl, rather than the last man, should have been the observing narrator, a revision that would have made the novel more believable as a prophecy. What is most noteworthy about this particular critique is that the reviewer shows himself to be a competent literary critic and a political conservative—a monarchist—as he laments the historical situation in *The Last Man*, in which the king of England has abdicated the throne and been replaced by a republic according to the will of the people. "The holy salt of royalty removed, what was to preserve the mass from corruption?"

UNSIGNED REVIEW FROM *THE LITERARY GAZETTE AND JOURNAL OF BELLES LETTRES* (1826)

This is a novel, of which the subject is sufficiently extraordinary. Two of the most successful poets of the day, Byron and Campbell, have dared only just to touch upon it in a few detached lines; and yet here we have three volumes of prose devoted to it by a female writer. Whether the bards were wise in their restricted flights, or whether this bolder undertaking could possibly succeed, we will not here inquire. The author, suffice it to say, is not unknown to the reading world, for her scarcely less bold, and certainly not altogether unsuccessful attempt under the title of Frankenstein. We shall, therefore, merely glance at the plan and conduct of the fable, and present a few extracts, as specimens of the manner in which it is executed. There is an Introduction, not very skillfully imagined, which gives us to understand that the work is to be looked upon as a sort of free translation of certain "Sibylline Leaves," picked up by a party of modern travellers in the (so called) cave of the Cumaen Sibyl, on the shores of the Bay of Naples: and the story (as the name indicates) relates to the life and fortunes of "the Last Man," who remains on the face of the earth after it has been desolated of its human inhabitants by a great plague, which rages during the last two or three years of the twenty-first century of our present era. The story, however, commences about the year 2073—thus affording scope for much matter not connected with the catastrophe, and enabling the writer to indulge in every possible (and impossible) flight of her anticipative imagination, touching the nature of human society, and of all other mundane matters, a hundred and fifty years hence!

The story is at first almost exclusively confined to a very few persons, who, for a while, figure in the highest circles of political life at the period in question. But the events related, and the scenes which are introduced to develop the characters, refer chiefly to the private life of those persons, and to that universal passion which woman is so well fitted to illustrate, and which, it appears, is to enjoy at least as much influence on human affairs in the year 2080 as it does now. It is not till the beginning of the second volume that the existence of plague is announced; and here commences the chief novelty of the design. Until the middle of this volume, *plague* confines its ravages to the eastern parts of the globe; though, from its extensive progress there, fears and misgivings are entertained every where, and corresponding precautions are taken. At length, however, it reaches England, and the whole narrative comes to be absorbed by a detailed account of its progress here—of the flight of those who are spared by it—of their melancholy journeyings from place to place of the almost-deserted world—and, finally, of the death of all, save and except the hero of the story, who survives alone—survives even the plague itself, and is left living and to live on the still productive earth—the Last Man.

Such is the monstrous fable. We shall now present our readers with a few extracts, to shew the manner in which the work is executed in its different departments of description of character and of passion. It appears that, in the days to come (according to these prophecies of our Cumaen Sibyl), we are to call for our balloon as we now do for our travelling chariot. Here is a short description of a journey in one:

"Every thing favoured my journey. The balloon rose half a mile from the earth, and with a favourable wind it hurried through the air, its feathered vans cleaving the unopposing atmosphere. Notwithstanding the melancholy object of my journey, my spirits were exhilarated by reviving hope, by the swift motion of the airy pinnace, and the balmy visitation of the sunny air. The pilot hardly moved the plumed steerage, and the slender mechanism of the wings, wide unfurled, gave forth a murmuring noise, soothing to the sense. Plain and hill, stream and corn-field, were discernible below, while we, unimpeded, sped on, swift and secure as a wild swan in his spring-tide flight. The machine obeyed the slightest motion of the helm; and the wind blowing steadily, there was no let or obstacle to our course. Such was the power over the elements—a power long sought, and lately won, yet foretold in bygone time by the prince of poets, whose verses I quoted, much to the astonishment of my pilot when I told him how many hundred years ago they had been written:—

"Oh human wit! thou canst invent much ill,
Thou searchest strange arts: who would think, by skill,
A heavy man like a light bird should stray,
And through the empty heavens find a way?"

They are to love in those days much as they do now. England, it appears, is to be a republic then; but the kingdom of Love is to remain an absolute monarchy, and its subjects are to be slaves. We quote a passage as superlative in the way of lady-metaphysics.

"Is there such a feeling as love at first sight? and if there be, in what does its nature differ from love founded in long observation and slow growth? Perhaps its effects are not so permanent; but they are, while they last, as violent and intense. We walk the pathless mazes of society vacant of joy, till we hold this clue, leading us through that labyrinth to paradise. Our nature dim, like to an unlighted torch, sleeps in formless blank till the fire attain it; this life of life—this light to moon, and glory to the sun. What does it matter, whether fire be struck from flint and steel, nourished with care into a flame, slowly communicated to the dark wick, or whether swiftly the radiant power of light and warmth passes from a kindred power, and shines at once the beacon and the hope? In the deepest fountain of my heart the pulses were stirred—around, about, beneath, the clinging memory, as a cloak, enwrapt me. In no one moment of coming time did I feel as I had done in time gone by. The spirit of Idris hovered in the air—her eyes were ever bent on mine—her remembered smile blinded my faint gaze, and caused me to walk as one not in eclipse, not in darkness and vacancy, but in a new and brilliant light, too novel, too dazzling for my human senses. On every leaf, on every small division of the universe, (as on the hyacinth AI is engraved), was imprinted the talisman of my existence—she is! she lives! I had not time yet to analyse my feeling, to take myself to task, and bask in the tameless passion—all was one idea, one feeling, one knowledge—it was my life!"

Were this not written by a woman, it would be sad, vapid impertinence: as it is written by a woman, we male critics do not know what it is. We wish we did! Who will teach us?

We intended to have given further extracts from that part of the work which precedes what may be said to comprise its direct object. But we had better go at once to the portion of it immediately connected with the catastrophe. The following description relates to the period immediately preceding the departure from England of its few remaining "people."

"On the twentieth of November, Adrian and I rode for the last time through the streets of London. They were grass-grown and desert. The open doors of the empty mansions creaked upon their hinges—rank herbage and deforming dirt had swiftly accumulated on the steps of the houses—the voiceless steeples of the churches pierced the smokeless air—the churches were open, but no prayers were offered at the altars—mildew and damp had already defaced their ornaments—birds and tame animals, now homeless, had built nests and made their lairs in consecrated spots. We passed St. Paul's. London, which had extended so far in suburbs in all direction, had been somewhat deserted in the midst, and much of what had in former days obscured this vast building was removed. Its ponderous mass, blackened stone, and high dome, had made it look not like a temple, but a tomb. Methought above the portico was engraved the *hic jacet* of England. We passed on eastwards, engaged in such solemn talk as the times inspired. No human step was heard or human form discerned. Troops of dogs, deserted by their masters, passed us; and now and then a horse, unbridled and unsaddled, trotted towards us, and tried to attract the attention of those which we rode, as if to allure them to seek like liberty. An unwieldy ox, who had fed in an abandoned granary, suddenly lowed, and shewed his shapeless form in a narrow doorway. Every thing was desert; but nothing was in ruin: and this medley of undamaged buildings and luxurious accommodation, in trim and fresh youth, was contrasted with the lonely silence of the unpeopled streets."

The finale approaches. What follows occurs at nearly the end of the last volume, when "the Last Man" has, for some time past, found himself literally alone in the world.

"As the fever of my blood increased, a desire of wandering came upon me. I remember that the sun had set on the fifth day after my wreck, when, without purpose or aim, I quitted the town of Ravenna. I must have been very ill. Had I been possessed by more or less delirium, that night had surely been my last; for as I continued to walk on the banks of the Mantone, whose upward course I followed, I looked wistfully in the stream, acknowledging that its pellucid waves could medicine my woes for ever, and was unable to account to myself for my tardiness in seeking their shelter from the poisoned arrows of thought, that were piercing me through and through. I walked a considerable part of the night, and excessive weariness at length conquered my repugnance to the availing myself of the deserted habitations of my species. The waning moon, which had just risen, shewed me a cottage, whose neat entrance and trim garden reminded me of my own England. I lifted up the latch of the door, and entered. A kitchen first presented itself, where, guided by the moonbeams, I found materials for striking a light. Within this was a bed room. The couch was furnished with sheets of snowy whiteness; the wood piled on the hearth, and an array as for a meal, might almost have deceived me into the dear belief that I had here found what I had so long sought—one survivor, a companion for my loneliness, a solace to my despair. I steeled myself against the delusion. The room itself was vacant: it was only prudent, I repeated to myself, to examine the rest of the house. I fancied that I was proof against this expectation; yet my heart beat audibly as I laid my head on the lock of each door; and it sunk again when I perceived in each the same vacancy. Dark and silent they were as vaults; so I returned to the first chamber, wondering what sightless host had spread the materials for my repast and my repose. I drew a chair to the table, and examined what the viands were of which I was to partake. In truth it was a death feast! the bread was blue and mouldy; the cheese lay a heap of dust. I did not dare examine the other dishes; a troop of ants passed in a double line across the table cloth; every utensil was covered with dust, with cobwebs, and myriads of dead flies: these were objects each and all betokening the fallaciousness of my expectations. Tears rushed into my eyes. Surely this was a wanton display of the power of the destroyer. What had I done, that each sensitive nerve was thus to be anatomised? Yet, why complain more now than ever? This vacant cottage revealed no new sorrow. The world was empty—mankind was dead—I knew it well—why quarrel, therefore, with an acknowledged and stale truth—yet, as I said, I had hoped in the very heart of despair, so that every new impression of the hard-cut reality on my soul, brought with it a fresh pang, telling me the yet unstudied lesson, that neither change of time nor place could bring alleviation to my misery; but that as I now was I must continue, day after day, month after month, year after year, while I lived."

The work closes shortly after this, leaving the unhappy subject of it to wander over the face of his earth, in a perpetual search after that companionship which he knows can never more be found.

When we repeat that these volumes are the production of a female pen, and that we have not ceased to consider Mrs. Shelley as a woman and a widow, we shall have given the clue to our abstinence from remarks upon them. That we must deem the tale altogether to be an instance of the strange misapplication of considerable talent, is most true. After the first volume, it is a sickening repetition of horrors, and a struggle after the display of morbid feelings which could not exist under the circumstances, nor even in the world as it now exists, with good and evil, joys and woes, mingled together. To hear a *last man* talking of having his "sensitive nerves anatomised" by any thing, is sheer nonsense: by the time a man had outlived his kind, Mrs. S. might be assured that the nervous system too was pretty nearly abolished. Then there is no keeping in any of the parts. In spite of the perfection of ballooning, people ride, and drive, and sail, as in the olden days, when aerial travelling was not so agreeable, when the remnant few of the world are all equal, of course—still, the principal characters hire chaises, have attendants, escorts, postillions! Really these are sad doings. We confess that we cannot get so seriously through the world in its last convulsions as we could wish; but there may be readers who can enter into the spirit of the thing, and to them the perusal of Mrs. Shelley's book may afford gratification. We will add, that there are some strong imaginings in it; and not the least cruel of these flights appears to us to be, the author's making the last human being an unfortunate gentleman. Why not *the last Woman*? she would have known better how to paint her distress at having nobody left to talk to: we are sure the tale would have been more interesting.

—Unsigned, from *The Literary Gazette
and Journal of Belles Lettres*, February
1826, pp. 102–103

Unsigned Review from
Monthly Review (1826)

Mrs. Shelley, true to the genius of her family, has found this breathing world and the operations and scenes which enliven it, so little worthy of her soaring fancy, that she once more ventures to create a world of her own, to people it with beings modelled by her own hand, and to govern it by laws drawn from the visionary theories which she has been so long taught to admire as the perfection of wisdom. She seems herself to belong to a sphere different from that with which we are conversant. Her imagination appears to delight in inventions which have no foundation in ordinary occurrences, and no charm for the common sympathies of mankind. We praise our most successful authors for the fidelity with which they paint the human character, for the simplicity which marks their representations of the living drama of life, and for the air of probability which they are sedulous to observe, even when they borrow most abundantly from the resources of imagination. If Mrs. Shelley is to be set down amongst our popular writers, she will owe her good fortune to the boldness of her departure for all the acknowledged canons of inventive literature; for the whole course of her ambition has been to pourtray monsters which could have existed only in her own conceptions, and to involve them in scenes and events which are wholly unparalleled by any thing that the world has yet witnessed.

This idea of 'The Last Man' has already tempted the genius of more than one of our poets, and, in truth, it is a theme which appears to open a magnificent and boundless field to the imagination. But we have only to consider it for a moment, in order to be convinced that the mind of man might as well endeavour to describe the transactions which are taking place in any of the countless planets that are suspended beyond our own, as to anticipate the horrors of the day which shall see the dissolution of our system. The utmost efforts of thought are absolutely childish, when they seek to fathom the abyss of ruin, to number the accumulation of disasters, to paint the dreadful confusion, which await that final scene. Every writer who has hitherto ventured on the theme has fallen infinitely beneath it. Mrs. Shelley, in following their example, has merely made herself ridiculous.

She generously permits our orb to roll on in its accustomed course until the year 2100, when the 'Last Man' is by her fiat left to perish. He is an Englishman, whom she names Verney and to whom, of course, she assigns a principal part in the conduct of her story, although he is originally brought up in the humblest of rural occupations. Her story commences about the year

2073, when the last of our kings is supposed to have abdicated 'in compliance with the gentle force of the remonstrances of his subjects, and a republic was instituted.' The view, however, which Mrs. Shelley gives of the practical effects of this system, is by no means an inviting one; the whole of the period which she described, is remarkable for civil strife, and so difficult did she find it to manage this part of her subject, that she was obliged to change the scene to Greece, in the final liberation of which she employs one of her heroes—for she has a number of them. This event accomplished (we hope, however, that this part of her tale will be anticipated even in our own times), her *dramatis personae* return to England, where pestilence soon destroys the whole population, with the exception of some fourteen or fifteen hundred souls who emigrate to Switzerland. On their way thither they find the continent also desolated, they themselves fall away like blighted ears of corn, till they are reduced to three individuals, two of whom perish by shipwreck. Verney survives them a few months to write this history, which Mrs. Shelley has obtained by some sort of magical incantation, in the mysteries of which we are not initiated.

There is nothing in the conduct, in the characters, in the incidents, or in the descriptive matter of this work, to which we feel any pleasure in referring. The whole appears to us to be the offspring of a diseased imagination, and of a most polluted taste. We must observe, however, that the powers of composition displayed in this production, are by no means of an ordinary character. They are indeed uncontrolled by any of the rules of good writing; but they certainly bear the impress of genius, though perverted and spoiled by morbid affectation. Mrs. Shelley frequently attempts to give her style a rhythmical conciseness, and a poetical colouring, which we take to have been the main causes of the bombast that disfigures almost every chapter of this unamiable romance.

The descriptions of the operations of the pestilence are particularly objectionable for their minuteness. It is not a picture which she gives us, but a lecture in anatomy, in which every part of the human frame is laid bare to the eye, in its most putrid state of corruption. In this part of her subject, as indeed in every other, she simplifies beyond all the bounds of moderation. We are reluctantly obliged to pronounce the work a decided failure.

—Unsigned, from *Monthly Review,*
March 1826, pp. 333–335

Unsigned Review from
The Knickerbocker (1833)

We suppose this lady to be the widow of the far famed poet and atheist Shelley. She has constructed a thrilling tale of much pathos, power, and horror; wilder, more extravagant, and remoter from probability, than ever entered the fevered brain of an expiring man, held back on this side the invisible country by the momentary stimulus of alcohol and laudanum. It is a sort of detailed and prose copy of Byron's terrible painting of darkness. Gloomy indeed must be the musings of the widow of a man so gifted and so horribly dark in his creed as Shelley, imagining herself alone in the universe. A love tale, and the usual incidents of a novel, the era of which is supposed in 2098, conduct Verney by the aid of earthquake, pestilence and shipwreck, to his dreary catastrophe of being THE LAST MAN—an unfortunate title, which we are sure ladies will not admire; for though men are filthy, smoking, spitting animals, with tough chins, yet they are useful in keeping off the dogs from ladies, and divers other offices of indispensable utility. Yet there is genius in these volumes; and many a sad mind will be arrested by the sombre eloquence and force of these paintings.

—Unsigned, from *The Knickerbocker,*
October 1833, p. 315

ADVENTURES OF PERKIN WARBECK

The first unsigned review of *Perkin Warbeck,* from *The Athenæum* of May 29, 1830, is quite favorable. The critic, despite reservations about the genre of historical romance and objections to the persistent doom and tragedy that interfere with the reader's enjoyment of the text, nevertheless believes this novel to be the work of an exceptional author who has clearly written with enthusiasm, the product of "a richly-endowed and vigorous intellect." Most particularly, he is full of praise for Mary Shelley's portrayal of Monina de Faro. In conclusion, this critic declares that the three volumes that comprise *Perkin Warbeck* are "calculated to enhance the reputation of their fair author."

In a second unsigned review of *Perkin Warbeck* from the *Edinburgh Literary Journal* of June 19, 1830, the critic praises the novel for its display of talent, though he finds it burdensome and weighed down by a preponderance of historical detail that interferes with an imaginative depiction of the characters. While maintaining that Mary Shelley offers a convincing argument that Perkin Warbeck is one and the same as the duke of York, the reviewer feels that the interlacing of fiction and historical romance does not work.

Unsigned Review from
The Athenaeum (1830)

To historical novels we confess ourselves to have a decided antipathy. They derogate from the dignity of history, by dragging her from the noble elevation where the sanction of ages has fixed her, to degrade her into a mere vehicle of romance. They cast the hue of falsehood over the glories of her truth, and rob her of her symmetry by a load of meretricious decoration. Characters which she has consecrated are abridged of their finest proportions by the merciless depredations of fiction; and those which she has consigned to everlasting infamy, are adorned in all the blazonry of romantic virtue. We scarcely know her under the gorgeous disguise. In spite, however, of our objection to historical romances, we are bound to confess that the volumes before us are the productions of no ordinary pen. It is manifest that a richly-endowed and vigorous intellect has directed the hand which traced them. They are written with a noble energy of thought—a deep concentration of feeling—a fervid glow of expression, and sweet purity of sentiment, which display in their author the very highest capabilities. The reader is hurried on from action to action with a spirit-stirring impulse, which never for a moment allows his excitement to abate; and the scenes which follow each other in such rapid succession, are wrought out with all the distinctness of a present reality. The characters are drawn with great vividness, and in some of them, especially, there is an originality which strikingly marks the powerfully-creative mind of the author of "Frankenstein."

Clifford, Frion, and Herman de Faro, we take to be very noble conceptions. The two first stand before us in the darkest hues of reckless depravity, whilst the latter is endowed with a dignity, which a peculiar mental idiosyncrasy often superadds to the natural elevation of virtue.

Mrs. Shelley's work contains simply what its title indicates—the fortunes of Perkin Warbeck, (whom our fair author presumes to be no impostor, but the true Plantagenet,) from his rescue from the Tower, when a child, to the sad termination of his career upon the scaffold.

The great defect in this romance appears to us to be the painful anticipation of disaster which is continually forced upon the reader, and which the mind cannot escape from, so that no pleasurable emotions are excited. It is painful to hurry through a succession of events which we know beforehand will all terminate unhappily. Warbeck's marriage with Lady Catherine Gordon is the only oasis amid the wilderness of misfortune through which he is doomed to wander. The interest of the reader is necessarily vastly diminished by his unavoidable knowledge, that every effort of the hero will fail, and that destruction must overtake him at the last.

We shall now let our fair author speak for herself—assured that she will fully vindicate her right to the merits which we have awarded her. We give her portrait of Monina de Faro:—

"Monina de Faro was, even in childhood, a being to worship and to love. There was a dreamy sweetness in her countenance—a mystery in the profound sensibility of her nature, that fascinated beyond all compare. Her characteristic was not so much the facility of being impressed, as the excess of the emotion produced by every new idea or feeling. Was she gay?—her large eyes laughed in their own brightness, her lovely countenance became radiant with smiles, her thrilling voice was attuned to lightest mirth, while the gladness that filled her heart, overflowed from her as light does from the sun, imparting to all around a share of its own essence. Did sorrow oppress her?—dark night fell upon her mind, clouding her face, oppressing her whole person, which staggered and bent beneath the freight. Had she been susceptible of the stormier passions, her subtle and yielding soul would have been their unresisting victim—but though impetuous—wild—the slave of her own sensations, her soft bosom could harbour no emotion unallied to goodness; and the devouring appetite of her soul, was the desire of benefiting all around her. Her countenance was the mirror of her mind. Its outline resembled those we see in Spanish pictures, not being quite oval enough for a northern beauty. It seemed widened at the forehead, to give space for her large long eyes, and the canopy of the darkly fringed and veined lid; her hair was not black, but of a rich sunny chestnut, finer than carded silk, and more glossy; her skin was delicate, somewhat pale, except when emotion suffused it with a deep pink. In person, she was not tall, but softly rounded; and her taper, rosy tipped fingers, and little feet, bespoke the delicate proportion that moulded her form to a beauty, whose every motion awakened admiration and love." i. 214–16.

The following picture of a bravo of the vindictive King of England is wrought with terrific distinctness:—

"In those times, when recent civil war had exasperated the minds of men one against the other, it was no difficult thing for a

Lancastrian King to find an instrument willing and fitting to work injury against a Yorkist. During Henry's exile in Britany, he had become acquainted with a man, who had resorted to him there for the sole purpose of exciting him against Richard the Third; he had been a favourite page of Henry the Sixth; he had waited on his son, Edward, Prince of Wales, that noble youth whose early years promised every talent and virtue; he had idolized the heroic and unhappy Queen Margaret. Henry died a foul death in the Tower; the gracious Edward was stabbed at Tewkesbury; the royal Margaret had given place to the widow Woodville: while, through the broad lands of England, the sons of York rioted in the full possession of her wealth. Meiler Trangmar felt every success of theirs as a poisoned arrow in his flesh; he hated them, as the mother may hate the tiger, whose tusks are red with the life-blood of her first-born; he hated them, not with the measured aversion of a warlike foe, but the dark frantic vehemence of a wild beast deprived of its young. He had been the father of three sons; the first had died at Prince Edward's feet ere he was taken prisoner; another lost his head on the scaffold; the third—the boy had been nurtured in hate, bred amid dire curses and bitter imprecations, all levelled against Edward the Fourth and his brothers—his mind had become distorted by the ill food that nurtured it: he brooded over the crimes of these men, till he believed that he should do a good deed in immolating them to the ghosts of the murdered Lancastrians. He attempted the life of the king—was seized—tortured to discover his accomplices: he was tortured, and the father heard his cries beneath the dread instrument, to which death came as a sweet release. Real madness for a time possessed the unhappy man, and when reason returned, it was only the dawn of a tempestuous day, which rises on the wrecks of a gallant fleet and its crew, strewn on the dashing waves of a stormy sea. He dedicated himself to revenge; he had sought Henry in Britany; he had fought at Bosworth, and at Stoke. The success of his cause, and the peace that followed, was at first a triumph, at last almost a pain to him. He was haunted by memories which pursued him like the hell-born Eumenides; often he uttered piercing shrieks, as the scenes, so pregnant with horror, recurred too vividly to his mind. The priests, to whom he had recourse as his soul's physicians, counselled him the church's discipline; he assumed the Franciscan habit, but found sack-cloth and ashes no refuge from the greater torture of his mind. This man, in various ways, had been recalled to Henry's mind, and now he selected him to effect his purpose." i. 247–51.

The meeting of the Duke of York with Jane Shore is a very sweetly-affecting passage:—

"Seated in the rude gipsy-cart, guided, protected, by the uncouth being into whose hands he had so strangely fallen, Richard for the first time felt the degradation and low fortune to which his aspirations, at variance with his means, made him liable. With a strong effort he dismissed these painful ideas, and fixed his contemplation on mightier objects, which gilded his mean estate, or were rather the 'gold o'erdusted' by such extraneous poverty. To rise from this lowliness to a throne were an emprise worthy of his ambition. Was he not a few hours ago a prisoner in the terror-striking Tower? And now he was free—free in his England; which, when the battle-day was come and past, would claim him for her own. A few words from Monina interrupted the silence: she sat at his feet, and they conversed in whispers in Spanish. Night had gathered round them; Monina, in all the innocence of her pure heart, was supremely happy: to be near her friend in his disasters, united to him in his peril, was a more rapturous destiny to her than the world's best pomp, and he absent. No busy conscience, no untoward thought, disturbed in her soul the calm of perfect bliss. She grew weary at last; her head sunk on Richard's knee, and, overworn with watching, she fell into a deep sleep. Richard heard her regular breathing; once or twice his fingers played among her dishevelled ringlets, while his heart whispered to him what a wondrous creation woman was—weak, frail, complaining, when she suffers for herself; heroic fortitude and untired self-devotion are hers, when she sacrifices herself for him she loves.

"The cart moved on, Richard saw not whither; they almost stuck in some flat low fields, and at last arrived at a solitary, miserable hut. Monina awoke, when they stopt, and the gipsy told them that this wretched dwelling was to be their asylum: the apartment they entered was poor beyond meanness—a bed of straw piled in one corner, a rude bench formed the furniture; the walls were ragged and weather stained, and the outer crumbling rafters were visible through the broken ceiling: there appeared to be neither food nor fire. The inhabitant of the hovel alone was there, a white-looking, emaciated female; yet with a look of such sweetness and patience, that she seemed the very enshrinement of Christian resignation, the type of sorrow and suffering, married to meek obedience to the supreme will. She had roused herself from slumber at the voice of the gipsy, and gathered her scant garments around her—scant and poor they were; her coarse woollen dress was tied by a girdle of rope round her slender waist; her head was wrapt in a kerchief; her feet were bare.

"'Jane,' said the old woman, 'you will not refuse the shelter of your roof to these poor wanderers?'

"Such an address seemed strange, for the rich attire of her guests ill-accorded with her poverty-stricken home; but she turned with a smile—she spoke—and then a throb of agony seemed to convulse her frame—her head swam; Richard rushed forward to prevent her falling, but she shrunk from him, and leaned on the old woman, who said with a look of triumph, 'I knew how it would be; it is vain to hide a bright light behind a veil of gauze! Yes, Jane, this is his son; and you may save him from danger and death.'

"Jane Shore, the once lovely mistress of King Edward, now the miserable outcast of the world's scorn, heard these words, as if they had been spoken to her in a dream. After the death of her royal lover, she had obeyed the impulse that made her cling to the soft luxuries of life, and yielded to solicitations which tended to guard her from the sharp visitation of the world. She had become the mistress of the Marquess of Dorset; but sorrow and penury were destined to pursue her in their worst shape—and wherefore? She had been good and humane; and in spite of her error, even the sternest moralist might have pitied her. But she was all woman, fearful of repulse, dreading insult; more willing to lie down and die, than, fallen and miserable, to solicit uncertain relief: squalid poverty, famine, and lonely suffering, were hers; yet in all she preserved an unalterable sweetness of disposition, which painted her wan face with its own soft colouring.

"The old woman went forth to seek for food, and the two friends were left for several hours alone with Jane. She gazed affectionately on the youthful Duke; she looked more timidly on Monina, whose sex could not be said to be disguised by her page's dress: the fallen woman fears woman, their self-sufficient virtues and cold

reprobation; yet the sensibility of Monina's countenance, and the soft
expression of her eyes, so all-powerful in their sweetness, could not
be mistaken; and her first shrinking from censure was exchanged for
even a more painful feeling. They were a lovely pair, these lone guests
of poverty; innocence sat on the brow of each, yet love beamed in
their aspect:—love! the two-edged sword, the flower-strewn poison,
the dread cause of every misery! More than famine and sickness Jane
feared love; for with it in her mind were linked shame and guilt, and
the world's unkindness, hard to bear to one, whose heart was 'open
as day to melting charity;' and she feared that she saw in this sweet
girl a bright reflex of her early days. Oh, might the blotted mirror
ne'er portray a change like hers! 'I am a living lesson of the woes
of love,' thought poor Jane; 'may this chance-visit to my hut, which
saves young Richard's life, ensure her innocence!' Thus impelled, she
spoke: she spoke of the danger of their solitary companionship; she
adjured York to fly the delusive charm—for love's own sake he ought
to fly; for if he made her his victim, affection would be married to
hate—joy to woe—her he prized to a skeleton, more grim than death.
Richard strove to interrupt her, but she misunderstood his meaning;
while Monina, somewhat bewildered, fancied that she only alluded
to the dangers she incurred in his cause, and with her own beaming
look cried, 'Oh, Mother, is it not better to suffer for one so noble;
than to live in the cold security of prosperity?'

" 'No, no,' said Jane: 'Oh, does my miserable fate cry aloud; no!
Edward, his father, was bright as he. Libertine he was called: I know
not if truly; but sincere was the affection he bore to me. He never
changed nor faltered in the faith he promised, when he led me from
the dull abode of connubial strife, to the bright home of love. Riches
and the world's pleasures were the least of his gifts, for he gave me
himself and happiness. Behold me now: twelve long years have
passed, and I waste and decay; the wedded wife of shame; famine,
sorrow, and remorse, my sole companions.'

"This language was too plain. The blood rushed into Monina's
face. 'Oh, love him not,' continued the hapless penitent; 'fly his love,
because he is beautiful, good, noble, worthy—fly from him, and thus
preserve him yours for ever.' " ii. 130–37.

Clifford's frustrated attempt at assassination is a vivid, but startling
picture:—

"War, held in leash during the army's march from Edinburgh, was now let loose; swift and barbarous he tore forward on his way; a thousand destructions waited on him; his track was marked by ruin: the words of Lord Surrey were fulfilled. What a sight for one, whose best hope in acquiring his kingdom, was to bestow the happiness of which the usurper deprived it. The English troops, about five hundred men, crossed the wide-spread plains in the immediate vicinity of Scotland; they entered a beaten track, where the traces of cultivation spoke of man: a village peeped from among the hedge-row trees—York's heart beat high. Would the simple inhabitants refuse to acknowledge him? A few steps disclosed the truth—the village had been sacked by the Scotch: it was half burnt, and quite deserted; one woman alone remained—she sat on a pile of ashes wailing aloud. The exiles dared not read in each other's eyes the expression of their horror; they walked on like men rebuked. This was England, their country, their native home; and they had brought the fierce Scot upon her. Passing forward, they met trains of waggons laden with spoil, droves of cattle and sheep. They overtook a troop roasting an ox by the burning rafters of a farmhouse, whose green palings, trim orchard and shaved grass-plat, spoke of domestic comfort; the house-dog barked fearfully: a Lowland archer transfixed him with his arrow.

"The English marched on; they dared not eye the ravagers; shame and hate contended—these were their allies; while the sarcasm and scornful laugh which followed them, drugged with wormwood the bitter draught. In vain, west or east or south, did they turn their eyes, a sad variety of the same misery presented itself on every side. A stout yeoman, gashed by an Highlander's claymore, was sometimes the ghastly stepping-stone passed over to enter his own abode; women and children had not been spared, or were only left to perish for want. Often during apparent silence, a fearful shriek, or the voice of lamentation, burst upon the air: now it was a woman's cry—now the shrill plaint of infancy. With the exception of these sufferers, the landscape was a blank. Where were the troops of friends Richard had hoped would hail him? Where the ancient Yorkists? Gone to augment the army which Surrey was bringing against the Scot; attached to these ill-omened allies, how could the Prince hope to be met by his partizans? He had lost them all; the first North Briton who crossed the Tweed trampled on and destroyed for ever the fallen White Rose.

"Resolutely bent on going forward till he should have advanced beyond the Scotch, on the following day York continued his march. They entered the ruins of another village; the desolation here was even more complete, although more recent; the flame was hardly spent upon the blackened rafters; the piles which the day before had been smiling dwellings, still smoked; a few domestic animals were skulking about. There was a church at the end of what had been a street; this was not spared. The English entered the desecrated aisle; an aged bleeding monk was lying at the altar's foot, who scowled even in death upon the soldiery; suddenly he recognized his countrymen; pleasure gleamed in his sunken eyes, 'Ye will avenge us! Deliver the land! The hand of God will lead ye on!'

"Plantagenet rushed forward, 'Father!' he cried, 'do I find you here?'

"The old man spoke, looked faintly; Edmund bent over him: 'My father, it is I, Edmund, your boy, your murde—'

" 'My son,' said the Monk, 'I behold you again, and die content! You are in arms, but by the blessing of the saints your sword's point is turned against the cruel invader. Not one, oh! not one Englishman will fall by his brother's hand, for not one will fight for that base deceit, the ill-nurtured Perkin, to whom God in his wrath has given such show of right as brings the Scot upon us. Once I thought—but no son of York would ally himself to these cruel border-robbers. God of my country, oh curse, curse him and his cause!' " ii. 299–303.

There is great spirit in the midnight attack on the city of Waterford:—

"Anon there came the splash of waters, the shout of men, the sentinels' startled cry, the sudden rush of the guard, the clash of swords, the scream, the low groan, the protracted howl, and the fierce bark of the watch-dog joining in: . . . yet honour, magnanimity, devotion filled the hearts of those who thus turned to hell a seeming paradise. Led by Richard and De Faro, while a party was left behind to ensure retreat, another rushed forward right through the town, to throw open the western gate, and admit Desmond, before the terrified citizens had exchanged their night-caps for helmets; in vain: already the market-place was filled with soldiers ready for the encounter; guided by a native, they endeavour to find a way through the bye-streets; they lost themselves; they got entangled in narrow alleys; the awakened citizens cast upon their heads tiles, blocks of wood, all they could lay hands upon; to get back to the square was their only salvation; although the storm and yell that rose behind, assured them that Desmond had commenced the attack. With diminished numbers York regained the market-place; here he was furiously attacked; the crowd still increased, until the knot of assailants might have been crushed, it seemed, by mere numbers; day, bright day, with its golden clouds and swift-pacing sun, dawned upon the scene. In one of those pauses which sometimes occur in the most chaotic roar, a trumpet was heard, sounding as it seemed Desmond's retreat from the walls. Richard felt that he was deserted, that all hope was over; and to secure the retreat of his men was a work of sufficient difficulty. Foot to foot the young hero and the veteran mariner fought; one by the quickness of his blows, the other by his tower-like strength, keeping back the enemy; while retreating slowly, their faces to the foe, they called on their men to make good their escape. They reached the quay—they saw the wide river, their refuge; their vessels near at hand, the boats hovering close, their safety was in sight, and yet hope of safety died in their hearts, so many and so fierce were those who pressed on them. Richard was wounded, weary, faint; De Faro alone— Reginald's old tower, which, dark and scaithless, frowned on them, seemed his type. They were at the water's edge, and the high tide kissed with its waves the very footway of the quay: 'Courage, my Lord, a few more blows and we are safe;' the mariner spoke thus, for he saw Richard totter; and his arm, raised feebly, fell again without a stroke. At that moment, a flame, and then a bellowing roar, announced that the tardy cannoneer had at last opened his battery on the fleet, from the tower. One glance De Faro cast on his caravel; the bolt had struck and damaged one of the vessels, but the Adalid escaped. 'Courage, my Lord!' again he shouted; and at that moment a blow was struck at Richard which felled him; he lay stretched at De Faro's feet. Ere it could be repeated, the head of the assailant was cleft by a Moorish scymitar. With furious strength, De Faro then hurled his weapon among the soldiers; the unexpected act made them recoil; he lifted up the insensible form of Richard with the power of an elephant; he cast him into the near waves, and leapt in after: raising him with one hand, he cut the waters with the other, and swam thus towards his vessel, pursued by a rain of missiles; one arrow glanced on Richard's unstrung helmet, another fixed itself in the joint at the neck; but De Faro was unhurt. He passed, swimming thus, the nearest vessels; the sailors crowded to the sides, imploring him to enter: as if it had been schoolboy's sport, he refused, till he reached the Adalid, till his own men raised Richard, revived now, but feeble, to her worn deck, and he, on board her well-known planks, felt superior to every sovereign in the world." iii. 45–8.

The description of the visit of the Queen and Lady Catherine Gordon to the dungeon of the condemned Duke of York, is powerfully affecting; but it is too long to transfer to our pages.

We must now close our notice of these interesting volumes, which are, in our opinion, calculated to enhance the reputation of their fair author. We have by no means selected the finest passages, as some of these were much too long for our columns: we have confined ourselves, therefore, to shorter extracts, and must refer our readers to the volumes themselves, if they wish to have an adequate idea of their merits.

—Unsigned, *Perkin Warbeck*, from
The Athenæum, no. 135, May 29, 1830,
pp. 323–325

Unsigned Review from
Edinburgh Literary Journal (1830)

This is a talented work, but, at the same time, a little tedious and heavy. Mrs Shelley informs us in the preface, that she studied the subject originally with a view towards historical detail, but that, becoming aware of its romance, she determined not to confine herself to the mere incorporation of facts narrated by the old Chroniclers. A good deal of the leaven of history, however, still remains; and though several fictitious characters have been introduced, a calm straight-forwardness of style characterises the whole book. The authoress sets out on the assumption that Perkin Warbeck was really the Duke of York, and consequently entitled to the throne of England and upon the death of his elder brother Edward the Fifth. Upon this disputed question it is unnecessary for us to enter farther, than to remark that sufficient plausibility attaches to Mrs Shelley's theory, to authorise her as a novelist to avail herself of it, although we are afraid that, in order to carry it through, she has been obliged, in more instances than one, to twist to her own interpretation the established facts of history. The chief fault we have to find with her production is, that it does not blend together with sufficient skill what is fictitious and what is true. The great use of an intermixture of fiction in an historical romance, is to relieve the reader from many dry details, and agreeably to fill up the interstices between those events which rivet the attention the more powerfully that they stand forth in bold and prominent contrast to the no less important occurrences of everyday life. Mrs Shelley, however, is contented to follow her hero's fortunes through thick and thin; and instead of fixing, as we should have advised her to do, on a few circumstances of acknowledged interest and moment, and contriving that all the narrative should tend towards them, she rather prefers patiently to act the part of a biographer, and with the utmost perseverance follows Warbeck through all his fortunes, whether his adventures be brilliant or stupid, fortunate or disastrous. Could every reader enter into the fate and character of her hero with the same enthusiasm as our authoress, there would be nothing tiresome in this minuteness of detail; but even though we were to grant that he was the veritable heir to England's crown, we fear that, with one or two exceptions, there was little in his career to warrant our devoting undivided attention to it through three long volumes. Unlike our own Prince Charles Stuart, Perkin Warbeck had never even the semblance of a kingly crown upon his head; and though received and acknowledged at various courts as a true Plantagenet, he does not appear to have had within himself genius enough to command his own fate. From the very first, he was driven about like a wreck from billow to billow. Wherever he came, it was as a mendicant; and however generously assisted, he was never able to better his condition. In Spain, in France, in the Netherlands, in Ireland, and in Scotland, he was continually involved in intrigues and petty insurrections; but he never once seriously disturbed the quiet of Henry the Seventh; and at last, when he fell into the hands of that monarch, the ignominious death which he died excited little sensation.

It is therefore to be regretted, we think, that Mrs Shelley has, in the present work, indefatigably gone through the whole of Perkin Warbeck's life. Many of the smaller adventures and unsuccessful attempts at rebellion should have been omitted, because they lead to nothing, and wear out without satisfying the mind; and because, moreover, they tend to diminish our respect for her hero, pointing him out as one continually borne down by adversity, and consequently one more to be pitied than admired. Had she, on the contrary, confined her story to one or two of the more striking parts of his career,—

such as his residence and marriage in Scotland, and subsequent fate,—she would have greatly strengthened her narrative; and by contracting her details into a narrower compass, given a solidity and compactness to them, in which they are at present deficient. To speak in the language of pointers, her novel has not a sufficiently powerful middle-distance and foreground. The objects introduced are too much diffused and scattered. She has taken us to the top of a hill, and when we expected a broad and beautiful lake to burst upon us at once, we see nothing but the long line of a canal, which is equally broad at the one end as it is at the other.

Though we have thus stated, pretty plainly, our objection to Mrs Shelley's novel, we must at the same time state, no less plainly, that it unquestionably bears the stamp of a powerful mind, and that no one can read it without feeling a conviction that the authoress need not fear a comparison with even the most talented of her sex. It is certain that Mrs Shelley is apt at times to be heavy, and assuredly her "Last Man" is, in many parts, abundantly so, yet we entertain a high respect for her abilities, and believe her worthy to have been the wife of the author of the "Cenci." There is much powerful writing in her "Perkin Warbeck," and several of the characters introduced—especially those of Sir Robert Clifford, Monina de Faro, and Catherine Gordon—are sketched with bold vigour and fine discrimination. It is not, however, in a facility of giving an intense individuality to the persons of her story that Mrs Shelley chiefly excels. We like her better in the narrative parts, interspersed as these always are with her own observations on men and manners, and coloured by her own peculiar imagination, feelings, and associations. We last week gave a short but favourable specimen of her style, and we shall now add one or two more. We like the following portrait of the companion of Perkin Warbeck's childhood—one who loved him deeply but hopelessly:

> "Monina de Faro was, even in childhood, a being to worship and to love. There was a dreamy sweetness in her countenance, a mystery in the profound sensibility of her nature, that fascinated beyond all compare. Her characteristic was not so much the facility of being impressed, as the excess of the emotion produced by every new idea or feeling. Was she gay—her large eyes laughed in their own brightness, her lovely countenance became radiant with smiles, her thrilling voice was attuned to lightest mirth, while the gladness that filled her heart, overflowed from her as light does from the sun, imparting to all around a share of its own essence. Did sorrow oppress her—dark night fell upon her mind, clouding her face, oppressing

her whole person, which staggered and bent beneath the freight. Had she been susceptible of the stormier passions, her subtle and yielding soul would have been their unresisting victim; but though impetuous—wild—the slave of her own sensations, her soft bosom could harbour no emotions unallied to goodness; and the devouring appetite of her soul was the desire of benefiting all around her. Her countenance was the mirror of her mind. Its outline resembled those we see in Spanish pictures, not being quite oval enough for a northern beauty. It seemed widened at the forehead, to give space for her large long eyes, and the canopy of the darkly-fringed and veined lid; her hair was not black, but of a rich sunny chestnut, finer than carded silk, and more glossy; her skin was delicate, somewhat pale, except when emotion suffused it with a deep pink. In person she was not tall, but softly rounded; and her taper, rosy-tipped fingers, and little feet, bespoke the delicate proportion that moulded her form to a beauty, whose every motion awakened admiration and love."

The following attempt, made by a creature of Henry the Seventh, upon Warbeck's life, is spiritedly told:

"The breeze had rather sunk towards sunset, but it arose again with the stars; the vessel's prow struck against the light waves, and danced gaily on, through the sea. One man stood at the helm; another, one of the Friar's hirelings, loitered near; the other kept out of the way. Still, beneath the thousand stars of cloudless night, the little bark hurried on, feeling the freshening of the wind; her larboard beam was deep in the water, and, close at the deck's leeward edge, Meiler and his intended victim paced. One thoughtless boy, high among the shrouds, whistled in answer to the wind. There was at once solitude and activity in the scene. 'This is the hour,' thought Richard; 'surely if man's sinful heart was ever touched with remorse, this man's may now. God's throne visible in all its beauty above us; beneath—around—the awful roaring waters, from which he lately so miraculously escaped!' He began to speak of England, of his mother, of the hopes held out to him by his companion; eager in his desire of winning a traitor to the cause of truth, he half forgot himself, and then started to find that, ever as he walked, his companion got him nearer to the brink of the slant, slippery deck. Seized with terror at this manifestation of the worst designs, yet scarcely daring to credit his suspicions, he suddenly stopt, seizing a rope that hung near, and steadying himself by winding his arm round it—an act that escaped his enemy's observation, for, as he did it, he spoke:—'Do you know, Father Meiler, that I suspect and fear you? I am an inexperienced youth, and if I am wrong, forgive me; but you have changed towards me of late from the kind friend you once were. Strange doubts have been whispered: do you reply to them! Are you my friend, or are you a treacherous spy?—the agent of the noble Yorkists, or Henry Tudor's hireling murderer?'

"As he spoke, the Friar drew still nearer, and the Prince recoiled further from him: he got on the sheer edge of the deck. 'Rash boy!' cried Trangmar, 'know that I am no hireling: sacred vengeance pricks me on! Son of the murderer! tell me where is sainted Henry? where Prince Edward? where all the noble martyrs of his cause? Where my brave and lost sons? There, even where thou shalt be quick—Look back, thy grave yawns for thee!'

"With these words he threw himself furiously on the Prince: the stripling sprung back with all the force lent him by the rope he held, and pushed at the same time Trangmar violently from him, as he cried aloud on the sailors, 'What ho! treason is among us!' A heavy splash of the falling Meiler answered his call; the strong man was cast down in his very pride; the waters divided, and sucked him in. In a moment the crew were on deck; Trangmar hireling, scared, cried out, 'He is King Henry's prisoner; seize him!' thus increasing the confusion. The friar, his garments floating, now appeared struggling among the waves; a rope was thrown to him; the vessel sped on meanwhile, and it fell far short; Richard, horror-struck, would have leapt in to save his enemy; but the time was gone—one loud shriek burst on the ear of night, and all was still; Trangmar, his misery, his vengeance, and his crimes, lay buried in the ocean's hoary caves."

We had marked other passages for quotation, but our space warns us that the above must suffice. We noticed briefly, about a fortnight ago, another novel which has just been published, bearing the same name; in nothing but the name, however, does it resemble that of Mrs Shelley, which is, in all respects, the superior of the two.

—Unsigned, *Perkin Warbeck*, from
*Edinburgh Literary Journal, or Weekly
Register of Criticism and Belles Lettres*,
June 19, 1830, pp. 350–352

LODORE

In an unsigned review from *Fraser's Magazine for Town and Country* of May 11, 1835, the critic begins with the statement that *Lodore* proves that Mary Shelley is the author of *Frankenstein*, which previously was not believed to be the product of a female author because of the "depth and sweep of thought" evidenced in the writing. He also feels that *Lodore* exhibits a profound understanding of human psychology, an awareness that distinguishes Mary Shelley from other female novelists. The author of the review then proceeds to enumerate the problems faced by her female counterparts. Praising *Lodore* for its simplicity and calmness, the critic approves of Shelley's adherence to the theme of love.

UNSIGNED REVIEW FROM *FRASER'S MAGAZINE* FOR *TOWN AND COUNTRY* (1835)

The publication of *Lodore* has gone a considerable way towards convincing us that Mrs. Shelley might have indeed been the author of *Frankenstein*—a work which we once believed could not possibly owe its existence to a female novelist, and this, not because there is a similitude between the structure and development of *Frankenstein* that fearful and fantastic dream of genius, and the love story before us, which is of the every-day world—its doings and its sufferings, but because there is common to both a depth and sweep of thought—a knowledge of human kind in its manifold relations with this earth—and a boldness and directness in penetrating to the recesses and displaying the motives and workings of the heart, its feelings and passions—not in woman only, but in man also—which we certainly should have imagined to be far beyond the scope and power of a lady. Yet is there, at the same time, nothing in these volumes which a lady might not have known, and felt, and written; nor can there be the slightest doubt that they are the production of a feminine mind, albeit one of robust culture and extraordinary vigour. In the form and course of thought, if not actually in the style of expression in many passages, and in the downright, unaffected, noble simplicity, with which, in *Lodore*, subjects are treated, in which the heart and senses play a subtly mingled part, we were oftentimes reminded of the confessions of that charming enthusiast, Madame Roland—the only politician and philosopher in petticoats we could ever bring ourselves to regard with affectionate respect. Like her, too, Mrs. Shelley has shewn, not only that she can unveil the soul of woman to its very uttermost recesses, but that she can divine, appreciate, and depict the character of men. The work is very unlike the generality of our modern novels; it does not contain a sweeping together of incidents from a long suite of stories, historic romantic, and burlesque; it does not present a faded anthology of *effête* jests, of shrivelled gallantries, and impossible sentimentalities. There is not a constant succession of the startling events, the outrageous griefs, the bloody battles, the atrocious catastrophes, which form the staple commodity of that farrago of elongated melodramas which so frequently constitutes a modern novel. Nor is that ingenious device resorted to which was originally borrowed by our novel-spinners from the festival scene in the pantomimes of having a number of persons, bedecked in the costume of great names, to stand by and assist at the multifarious performances of the regular actors in the scene—pseudo-representatives of kings and Caesars, beauties and heroes, wits and sages—to witness, as it were, the vigour of Harlequin and the agility of Columbine to say nothing of the parts of the Clown and Pantaloon. Nor is that vile expedient put in use of pretending to gratify the prurient curiosity of the vulgar by the introduction of real characters who have rendered themselves either distinguished or notorious on the stage of life. No! nor is the plot "perplexed in the extreme;" nor are the characters multitudinous, like the waves of the sea; nor are they ever suffered in obedience to some immediate necessity of the author, to obey the magical injunction,

"Come like shadows.
So depart;"

nor, moreover, do we, from first to last, find a single being who is absolutely exalted above, or depressed below humanity.

The story is simple—its theme is

"Love, still love!"

It treats of the hopes and fears, the joys and sorrows, the delights and dangers, the blessings and the evils, of the fierce and tender passion. A healthy moral pervades her whole treatment of the subject. She might as well, perhaps, have taken for her motto the following lines of her husband, as those she has selected from Ford:

"Those who inflict must suffer, for they see
The work of their own hearts; and that must be
Our recompense or wretchedness."

Yet her motto is also fine:

"In the turmoil of our lives,
Men are like politic states or troubled seas,
Tossed up and down with several storms and tempests,
Change and variety of wrecks and fortunes;
Till labouring to the havens of our homes,
We struggle for the calm that crowns our ends."—FORD.

Do not imagine, however, from this, that there is the slightest touch of fatalism in her novel; on the contrary, the principle she would fain inculcate seems to be, that men hold their destinies in their own hands, and that our own evil passions are our only potent enemies. The execution of the work is, upon the whole, extremely good—it is quite worthy of the design. The impress of an original and thoughtful mind is visible throughout, and there are many passages of exceeding gracefulness, of touching eloquence, and of intense feeling. Her most obvious faults are that of occasionally introducing, by way of illustration, wild and quaint imagery—we might say, in some instances, imagery which is quite incongruous with that it is intended to illustrate; and, secondly, that of analysing and detailing too minutely each and every one of the sensations, intermingled or successive, which, when operating in mass (so to speak) constitute a feeling or a passion. The result of this extreme elaborateness is often to weary, and always by refining away, to injure the general effect. These faults, however, we apprehend, may be with her either the results of education, or the pious faults of imitation; for her husband has fallen into the first in several of his poems, her father is remarkable for the other.

Mrs. Shelley has not like a weak and ambitious artist, crowded her canvass with figures. Her characters are few—they were well-considered, perfectly individualised, and in happy contrast. There is no attempt at a violent opposition of colours to produce startling effects. In the calm consciousness of power, she has dispensed altogether with a villain who, in many a grand modern novel is made to serve the same purpose, as a daub of black in one of Martin's monster-pictures. All the characters are excellently drawn: the greater number are very elaborately wrought forth, the rest are firmly sketched. We have said that Mrs. Shelley has not condescended to play the pander to the appetite for private scandal to introducing "fashionables" notorious for good or evil, into her work; yet has she availed herself of her experience, on the quality and nature of which, we do maintain, does the value of the novel mainly depend: nothing can compensate in the novel for want of experience. And therefore is it, that the attempt of ladies generally to write of "many-figured life," is so utterly cold, incapable, and ridiculous.

The best fashionable stuff of the day bears the same relation to a true novel as the idle, aimless sonata does to the passion-breathing, soul-fraught melody. "*Que me veux tu Sonate?*" exclaimed Rousseau;—"What are you after, Listonia Bulweria Wigetta?" exclaims the reader to the mocking-bird she-novelist;—and even accommodating echo can only furnish an eh! or an ah! in the guise of a reply to either of these interesting enquiries. But neither the vigorous but vague *whinney* of the eh! or the desponding expectoration of the ah! at all effect Mrs. Shelley. In this novel she has availed herself of her association with greatest men. We have some allusions to their story, some fine and sweet touches of their character: rather, let us say, of their idiosyncracy. This is, to those who have known them through their works, coming from a devoted, but too wise to be a superstitious worshipper, altogether delightful. But of this anon: we will now turn to the story.

Lodore is the son of a gentleman, ennobled for his exploits during the American war. He has passed a number of years abroad, to the great grief of his father and family, who cannot imagine why he should continue to absent himself from the dear paternal roof tree. But he has formed an unfortunate attachment abroad—a *liaison avec une femme mariée*; which, although apparently the most easy, is yet in truth, one of the most difficult liaisons possible to break. The fact is, he gets very tired—(it is not declared, but it is clearly intimated in the novel)—and he returns to England. He is now at that "most damnable of middle ages," the middle age of man; he is not acquainted with the course of fashionable life—he is at once too full of pride himself, and too ignorant of the utter meanness of others, to make his way there. He fails, too, like Byron, in politics; and he retires from the busy struggles of ambition, fantastical or political. He goes to Wales, and there he commits the horrible but common fault of the morbid sentimentalist of marrying a mere juvenile piece of womanhood, who has nothing to recommend her except the freshness of sixteen, with a pretty face, and, as he fancies, an undiscriminating docility. He marries her, and she might be very well; but in the absence of all other earthly possessions, with the exception of that which old Adam was good enough to entail upon his daughters, she had a mother—a low-born, vulgar, but clever mother—and she contrives to embitter his whole existence. Unfortunately, the tenderling he has wedded induces him to take the "old serpent" into his house. Thenceforth for him there is no peace. His young wife learns to regard him first as a humourist, then as a tyrant; he loves her against his judgment, she hates him in spite of her vow. At length a child is born to them, and then Lodore is delighted: he has now something that he may love, and teach, by his very excess of affection, to love him in return. But even this last resource of an expansion of kindly feeling, so dear to the desolate, is denied to him; the arrival of his old mistress, a Polish countess, with *his* son, is the means of utterly dissipating the last shadows which his dream of joy had cast forth. His young son and his young wife enter into a palpable flirtation, and, in a paroxysm of jealousy and rage, he strikes the boy, and then determines to abandon name and fame rather than to stigmatise his high-born mistress and her son. He determines on leaving England forthwith. He invites, in the most intense earnestness of feeling, his wife to accompany him: under the chilling auspices of her mother she refuses, and he departs with his child. The wife and husband are thenceforth parted: they never were allowed the opportunity of understanding each other's hearts through the formality of the wife's heart, which had been disciplined into coldness, and the sensitive pride of the husband. He retires to America, turns settler, and his whole delight is the culture of his daughter. The feeling is holy, the occupation sacred—he rears her as a lady. At length, like a wise man, he feels it necessary, from the very love of his *innocent* girl, to leave the solitude in which he fancied she was all safe. We subjoin an outline of the circumstances and reason; Whitelock, be it observed, is a young artist, who has come to the settlement, and commenced making love to Lodore's daughter:

"Ethel knew nothing of the language of love; she had read of it in her favourite poets, but she was yet too young and guileless to apply any of its feelings to herself. Love had always appeared to her blended with the highest imaginative beauty and heroism, and thus was, in her eyes, at once awful and lovely. Nothing had vulgarised it to her. The greatest men were its slaves, and according as their choice fell on the worthy or unworthy, they were elevated or disgraced by passion. It was the part of a woman so to refine and educate her mind, as to be the cause of good alone to him whom fate depended on her smile. There was something of the Orondates' vein in her ideas, but they were too vague and general to influence her actions. Brought up in American solitude, with all the refinement attendant on European society, she was aristocratic, both as regarded rank and sex; but all these were as yet undeveloped feelings—seeds planted by the careful maternal hand, not yet called into life or growth.

"Whitelock began his operations, and was obliged to be explicit to be at all understood. He spoke of misery and despair; he urged no plea, sought no favour, except to be allowed to speak of his wretchedness. Ethel listened—Eve listened to the serpent, and since then her daughters have been accused of an aptitude to give ear to forbidden discourse. He spoke well, too, for he was a man of unquestioned talent. It is a strange feeling for a girl, when first she finds the power put into her hand of influencing the destiny of another to happiness or misery. She is like a magician holding for the first time a fairy wand, not having yet had experience of its potency. Ethel had read of the power of love; but a doubt had often suggested itself, of how far she herself should hereafter exercise the influence which is the attribute of her sex. Whitelock dispelled that doubt. He impressed on her mind the idea that he lived or died through her fiat.

"For one instant vanity awoke in her young heart, and she tripped back to her home with a smile of triumph on her lips. The feeling was short-lived. She entered her father's library, and his image appeared to rise before her to regulate and purify her thoughts. If he had been there, what could she have said to him—she who never concealed a thought? or how would he have received the information she had to give? What had happened had not been the work of a day; Whitelock had for a week or two proceeded in an occult and mysterious manner: but this day he had withdrawn the veil, and she understood much that had appeared strange in him before. The dark, expressive eyes of her father she fancied to be before her, penetrating the depths of her soul, discovering her frivolity, and censuring her lowly vanity, and, even though alone, she felt abashed. Our faults are apt to assume giant and exaggerated forms to our eyes in youth, and Ethel felt degraded and humiliated; and remorse sprung up in her gentle heart, substituting itself for the former pleasurable emotion.

"The young are always in extremes. Ethel put away her drawings and paintings. She secluded herself in her home; and arranged so well, that, notwithstanding the freedom of American manners, Whitelock contrived to catch but a distant glimpse of her during the one other week that intervened before her father's return. Troubled at this behaviour he felt his bravery ooze out. To have offended Fitzhenry was an unwise proceeding, at best; but when he remembered the haughty and reserved demeanour of the man, he recoiled, trembling, from the prospect of encountering him.

"Ethel was very concise in the expressions she used to make her father, on his return, understand what had happened during his absence. Fitzhenry heard her with indignation and bitter self-reproach. The natural impetuosity of his disposition returned on him, like a stream which had been checked in its program, but which had gathered strength from the delay. On a sudden, the future, with all its difficulties and trials presented itself to his eyes; and he was determined to go out to meet them, rather than to await their advent in his seclusion. His resolution formed, and he put it into immediate execution: he would instantly quit the Illinois. The world was before him; and while he paused on the western shores of the Atlantic, he could decide upon his future path. But he would not remain where he was another season. The present, the calm, placid present, had fled like morning mist before the new-risen breeze: all appeared dark and turbid to his heated imagination. Change alone could appease the sense of danger that had risen within him—change of place, of circumstances, of all that for the last twelve years had formed his life. 'How long am I to remain at peace?'—the prophetic voice heard in the silence of the forests recurred to his memory, and thrilled through his frame. 'Peace! was I ever at peace? Was this unquiet heart ever still, as, one by one, the troubled thoughts which are its essence have risen and broken against the barriers that embank them? Peace! My own Ethel! all I have done—all I would do—is to gift thee with that blessing which has for ever fled the thirsting lips of thy unhappy parent.' And thus, governed by a favored fancy and untamed passions, Fitzhenry forgot the tranquil lot which he had learnt to value and enjoy; and quitting the haven he had sought, as if it had never been a place of shelter to him, unthankful for the many hours which had blessed him there, he hastened to reach the stormier seas of life, whose breakers and whose winds were ready to visit him with shipwreck and destruction."

Reader! are not these pages beautiful as true? But to go on with the story. Lodore arrives at New York with Ethel, and is shortly after shot in a duel by a Yankee, who had denounced him as a coward.

Ethel passes over to England, and is received by a maiden aunt: Lodore had in his will especially exempted her from the guardianship of her mother. She is accompanied by the daughter of an old schoolfellow of Lodore's, and by Mr. Villiers, a young English gentleman, who had acted as her father's friend in the fatal duel. Ethel and he fall in love with each other, and are after a time married; and all is happiness until poverty besets their path, but is powerless against the strength of their affections. Nothing, in sooth, can be more exquisitely told than the whole story of their loves. They are perfectly happy, and continue to be happy, without the zest of sin. The tale is as fervently and as beautifully told as that of the sunny existence of unfailing love led by Trelawney's hero, and his Arab bride, in that work of passion, and power, and genius, styled *The Adventures of a Younger Son*. The feeling in either is true, and therefore the same in both. The scene only, with its figures and accessories, is different: the one is laid within the precincts of savagery, the other within the limits of Civilisation.

At length these married lovers are rescued from misery and confinement by an act of glorious generosity upon the part of her mother—an act of which nobody would have supposed the fashionable Lady Lodore capable. Pride and a cold-hearted, vulgar mother have spoiled Lady Lodore, and troubled the whole current of her life; pride caused her separation from her husband; pride prevented her from marrying a certain Horatio Saville, in whose person and character we recognise many traits of our beloved Shelley—of him who was, in his own sweet words,

"Gentle, and brave, and generous;
The child of Grace and Genius."

Witness the following sketch:

"It was very late at night when they reached their hotel, and they were heartily fatigued; so that it was not till the next morning that, immediately after breakfast, Villiers left Ethel, and went out to seek the abode of his cousin.

"He had been gone some little time, when a waiter of the hotel, throwing open Ethel's drawing-room door, announced 'Signor Orazio.' Quite new to Italy, Ethel was ignorant of the custom in that country of designating people by their Christian names; and that Horatio Saville being a resident in Naples, and married to a Neapolitan, was known every where by the appellation which the servant now used. Ethel was not in the least aware that it was Lucy's brother who presented himself to her. She saw a gentleman, tall, very slight in person, with a face denoting habitual thoughtfulness, and stamped by an individuality which she could not tell whether to think plain, and yet it was certainly open and kind. An appearance of extreme shyness, almost amounting to awkwardness, was diffused over him, and his words came hesitatingly; he spoke English, and was an Englishman—so much Ethel discovered by his first words, which were, 'Villiers is not at home?' And then he began to ask her about her journey, and how she liked the view of the bay of Naples, which she beheld from her windows. They were in this kind of trivial conversation when Edward came bounding up-stairs, and with exclamations of delight greeted his cousin. Ethel, infinitely surprised, examined her guest with more care. In a few minutes she began to wonder how she came to think him plain. His deep-set dark grey eyes struck her as expressive, if not handsome. His features were delicately moulded, and his fine forehead betokened depth of intellect; but the charm of his face was a kind of fitful, beamy, inconstant smile, which diffused incomparable sweetness over his physiognomy. His usual look was cold and abstracted—his eye speculated with an inward thoughtfulness—a chilling seriousness sat on his features, but this glancing and varying half-smile came to dispel gloom, and to invite and please those with whom he conversed. His voice was modulated by feeling, his language was fluent, graceful in its terms of expression, and original in the thoughts which it expressed. His manners were marked by high breeding, yet they were peculiar. They were formed by his individual disposition, and under the dominion of sensibility. Hence they were often abrupt and reserved. He forgot the world around him, and gave token, by absence of mind, of the absorbing nature of his contemplations. But at a touch this vanished, and a sweet earnestness, and a beaming kindliness of spirit, at once displaced his abstraction, rendering him attentive, cordial, and gay.

We have only left ourselves space to say that Lady Lodore is at last married to Horatio, and that with her change of name ends *Lodore*, one of the best novels it has been of late years our fortune to read. We are very happy to be able to confer this praise on Mrs. Shelley, whose name is dear to us (as we doubt not from "the late remorse of love," it is to the public), for the sake alike of the dead or the living—her illustrious husband, and her living son, who was born in his image.

—Unsigned, from *Fraser's Magazine*
for Town and Country, May 11, 1835,
pp. 600–605

Unsigned Review from *Leigh Hunt's London Journal and The Printing Machine* (1835)

We congratulate Mrs Shelley on the appearance of this her latest and most agreeable work. It has not the inventive genius of 'Frankenstein.' That is a thing to happen only once in many years. But then it is not mixed up, like that work, with matter of doubtful attraction; neither has it the uneasiness of her subsequent novels, either in story or style. Her spirits appear not to have been well settled when she wrote those novels, and, from not being perhaps quite in earnest, her style was overwrought. Nothing can be more agreeable, yet forcible, than the language of the production before us. Mrs Shelley has a decided ear for the musical in writing. Even the name of her work, we suspect, was selected merely from its noble and harmonious sound; for it has nothing to do with its namesake the lake, though the "falls" of Lodore are something analogous to her hero's grand and impetuous spirit, and his proneness to mingle with his mother earth. There is a good deal of pain and sorrow in the book, as will be guessed by this allusion to the principal character; but then it is relieved, as life is, by charming contrasts of pleasure, and patience, and contentment; the most painful of the characters, not being fools, grow better and kinder as they grow older; and above all, though everybody does not end happily, yet the book itself does; and the salutary impression is left upon the reader, that effort is not in vain, nor life a thing ignoble and cheerless. Furthermore, the work has more unexpected yet natural turns of incident than any we have seen for a long time; we read it, without intermission, and with gratified curiosity, at what might be called one sitting, making, allowance for a night's rest, and awoke next morning, like the Sultan, anxious to hear how the lady "continued." It is interesting to see Mrs Shelley quote her husband so often at the top of her chapters; and though her characters are laid in high life, and she makes the best of the conventionalities, yet she sympathises with the truly great world throughout, not merely the little great world of St James's. She has even ventured, in the spirit of the novelists of the last century, to put her favourite hero and heroine, a married couple, into a lock-up house, which, with the beautiful self-sufficingness of youth and love, and in spite of frightful cares, they convert into a *pro tempore* bower of bliss. We only think she has done Lady Mary Wortley a little too much honour in quoting her on the occasion; for though "champagne and a chicken" are very good things, and "lips though rosy (as the poet says) must still, be fed," yet Mrs Shelley's lovers, true to nature as they are, are truer also to sentiment than any which Lady Mary ever fancied or could comprehend; and would hardly have enumerated such things as part of the climax of a happy meeting. It is curious, by the way, how capitally well the two cousins jumped together in that particular,—Lady Mary and Fielding;—for he was her kinsman, and is mightily fond of making his lovers eat and drink. We are not sure whether the verses in which she speaks of meeting

"—With champagne and a chicken *at last*"

were not addressed to him. Or was it to Congreve? another gentleman, not overburthened with the sentimental?

Next week we shall give our extracts.

—Unsigned, from *Leigh Hunt's London Journal and The Printing Machine*, vol. II, 1835

FALKNER

A favorable review of *Falkner* appeared in *The Literary Gazette and Journal of Belles Lettres* of February 4, 1837. Praising Mary Shelley again for her ability to convey sympathy and pathos, the critic identifies *Falkner* as a romance—a highly imaginative work—in terms of both character and events, rather than conforming to a portrait of actual life, which is expected with a work classified as a novel. In a word, he declares Mary to be a "genius" in expressing emotions. "Her description of the orphan Elizabeth, whose father and mother have died, and are buried in the churchyard of a remote sea-bathing village in Cornwall, is very affecting."

In an unsigned review from the *Monthly Review* of March 1, 1837, the critic extols *Falkner* as Mary Shelley's finest novel in terms of sentiment and pathos, arguing that even the principal culprit elicits our sympathy. He also states that Mary Shelley's profound psychological insight differentiates her from her unhappy father, William Godwin. In his discussion of Percy Bysshe's influence, the reviewer also finds that, while Percy's aesthetic influence is evident, Mary Shelley has found the proper balance between imagination and truth so as to stay within the boundary lines of the credible.

Unsigned Review from
The Athenæum (1837)

We have always admired Mrs. Shelley's novels as breathing more of the spirit of romance than the generality of works which see the light in these matter-of-fact days. Even where their scene is laid in our country—when their actors are drawn from the class to which we ourselves have long—we recognize an elevation of tone in their conception—a constant appeal to our more generous sympathies—a constant display of the fine affections, which raise them above the common level of tales of every-day life, though they are somewhat deficient, perhaps, in that vitality which characterizes other contemporary works. They are, in short, stories of thought and feeling, rather than of manners and character; and the one before us is among the best, if not quite the best, of the number.

A slight outline of the plot of 'Falkner" will, we think, bear out our judgment. The tale begins in Cornwall, with a little orphan girl (who is indebted to the coarse charity of a cottager for her food and clothing,) saying her prayers upon her mother's grave in a lonely churchyard—nothing, of its kind, can be much more tender or graceful than the whole picture. To this lonely place a conscience-stricken man comes with the intent of putting an end to his existence: the child, too young and too innocent to understand his purpose, arrests it, and, her fortunes, by romantic chance, proving in somewise linked with his,—becomes subsequently his companion and the child of his adoption, growing up fair and gracious—and, though womanly and delicate, endowed with such strength of purpose and principle as is rarely developed in those whose youth has been passed more according to the common fashion. They travel together, Falkner still bearing about with him a hidden sorrow and remorse, which darken the sunshine of his life, and urge him from place to place. At length a series of casual, and, it would seem, fated encounters with the hero of the tale Gerard Neville—who is as noble and unworldly a creature as its heroine—forces his secret from him. Falkner had loved this Neville's mother before her marriage, and, on finding that she had given her hand away during his absence from England, sought her out to reproach her—was admitted to a few secret interviews, and, in a moment of passion, (her fidelity to her formal suspicious husband remaining unshaken,) conceived and executed the wild plan of carrying her off. She died on the journey—was buried secretly; and it was the remorse consequent on her death which had driven him to resolve on suicide. On Mrs. Neville's flight being discovered, Sir Boyvill, her husband, had instituted a suit for divorce, (not being able positively to ascertain her fate,) and forced her son, the hero aforesaid, to the bar of the House of Lords to bear witness to his mother's criminality. The result of Gerard's obdurate incredulity, which grew up with him, was ill-usage and estrangement on the part of his father, and an intense and holy purpose on his own, to justify his mother's memory—to discover her fate—and to avenge himself on her destroyer. Chance—that Archimago of all novelists—throws him into Elizabeth Falkner's way; he falls desperately in love with her, ere he discovers that the guardian, to whom she clings with more than a daughter's affection, is the man he has so long sought; he then—

Gentle reader, we have done; we have thus imperfectly shadowed out the mystery of the novel, but we must leave the unraveling of it to Mrs. Shelley,— satisfied, that if you put yourself under her guidance, you will own that your labour has not been in vain.

—Unsigned, from *The Athenæum*,
no. 484, February 4, 1837, pp. 74–75

Unsigned Review from *The Literary Gazette and Journal of Belles Lettres* (1837)

Mrs. Shelley wields a powerful pen for a female hand. Energy and highly wrought passion are her most characteristic features; and when she smiles, it is very Cassius-like. The relief of playfulness does not suit her pictures; and she therefore rarely attempts that variation, but substitutes, instead, passages of tenderness and pathos. The whole becomes a production of highly wrought excitement, with only the repose—if repose it can be called—of some natural touches of infantile and common feelings; and thus, though forcible in detail and general effect, the prevailing colours are sombre and gloomy.

Falkner bears a near resemblance to Sir Edward Mortimer; and Elizabeth Raby, the heroine, his adopted daughter, reminds us (only that she is of another sex) of the general construction of the plot and the incidents of the "Iron Chest." The principal characters, as well as the leading events of the story, belong rather to the regions of romance than to that representation of actual life which we understand by the term, "Novel," and the reader, without being much at a loss to guess the mystery enveloped in the narrative, or the way in which affairs will end, is led along by the talent of the writer through certain walks of imagination, till her task is completed, and the *dénouement* allowed.

With these few remarks we shall (without removing any of the veil which covers the plot) give a few examples of Mrs. Shelley's genius, in different lights. Her description of the orphan Elizabeth, whose father and mother have died, and are buried in the churchyard of a remote sea-bathing village in Cornwall, is very affecting.

> "The little orphan grew, meanwhile, as a garden-rose that accident has thrown amidst briers and weeds—blooming with alien beauty, and unfolding its soft petals, and shedding its ambrosial odour beneath the airs of heaven, unharmed by its strange position. Lovely as a day of paradise, which, by some strange chance, visits this nether world to gladden every heart, she charmed even her selfish protectress; and, despite her shabby attire, her cherub smiles, the free and noble steps which her tiny feet could take even now, and the music of her voice, rendered her the object of respect and admiration, as well as love, to the whole village. The loss of her father had acquainted the poor child with death. Her mother had explained the awful mystery as well as she could to her infantile intellects, and,

indulging in her own womanish and tender fancies, had often spoken of the dead as hovering over and watching around his loved ones, even in the new state of existence to which he had been called. Yet she wept as she spoke. 'He is happy,' she exclaimed; 'but he is not here! Why did he leave us? Ah! why desert those who loved him so well, who need him so dearly? How forlorn and castaway are we without him!' These scenes made a deep impression upon the sensitive child; and when her mother died too, and was carried away and placed in the cold earth beside her husband, the orphan would sit for hours by the graves, now fancying that her mother must soon return, now exclaiming, 'Why are you gone away? Come, dear mamma, come back—come quickly!' Young as she was, it was no wonder that such thoughts were familiar to her. The minds of children are often as intelligent as those of persons of maturer age, and differ only by containing fewer ideas; but these had so often been presented to her, and she so fixed her little heart on the idea that her mother was watching over her, that at last it became a part of her religion to visit, every evening, the two graves, and saying her prayers near them—to believe that her mother's spirit, which was obscurely associated with her mortal remains reposing below, listened to and blessed her on that spot. At other times, neglected as she was, and left to wander at will, she conned her lesson, as she had been accustomed at her mother's feet, beside her grave. She took her picture-books there, and even her playthings. The villagers were affected by her childish notion of being 'with mamma,' and Missy became something of an angel in their eyes; so that no one interfered with her visits, or tried to explain away her fancies. She was the nursling of love and nature: but the human hearts which could have felt the greatest tenderness for her beat no longer, and had become clods of the soil,—

'Borne round in earth's diurnal course,
With rocks, and stones, and trees.'

There was no knee on which she could playfully climb, no neck round which she could fondly hang, no parent's cheek on which to print her happy kisses: these two graves were all of relationship she knew upon the earth; and she would kiss the ground and the flowers, not one of which she plucked, as she sat embracing the sod. 'Mamma' was every where around. 'Mamma' was there beneath and still she could love and feel herself beloved. At other times she played gaily with her young companions in the village, and sometimes she fancied that she loved some one among them. She made them presents of books and toys, the relics of happier days; for the desire to benefit, which springs up so naturally in a loving heart, was strong within her, even in that early age: but she never took any one with her in her churchyard visits—she needed none while she was with mamma. Once, indeed, a favourite kitten was carried to the sacred spot; and the little animal played amidst the grass and flowers, and the child joined in its frolics. Her solitary gay laugh might be heard among the tombs—she did not think it solitary: mamma was there to smile on her as she sported with her tiny favourite."

The love of children is well illustrated in the annexed:—

"We human beings are so unlike one to the other, that it is often difficult to make one person understand that there is any force in an impulse which is omnipotent with another. Children, to some, are mere animals, unendued with instinct, troublesome, and unsightly—with others they possess a charm that reaches to the heart's core, and stirs the purest and most generous portions of our nature."

The young hero, Neville, is perhaps drawn too strongly for his tender years. At sixteen, this seems to be more of creative fiction than truth:—

"He was wondrously handsome; large, deep-set hazel eyes, shaded by long dark lashes—full at once of fire, and softness; a brow of extreme beauty, over which clustered a profusion of chestnut-coloured hair; an oval face; a person, light and graceful as a sculptured image—all this, added to an expression of gloom that amounted to sullenness, with which, despite the extreme refinement of his features, a certain fierceness even was mingled, formed a study a painter would have selected for a kind of ideal poetic sort of bandit stripling."

Then Elizabeth, at thirteen, is equally premature:—

"Every other arrangement for their voyage was quickly made, and it remained only to determine whether Miss Jervis should accompany them. Elizabeth's mind was divided. She was averse to parting with an unoffending and kind companion, and to forego her instructions—

though, in truth, she had got beyond them. But she feared that the governess might hereafter shackle her conduct. Every word Falkner had let fall concerning his desire to die, she remembered and pondered upon. To watch over and to serve him was her aim in going with him. Child as she was, a thousand combinations of danger presented themselves to her imagination, when her resolution and fearlessness might bring safety. The narrow views and timid disposition of Miss Jervis might impede her grievously."

We conclude with the original sketch of the last representative of one of the oldest families in England, the grandfather of Elizabeth; to whose protection, Falkner, for urgent reasons, is most desirous to consign her.

"The first step he took, in furtherance of this new resolution, was to make inquiries concerning the present state of Elizabeth's family; of which, hitherto, he knew no more than what he gathered from her mother's unfinished letter: and this was limited to their being a wealthy Catholic family, proud of their ancestry, and devoted to their faith. . . . The present head of the family was an old man; he had long been a widower, left with a family of six sons. The eldest had married early, and was dead, leaving his widow with four daughters and one son, who was heir of the family honours and estates, and resided with his mother, for the most part, at the mansion of his grandfather. Of the remaining sons, little account could be gained. It was the family custom to concentrate all its prosperity and wealth on the head of the eldest son; and the younger, precluded by their religion, of that time, from advancement in their own country, entered foreign service. One only had exempted himself from the common lot, and become an outcast, and, in the eyes of his family, a reprobate. Edwin Raby had apostatised from the Catholic faith; he had married a portionless girl of inferior birth, and entered the profession of the law. His parents looked with indignation on the dishonour entailed on their name through his falling off; but his death relieved their terror—he died, leaving a widow and an infant daughter. As the marriage had never been acknowledged, and female offspring were held supernumerary, and an encumbrance in the Raby family, they had refused to receive her, and never heard of her more."

Falkner proceeds to Northumberland to restore the orphan, his adopted daughter.

"At length he arrived at his destination, and reached the entrance to Belleforest. The mansion, a fine old Gothic building, adorned by the ruins of an ancient abbey, was in itself venerable and extensive, and surrounded by a princely demesne. This was the residence of Elizabeth's ancestors—of her nearest relatives. . . . Every thing around denoted grandeur and wealth: the very circumstance that the family adhered to the ancient faith of the land—to a form of worship which, though evil in its effects on the human mind, is to the eye imposing and magnificent—shed a greater lustre round the place. On inquiry, Falkner heard that the old gentleman was at Belleforest—indeed, he never quitted it; but that his daughter-in-law, with her family, were in the south of England. Mr. Raby was very accessible: on asking for him, Falkner was instantly ushered in. He entered a library of vast dimensions, and fitted up with a sort of heavy splendour; very imposing, but very sombre. The high windows, painted ceiling, and massy furniture, bespoke an old-fashioned, but almost regal taste. Falkner, for a moment, thought himself alone, when a slight noise attracted his attention to a diminutive, and very white old gentleman, who advanced towards him. The mansion looked built for a giant race; and Falkner, expecting the majesty of size, could hardly contract his view to the slender and insignificant figure of the present possessor. Oswi Raby looked shrivelled, not so much by age as the narrowness of his mind, to whose dimensions his outward figure had contracted itself. His face was pale and thin; his light-blue eyes grown dim: you might have thought that he was drying up and vanishing from earth by degrees. Contrasted with this slight shadow of a man, was a mind that saw the whole world almost concentrated in himself. He, Oswi Raby; he, head of the oldest family in England, was first of created beings. Without being assuming in manner, he was self-important in heart; and there was an obstinacy, and an incapacity to understand that any thing was of consequence except himself, or rather, except the house he represented, that gave extreme repulsion to his manners. It is always awkward to disclose an errand such as Falkner's; it was only by plunging at once into it, and warming himself by his own words, that he contrived to throw a grace round his subject. A cloud gathered over the old man's features; he grew whiter, and his thin lips closed as if they had never opened except with a refusal. 'You speak of very painful circumstances,' he said; 'I have sometimes feared that I should be intruded upon in behalf of this person; yet, after so many years, there is less pretence than ever for encroaching upon an injured family.' Edwin himself broke the tie. He was rebellious and apostate. He had talents, and might have distinguished himself to his honour: he preferred irreparable disgrace. He abandoned the religion which we consider as the most precious part of our inheritance, and he added imprudence to guilt, by, he being himself unprovided for, marrying a portionless, low-born girl. He never hoped for my forgiveness; he never even asked it. His death—it is hard for a father to feel thus—but his death was a relief. 'We were applied to by his widow; but with her we could have nothing to do. She was the partner of his rebellion—nay, we looked upon her as its primal cause. I was willing to take charge of my grandchild, if delivered entirely up to me. She did not even think proper to reply to the letter making this concession. I had, indeed, come to the determination of continuing to her a portion of the allowance I made to my son, despite his disobedience; but from that time to this no tidings of either mother or daughter have reached us.' 'Death must bear the blame of that negligence,' said Falkner, mastering his rising disgust. 'Mrs. Raby was hurried to the grave but a few months after your son's death, the victim of her devoted affection to her husband. Their innocent daughter was left among strangers, who did not know to whom to apply. She, at least, is free from all fault, and has every claim on her father's family.' 'She is nothing, and has no claim,' interrupted Mr. Raby, peevishly, 'beyond a bare maintenance, even if she be the person you represent. I beg your pardon, sir, but you may be deceived yourself on this subject; but, taking it for granted that this young person is the daughter of my son, what is she to me?' 'A grand-daughter is a relation,' Falkner began; 'a near and dear one—' 'Under such circumstances,' interrupted Mr. Raby,—'under the circumstances of a marriage to which I gave no consent, and her being brought up at a distance from us all, I should rather call her a connexion than a relation. We cannot look with favour on the child of an apostate, educated in a faith which we consider pernicious. I am an old-fashioned man, accustomed only to the society of those whose feelings coincide with mine, and I must apologise, sir, if I say any thing to shock you, but the truth is self-evident: a child of a discarded son may have a slender claim for support—none for favour or countenance. This young person has no right to raise her eyes to us; she must regulate her expectations by the condition of her mother, who was a sort of servant, a humble

companion or governess, in the house of Mrs. Neville of Dromore.'
Falkner grew pale at the name, but, commanding himself, replied, 'I
believe she was a friend of that lady. I have said I was unacquainted
with the parents of Miss Raby; I found her an orphan, subsisting on
precarious charity. Her few years, her forlorn situation, her beauty
and sweetness, claimed my compassion: I adopted her—' 'And would
now throw her off,' again interrupted the ill-tempered old man. 'Had
you restored her to us in her childhood; had she been brought up in
our religion among us; she would have shared this home with her
cousins. As it is, you yourself must be aware that it will be impossible
to admit, as an inmate, a stranger—a person ignorant of our peculiar
systems—an alien from our religion. Mrs. Raby would never consent
to it; and I would on no account annoy her, who, as the mother and
guardian of my heir, merits every deference. I will, however, consult
with her, and with the gentleman who has the conduct of my affairs;
and, as you wish to get rid of an embarrassment, which, pardon me if
I say you entirely brought on yourself, we will do what we judge due
to the honour of the family: but I cannot hold out any hopes beyond a
maintenance—unless this young person, whom I should then regard
as my grand-daughter, felt a vocation for a religion out of whose pale
I will never acknowledge a relation.' At every word Falkner grew more
angry. He always repressed any manifestation of passion, and only
grew pale, and spoke in a lower, calmer voice. There was a pause; he
glanced at the white hair and attenuated form of the old man, so as
to acquire a sufficient portion of forbearance; and then replied,—'It is
enough: forget this visit; you shall never hear again of the existence of
your outraged grandchild. Could you for a moment comprehend her
worth, you might feel regret at casting from you one whose qualities
render her the admiration of all who know her. Some day, when the
infirmities of age increase upon you, you may remember that you
might have had a being near, the most compassionate and kind that
breathes. If ever you feel the want of an affectionate hand to smooth
your pillow, you may remember that you have shut your heart to one
who would have been a daily blessing.'

—Unsigned, *Falkner*, from *The Literary*
Gazette and Journal of Belles Lettres,
February 4, 1837

UNSIGNED REVIEW FROM
MONTHLY REVIEW (1837)

Falkner is perhaps the finest and most powerful, in regard to sentiment, of
Mrs. Shelley's novels. Tenderness, pathos, and romantic elevation of feeling
characterize all her productions. There is not much of real life in her stories,
but a vast amount of thought and pensive meditation. Her colouring is for
the most part sombre, but yet refining, and when she probes to the source
of human action, though it be with much of her father's discernment, it is
not with his misanthropic tendency, but with a generous sympathy with
and for her kind. In the present instance, for example, her Falkner bears a
close resemblance to his Sir Edward Mortimer; but there is also enough of
dissimilarity to remove her portrait to a wide distance from coming under
the charge of imitation, or being blamed for inculcating that scepticism
as to the existence of human virtue and disinterested goodness, which her
father's creations too potently taught. She seems also to have imbibed much
of her husband's poetic temperament, its singular loveliness and delicacy, but
to have shorn it of those extravagant visions and emotions which led him
beyond the province of truth, and the dictates of a well-regulated judgment,
which certainly are as essential to poetic excellence, as are the flights of an
ardent or sensitive imagination.

We have said that Mrs. Shelley's colouring is for the most part sombre; but
it should rather, perhaps, be asserted that her themes being gloomy, and her
characters closely connected with some mystery of extraordinary weight and
depth, there is necessarily established very early in the story over the mind of
the reader, that brooding foreboding of evil and of terrible things, that cannot
be playfully dealt with. But it is to the honour of her genius, and to the force
as well as delicate beauty of her minute delineations, that this gloominess is
never felt to be unwelcome, but of a soft and melancholy cast. Falkner, for
example, is a tale in which crime, dark deeds, and remorse form prominent
parts. There is great suffering also entailed upon the innocent. And yet not
only is the story one of arresting power, but the chief criminal himself, who
is the hero, engages the heart, and fain would we see him restored to mental
comfort, and hear of him being forgiven. Along with this absorbing interest
in behalf of Falkner—(which is established by nothing like meretricious or
morbid sentiments, but by an acute and delicate dissection of motives and
temptations, and an unmitigating picture of the consequences of crime, even
in this world, as also the penitent's desire to atone for his great offences, were
it but by enduring the punishment which his guilt has incurred)—there are so

many charming characters, incidents, and feelings portrayed as to render this romantic story rather pathetic than gloomy, rather the vehicle of melancholy reflections than of horror. We are not going to lift the veil from the plot, nor to specify the part which any of the leading characters perform; but we may safely declare that Elizabeth Raby is one of the loveliest and most winning creatures that ever graced the earth through the enchantment of painter or poet. Her lover is a suitable portrait; but we must not longer stand on the threshold. We therefore enter and help ourselves without any great regard to selection, confining our extracts to one sketch, for it is impossible to take up any separate morsel without feeling assured that there is behind much that is more precious, although of a similar mould and beauty. Those who delight to contemplate the innocence, the guileless ways of childhood, the affection, the intelligence, and loveliness of those who have been properly cared for, let them study the portrait we now introduce. The locality is a sea-bathing village in Cornwall.

"A little girl, unnoticed and alone, was wont, each evening, to trip over the sands—to scale, with light steps, the cliff which was of no gigantic height, and then, unlatching the low white gate of the churchyard, to repair to one corner, where the boughs of the near trees shadowed over two graves—two graves, of which one only was distinguished by a simple head-stone to commemorate the name of him who mouldered beneath. This tomb was inscribed to the memory of Edwin Raby, but the neighbouring and less-honoured grave claimed more of the child's attention—for her mother lay beneath the unrecorded turf.

"Beside this grassy hillock she would sit and talk to herself, and play, till, warned home by the twilight, she knelt and said her little prayer, and with a 'Good night, mamma,' took leave of a spot with which was associated the being whose caresses and love she called to mind, hoping that one day she might again enjoy them. Her appearance had much in it to invite remark, had there been any who cared to notice a poor little orphan. Her dress, in some of its parts, betokened that she belonged to the better classes of society; but she had no stockings, and her little feet peeped from the holes of her well-worn shoes. Her straw bonnet was dyed dark with sun and sea spray, and its blue ribbon faded. The child herself would, in any other spot, have attracted more attention than the incongruities of her attire. There is an expression of face which we name angelic, from its purity, its tenderness, and, so to speak, plaintive serenity, which we oftener see in young children than in persons of a more advanced age. And such was hers: her hair, of a light golden brown, was parted over a brow fair and open as day: her eyes deep set and earnest, were full of thought and tenderness; her complexion was pure and stainless, except by the roses that glowed in her cheek, while each vein could be traced on her temples, and you could almost mark the flow of the violet-coloured blood beneath: her mouth was the very nest of love: her serious look was at once fond and imploring; but when she smiled it was as if sunshine broke out at once, warm and unclouded: her figure had the plumpness of infancy; but her tiny hands and feet, and tapering waist, denoted the faultless perfection of her form. She was about six years old—a friendless orphan, cast, thus young, pennyless on a thorny, stony-hearted world. . . .

"The orphan would sit for hours by the graves, now fancying that her mother must soon return, now exclaiming, 'Why, are you gone away? Come, dear mamma, come back—come quickly!' Young as she was, it was no wonder that such thoughts were familiar to her. The minds of children are often as intelligent as those of persons of maturer age—and differ only by containing fewer ideas—but these had so often been presented to her—and she so fixed her little heart on the idea that her mother was watching over her, that at last it became a part of her religion to visit, every evening, the two graves, and saying her prayers near them, to believe that her mother's spirit, which was obscurely associated with her mortal remains reposing below, listened to and blest her on that spot.

"At other times, neglected as she was, and left to wander at will, she conned her lesson, as she had been accustomed at her mother's feet, beside her grave. She took her picture-books there—and even her playthings. The villagers were affected by her childish notion of being 'with mamma;' and Missy became something of an angel in their eyes, so that no one interfered with her visits, or tried to explain away her fancies. She was the nursling of love and nature: but the human hearts which could have felt the greatest tenderness for her beat no longer, and had become clods of the soil—

Borne round in earth's diurnal course
With rocks, and stones, and trees.

"There was no knee on which she could playfully climb—no neck round which she could fondly hang—no parent's cheek on which to print her happy kisses—these two graves were all of relationship she knew upon the earth—and she would kiss the ground and the flowers, not one of which she plucked—as she sat embracing the sod. 'Mamma' was everywhere around. 'Mamma' was there beneath, and still she could love and feel herself beloved.

"At other times she played gaily with her young companions in the village—and sometimes she fancied that she loved some one among them—she made them presents of books and toys, the relics of happier days; for the desire to benefit which springs up so naturally in a loving heart was strong within her, even in that early age. But she never took anyone with her in her church-yard visits—she needed none while she was with mamma. Once, indeed, a favourite kitten was carried to the sacred spot, and the little animal played amidst the grass and flowers, and the child joined in its frolics—her solitary gay laugh might be heard among the tombs—she did not think it solitary; mamma was there to smile on her, as she sported with her tiny favourite."

When alluding to the love of children, Mrs. Shelley says, "we human beings are so unlike one to the other, that it is often difficult to make one person understand that there is any force in an impulse which is omnipotent with another. Children, to some, are mere animals, unendued with instinct, troublesome, and unsightly; with others they possess a charm that reaches to the heart's core, and stirs the purest and most generous portions of our nature." It is easy to understand to which of these classes this elegant writer belongs; but to all who range in the other rank, her delineations of young life will seem extravagance, and be a mystery.

Here is a very different picture, and yet it is of one who stands so near as grandfather to the orphan.

"On inquiry, Falkner heard that the old gentleman was at Belleforest—indeed, he never quitted it; but that his daughter-in-law with her family, were in the south of England. Mr. Raby was very accessible: on asking for him, Falkner was instantly ushered in. He entered a library of vast dimensions, and fitted up with a sort of heavy splendour; very imposing, but very sombre. The high windows, painted ceiling, and massy furniture, bespoke an old-fashioned, but almost regal taste. Falkner, for a moment, thought himself alone, when a slight noise attracted his attention to a diminutive, and very white old gentleman, who advanced towards him. The mansion looked built for a giant race; and Falkner, expecting the majesty of size, could hardly contract his view to the slender and insignificant figure of the present possessor. Oswi Raby looked shrivelled, not so much by age as the narrowness of his mind, to whose dimensions his outward figure had contracted itself. His face was pale and thin; his light-blue eyes grew dim: you might have thought that he was drying up and vanishing from the earth by degrees. Contrasted with this slight shadow of a man, was a mind that saw the whole world almost concentrated in himself. He, Oswi Raby, he, head of the oldest family in England, was first of created beings. Without being assuming in manner, he was self-important in heart; and there was an obstinacy, and an incapacity to understand that anything was of consequence except himself, or rather, except the house he represented, that gave extreme repulsion to his manners."

Falkner's errand to this repulsive personage was to restore to him the orphan, whom he (Falkner) had adopted some years before as his own daughter. But the shrivelled grandfather has no compassion and no affection; thinking that his son's relinquishing the faith of his ancestors, and marrying a lowly born woman, were sufficient grounds for neglecting their only child. The ill-tempered and heartless old man, in the course of the colloquy, obdurately abides by his usual methods of thinking, and among other reasons for his opinion and conduct, says—

"'Had you restored her to us in her childhood; had she been brought up in our religion among us; she would have shared this home with her cousins. As it is, you yourself must be aware that it will be impossible to admit as an inmate, a stranger—a person ignorant of our peculiar systems—an alien from our religion. Mrs. Raby would never consent to it; and I would on no account annoy her, who, as the mother and guardian of my heir, merits every deference. I will, however, consult with her, and with the gentleman who has the conduct of my affairs; and, as you wish to get rid of an embarrassment, which, pardon me if I say you entirely brought on yourself, we will do what we judge due to the honour of the family: but I cannot hold out any hopes beyond a maintenance—unless this young person, whom I should then regard as my grand-daughter, felt a vocation for a religion out of whose pale I will never acknowledge a relation.' At every word Falkner grew more angry. He always repressed any manifestation of passion, and only grew pale, and spoke in a lower, calmer voice. There was a pause; he glanced at the white hair and attenuated form of the old man, so as to acquire a sufficient portion of forbearance, and then replied—'It is enough: forget this visit; you shall never hear again of the existence of your outraged grandchild. Could you for a moment comprehend her worth, you might feel regret at casting from you one whose qualities render her the admiration of all who know her. Some day, when the infirmities of age increase upon you, you may remember that you might have had a being near, the most compassionate and kind that breathes. If ever you feel the want of an affectionate hand to smooth your pillow, you may remember that you have shut your heart to one who would have been a daily blessing.' "

Just as we had got this length with the novels of the month, and exhausted fully more than the space which extracts from them can righteously demand, in comes Paynell, the Disappointed Man, and desires to have a corner in our apartment, and a forward station among his tribe. We are sorry, however, that he can only be allowed a narrow space in the particular circumstances now alluded to, although had he made his entrance at an earlier hour, there could have been no objection to giving him his due precedence. But it matters the less that he should once more be *disappointed*, in as far as he is denied an opportunity of laying before fiction's conclave, some of his experience of the "stale and unprofitable uses of this world"—because in a few words, we are able to convey a much more accurate account of him, than could have been done had he not come after Mr. Falkner. The truth is, that the two belong to the same family, bearing, of course, this distinctive and individual feature—that is to say, that crime and woeful deeds mark the career of each of the heroes, although Mr. Paynell is most closely related to the Byron branch, while the other claims kindred with that of Mr. Godwin. There is one great advantage, however, according to our opinion, which Mrs. Shelley's novel has over that of Mr. Stapleton—it is thus, that the former's hero claims our sympathies, while the latter repels them; the one's history has an elevating and refining influence upon the reader: that of the other is revolting.

—Unsigned, *Falkner*, from *Monthly Review*,
March 1, 1837, pp. 376–380

Chronology

1797   Mary Wollstonecraft Godwin is born on August 30 at Somers Town to William Godwin and Mary Wollstonecraft (who dies shortly after her daughter's birth).

1801   William Godwin marries Mary Jane Clairmont, who has a daughter, Claire, and a son, Charles.

1803   Mary Jane Godwin gives birth to William Godwin, Jr.

1805   William and Mary Jane Godwin open a publishing firm and shop that sells children's books.

1811   Percy Shelley marries Harriet Westbrook.

1812   Percy Shelley and Mary Godwin meet for the first time while Shelley studies with William Godwin.

1813   Percy Shelley separates from Harriet.

1814   Mary and Shelley meet again and fall in love; Mary declares her love for Percy at her mother's grave. William Godwin forbids Mary to see Percy. Mary and Percy elope with Mary's stepsister, Claire. Mary begins her novel *Hate*. They return to England. Shelley's estranged wife, Harriet, gives birth to his son, Charles.

1815   Mary gives birth to a daughter, who dies.

1816   Mary gives birth to son William. Claire begins an affair with Lord Byron. Mary, Percy, and Claire meet Byron in Geneva. At the Villa Diodati, Byron, Percy, Mary, and Polidori write ghost stories. Mary begins *Frankenstein*. Percy, Mary, and Claire return to England, where Harriet's suicide makes Mary and Percy's marriage possible.

1817 The Shelleys spend the year at Marlow. Mary gives birth to daughter Clara. She completes *Frankenstein* and writes, with Percy, *History of a Six Weeks' Tour.*

1819 Son William dies in Rome. Mary writes *Mathilda,* which was not published in her lifetime. Mary gives birth to son Percy Florence.

1820 The Shelleys move to Pisa. Mary writes verse dramas *Proserpine* and *Midas.*

1822 The Shelleys live at Casa Magni at Lerici. Mary miscarries and nearly dies. Percy Shelley drowns when the boat he is sailing on is lost at sea. Mary writes "The Choice."

1823 Mary publishes *Valperga.* She returns to England with Claire and Percy Florence. She revises *Frankenstein.* Mary collects and edits Percy's unpublished poems into one volume titled *Posthumous Poems of Percy Bysshe Shelley.*

1824 Byron dies. Mary begins to write *The Last Man.*

1826 *The Last Man* is published. Harriet and Percy's son, Charles, dies, which makes Percy Florence the heir to his grandfather Sir Timothy Shelley.

1828 Mary writes "The Sisters of Albano" for *The Keepsake,* an annual journal.

1830 Mary publishes *Adventures of Perkin Warbeck.*

1831 Revised edition of *Frankenstein* is published with an introduction by Mary.

1835 Mary publishes *Lodore.*

1836 Mary's father, William Godwin, dies.

1837 Mary publishes *Falkner.*

1838 Mary publishes essays in *Lives of the Most Eminent . . . Men of France.*

1839 Mary edits Percy's *Poetical Works* and *Essays.*

1844 Sir Timothy dies; Percy Florence inherits his title and estates. *Rambles in Germany and Italy* is published.

1848 Sir Percy marries Jane St. John.

1851 Mary Shelley dies in London on February 1.

1959 *Mathilda* is published.

Index

Characters in literary works are indexed by first name (if any), followed by the name of the work in parentheses